Lucius Seth Huntington

Professor Conant

A Story of English and American Social and Political Life

Lucius Seth Huntington

Professor Conant
A Story of English and American Social and Political Life

ISBN/EAN: 9783337070427

Printed in Europe, USA, Canada, Australia, Japan

Cover: Foto ©Suzi / pixelio.de

More available books at **www.hansebooks.com**

PROFESSOR CONANT:

A STORY OF ENGLISH AND AMERICAN SOCIAL AND POLITICAL LIFE.

BY

HON. L. S. HUNTINGTON, Q.C.,
(LATE POSTMASTER-GENERAL OF CANADA, &C., &C., &C.)

> It is not that I adulate the people;
> Without *me* there are demagogues enough,
> And infidels to pull down every steeple,
> And set up in their stead some common stuff.
> * * I do not know—I wish men to be free,
> As much from mobs as kings—from you as me.
> — LORD BYRON.

NEW YORK:
R. WORTHINGTON, 770 BROADWAY.
1884.

COPYRIGHT, 1884,
BY R. WORTHINGTON.

PRESS OF J. J. LITTLE & CO.,
NOS. 10 TO 20 ASTOR PLACE, NEW YORK.

TO

PROFESSOR GOLDWIN SMITH, D.C.L.,

I Dedicate this little Story,

BY PERMISSION,

AS A TRIBUTE OF RESPECT FOR HIS GREAT REPUTATION
AS
AN EMINENT PUBLICIST,

AN ACUTE AND LIBERAL THINKER,

AND A BRILLIANT WRITER,

AND AS A TOKEN OF

PERSONAL ESTEEM AND FRIENDSHIP.

THE AUTHOR.

159 W. 46TH ST.,
NEW YORK, APRIL, 1884.

PREFACE.

The characters that flit along these pages were pleasant companions of the author's enforced seclusion during the weeks in which they were written. Some of them should be careful thinkers in their various walks of life; and they should all be good talkers, for they are well instructed and they have seen the world. Their discussions are, of course, cursory, for they pick up topics and lay them down again, in rapid succession. If we listen sometimes to an enthusiast, a cool conservative is at hand to reply. The author assumes only the rôle of a reporter, and the public will judge if he does his work well. He is not responsible for what his characters say, but only for giving them the opportunity to say it.

Their loves and exultations, their griefs and perils, the modest "talks," in which they discuss their plans, and their theories of religious, political and social life became strangely real to him who wrote. The story ceases to be fiction when the great English Lord is found at the feet of the American girl, and when the great English scholar pursues his inquiries among Massachusetts farmers and generally studies Democracy as the countries of America are teaching it. We must all learn that lesson, kings and people, or suffer for not comprehending it. Carlyle says: "Universal Democracy, whatever we may think of it, has declared itself, as an inevitable fact of the days in which we live," and a greater than Carlyle has ordained that to study the loves of men and women is to court enchantment and infatuation.

The author has thus woven a little romance with characters English, American and Colonial, and has ventured thereby to suggest that fealty to Liberty which Society should exact from those who love and would maintain political freedom; in the faith, that the more nearly England and America are drawn together in every relation which promotes human happiness, the better service will they render mankind.

CONTENTS.

CHAPTER		PAGE
I.	A Dinner at the Tower of London	1
II.	Lords and Ladies	5
III.	Blood is Thicker than Water	12
IV.	The Plot Thickens	23
V.	The American Cousin Dazzles my Lord	33
VI.	A Voice from the Trossachs	47
VII.	The Jolliest Trip ever Projected	62
VIII.	Going Down to the Sea in Ships	68
IX.	All went Merry as a Marriage Bell	77
X.	Coming into the Track of a Storm	88
XI.	De Luynes Discusses Burning Questions	97
XII.	Ave Sanctissima	111
XIII.	Who Could Foresee Perils?	127
XIV.	The King of Terrors	141
XV.	De Luynes Honored in Death	156
XVI.	The Flags Blend with Graceful Harmony	171
XVII.	The Jesuit and the Orangeman	183
XVIII.	The Professor Visits Boston	190
XIX.	We are Massachusetts Farmers	203
XX.	The People's King in America	227
XXI.	Homeward Bound	250
XXII.	Thine and Mine	255
XXIII.	The British Lion Fondles the Professor	273
XXIV.	Gathering in the Threads	280
XXV.	Nous Verrons	290

PROFESSOR CONANT.

CHAPTER I.

A DINNER AT THE TOWER OF LONDON.

"Oh, the fool!" said Tom Conant, "to sell himself to Hymen for an ugly woman and two thousand a year. Why not have gone to America, where, I am told, pretty women abound, handsome and rich too, by Jove, who are crying their eyes out for foreigners of high birth?"

"Not so fast, young man," replied the person addressed, "she was a pretty girl and is a most interesting woman; I only thought her a little exacting, and that George was somewhat under restraint. Pray, don't quote me as an authority if you are to say these naughty things. Mrs. George is a prophetess as well as an heiress, and there are little birds to carry, far into the North, the story of our confabulating here. I'll wager you that when we next meet her she will wear an odd smile of contempt for our opinions."

"Nonsense, Edgar, I am too much in earnest to heed your *badinage*. Poor Wallace is the type of a class; a brave soldier, an impecunious gentleman, beloved by his friends and crazed by the usurers. He wins the usual distinctions of a fast life—debts and other doubtful things, and then he sells out and marries."

"Well, Tom, that seems to me better than suicide.

If George might have done better he might have done
worse; and, after all, the bonnie bride may even run
more risk than her Lord. My sojourn was very pleasant
in Scotland; but the Scotch are a canny, clannish people.
It was my first visit, and they could scarcely understand
my early neglect of their country. 'Did I know,' they
asked, 'when I first stepped foot in Glasgow, that I was
in the second city of the Empire? And what had I
thought when I saw the crowds pouring towards George's
Square?' I bethought me of the Cockney's answer, but
I dared not repeat it. What did I think? Why, I
thought what numbers of Scotchmen there are still to
come South!" Tom laughed.

"That's a good joke. But, if you put it in a book, only
London Scotchmen will understand it. I will not quote
the familiar slander about a surgical operation; but
look at his Lordship now, to come near home, and tell
me if you think he would take it in!"

"Ah, no," replied Col. Lyons, "his Lordship never
laughs at anything Scotch. He told me himself that he
thought Dean Ramsay's 'Reminiscences' an utter waste
of powder and shot. But he's no fool, though he is
peculiar. I believe, like Dundreary, he might be still
in doubt as to whether a certain nondescript young
lady likes cheese; but he's a good fellow, all the same,
and now he comes——"

A tall, slight man with an uncertain gait and a nervous
manner approached the group. He was reserved but
gentle, and you saw that he was welcome and among
friends.

"Is Tom in mischief to-night as usual?" he asked,
good humoredly; but he was only answered with a laugh
and a protest from Capt. Conant.

Lord Bolton was older than his companions, though still in the freshness and vigor of life. He never talked of his age; he never encouraged others to speak of it. He might regret the days of his early youth, or he might dread the knowledge of good and evil that comes with years. Dr. Blair somewhere remarks that "at thirty a man suspects himself a fool, at forty he knows it." My Lord never enlightens you about his suspicions. "Don't speak of birthdays," he would say, "their admonitions are unpleasant."

His finely formed head was "silvered o'er," but you knew it was not the frost of age; and, if his pleasing face seemed a little weary, you saw it was still young, and had not been worn with years of labor. He spoke, at first, with a slight lisp, and with a diffident manner; but he had been known to display earnestness, and at times eloquence. His perceptions were not quick, but his good sense was proverbial. Perhaps his sayings would pass into proverbs more readily than those of humbler folk. Some of his young friends were critical, and they found him a laggard in love and slow to interpret a joke. All this may change as we see and hear more of him. His associates might differ as to his eccentricities, but he had a kindly word for them all.

Our friends are guests of Col. Lyons, of the —— Guards, whose regiment had been lately detailed for garrison duty at the old Tower of London. A party of young officers and their friends have assembled and are awaiting dinner in the mess-room, once sacred to the sorrows of great prisoners of State. On the walls around might still be seen lines traced by the delicate hand of the Lady Jane Grey, in the dismal solitude of her last imprisonment.

The great fortress slept, with all her landmarks and trophies, her memories of generations of cruelty, and the contests—now glorious, anon reeking with infamy—through which the fabric of British liberty was built up.

The place calls up many reminiscences to-night, for the Lord High Constable is among the guests, but few of them are contemplating the past. The speculations of the antiquaries, if there be any among the present gathering, are not concerned with the early morning of history. Contemplation may come with the morrow; just now the guests are drowning thought in their happy revels, and their boisterous laughter provokes no echo of remonstrance, or reproach from the illustrious shadows that have so long hovered over the mysteries of the Tower.

CHAPTER II.

LORDS AND LADIES.

The painter in oil and the sculptor in marble produce the form, the pose, perhaps even the expression of features, which it is only left for the word-painter to describe.

The mass of men think so much by images that they need a palpable figure, a material copy, to create an impression, while the word-painter seldom achieves more than the musical jingle of his words. The advantages are reversed when we come to describe qualities instead of things; the spiritual, instead of the material, agencies of being; not because the word-picture is perfect, but because art cannot scan the domain of the immaterial, nor, within it, can she "hold nature up to nature's God." And yet, it does not follow that one should never paint in words what can be photographed by the sun. Enough may be fairly deduced to shorten many pen-and-ink sketches, and perhaps lighten the labor, and sometimes even the sin, of many readers; some of whom weary over much description, and others, alas! wickedly vault it altogether.

Tom Conant was the son of an Oxford professor of distinction, who had lately added to a life of scholastic honors the dignities of a member of Her Majesty's House of Commons. He was an author of repute, and a gentleman of undoubted culture and *bonhomie*. Though he still loved his Alma Mater, and maintained his nominal connection with her, he was an ardent Liberal, and gave the best powers of his well-stored mind to his country's service. A "young member," as the phrase goes, he had taken high position in the House, and his learning and industry had been recognized by the appointment to many chairmanships, while his careful and intelligent discussion of questions relating to the higher work of administration was rapidly increasing his influence both in the House and the country.

Tom was his father's especial weakness. He was proud of the boy's fine qualities, and he knew better than Tom dreamed about his faults, which he regarded as venial, and which he said "Tom would manage in time." "The boy is his mother's son," he would say, "full of nervous energy and faith. He is generous, and perhaps extravagant, but look at what temptations he has in the Guards. He will have sown his wild oats at a younger age than most boys; yet he has not sown them very thick, if I know him truly. I believe he has kept few secrets from me. Dear me! Tom will be a man soon. He is twenty-two, if he is a day."

Tom, on the other hand, was passionately fond of his father. The two were often, so to speak, confidential when they were alone together—but when the world was about them, they were men. Did they dream what labors and triumphs each would yet sustain in the other's life?

Lord Bolton was heir to a peer of the realm. His ancestors were with William the Conqueror—erroneously so-called, because he only conquered the usurper, Harold—and negotiated terms with the nation whose laws he swore to maintain. My Lord never knew what had been the station of his great progenitor under the Norman monarch. It was enough that he "came over," and, for the rest, he might have been prince or beggar. His family had been ennobled, and, on one side or other, had served England bravely in all her great struggles of war or peace. His grandfather had been a favorite of George the Fourth, and his father was at one time Prime Minister of England. On his mother's side had descended the glories of Blenheim in that direct family-line which for nigh two hundred years has absorbed the national benefactions. His ample estates testified to his substantial lineage, and he was to inherit his father's boundless wealth, including his "cattle on a thousand hills." What need my Lord care for wits, their jokes or their methods? If he was sometimes dull, might he not be a patron, and in his train have a retinue of punsters and poets and painters? What could be denied him, this great Lord, with his mighty name and his vast possessions? True, the times might change; they were changing. One could submit to competition from a Rothschild, though the finger-marks of commerce were seen on his doors. A Lord Mayor might be forgiven ducal splendors, for he rules over millions and speaks with the voice of the law. But Commerce levels all things. The costermonger of to-day may be His Grace the Duke de *Chemin-de-fer* of the near decade; even now, wealth has no monopoly of rank, for the commonest people are invested with it; and with all this distribution of wealth, titles themselves may lose *prestige* in England.

"They must be a strange people in America," said my Lord, "if one may judge from the Americans I have met in my travels. They love titles there, I am told, though they are growing to be debatable blessings at home. One might do worse than go across. I am going to America, Tom," said my Lord. "Will you come?"

Tom did not suppress any involuntary surprise as he answered: "Thanks! That *would* be jolly, indeed; but I must first see my father, and will you bid me try and persuade him to join us? He needs rest."

"All right," said my Lord, as if he had been a railway guard, and not the titled possessor of millions.

That night, before Tom retired, he sought his father, and pressed him to be one of Lord Bolton's party.

"I really need the rest, Tom," said the Professor, "and I have not been in America these ten years. The pleasure of going with you, my boy, would be an additional incentive."

"Thanks, father," Tom answered gayly; "Bolton is of the salt of the earth, say what they will about him. I was annoyed by an ill-natured remark of Fred Cuthbert to-night," continued Tom; "Bolton will fulfil his mission in life," Fred had said. "How's that?" I asked, half absently. "He will prove that talent is not hereditary," was the rejoinder.

"Fred will not prove that it *is*," said the professor, dryly, "if he pretends to inherit his gifts from Sir John Cuthbert."

Tom Conant went to Brighton to spend the Sunday with his mother and some friends. They had just returned from church where a great New York preacher had much interested and a little disturbed them.

"You see," said Tom, "the theme was grand, and the discourse was full of noble thoughts, presented with the skill of a master; but there was a vein of levity here and there, which we don't look for in the pulpit. One felt there was a charm which one ought to resist. Sometimes I wanted to cheer. Do you remember that story of the old woman who heard the Choral Litany for the first time, and who said it was 'sweet, but it was an awful way to spend the Sabbath?'"

"Yes," said Tom's mother, "we are accustomed to a certain solemnity in the treatment of sacred things. But vivacity gives warmth and life, and the preacher, no doubt, finds great wealth of illustration in the most familiar fields. There ought to be a *via media* between the humdrum and the sensational. Worship is an act of adoration; it is emotional as well as reverent. I like Doctor Elmwood, and have invited him and his niece to lunch with us. The young lady is shy, but you will find the Doctor an intelligent and interesting man."

"Whew!" thought Tom, "An American girl!" But he answered, "Yes, mother, I am sure I shall be delighted to meet him." So saying, Tom kissed his mother, and retired to his room.

"I wonder what she is like," he soliloquized, "this American niece of an American parson!" And striding up and down his room, he hummed to a pensive air:—

> "Or soft black eyes, or melting blue,
> Which has the darling of the two?"

Tom Conant had not lost the freshness of his boyhood, though he had come to man's estate. Without being a great scholar he was well educated, both by study and travel. He had taken a respectable position both at school and college, even a brilliant one, wherever hard knocks could be dispensed with, and native talent pulled him through.

His father, who had been a great worker, had been willing to spare the son the drudgery he had endured; and if he had not altogether approved Tom's choice of the army, he had seen in it a relief from the unremitting strain of his own occupations. "Tom's tastes do not lead him my way," he said, "and without love for the work, the burden of it would be intolerable." And so the son was left to be what we have found him, an accomplished, generous, impulsive young man of the world.

America had been to Tom the usual *terra incognita* of Britons. The geography of the New World he had been taught, but its people he had never seen; moreover, what he had read was generally inconsistent, and very often uncomplimentary. He knew they were fifty millions—a multitudinous people. They had lately emerged from a great war, with a million of men in arms. But the Chinese had numbers, and the society-journals were discussing the points of resemblance between them and his cousins across the sea.

Notwithstanding the humors of the critics, he remembered that the people of this mysterious western land were but an offshoot of the old stock—Britons modified, if not improved; and he had a profound regard for their history and their achievements. But, at the present moment, it was not with Tom a question of vital or political statistics. He would look into graver questions later. If the truth must be told, Tom, to-day, was neither natural nor characteristic. But we all have had moods we could not explain, and our follies, even consciously to ourselves, have had a beginning. Had the new preacher so impressed him, or was he surrendering to the young American girl, whom he had not seen?

Tom's thoughts pursued him in his dreams. He dared not acknowledge to himself how often his imagination had woven fascinating visions, which might be no longer myths, now that this little stranger had come across the sea. How did he know she was little? His mother had said she was shy; that was all he knew about her. If she was shy, she ought to be young. And was she pretty? Was she his fate, and should he hate her? She could not be rich, but he did not care for that.

He awoke and shortly after rose, exclaiming to himself, "What a fool I am!"

CHAPTER III.

BLOOD IS THICKER THAN WATER.

"A ROAST of beef and *entremets*," comprised what Mrs. Conant called her "quiet Sunday dinner." The Professor, as Mrs. Conant explained to Dr. Elmwood, had been unwillingly detained in London. Tom shared the honors with his mother; on his right hand sat Miss Agnes Winthrop, of Boston, a young lady of seventeen summers, who was passing her last year at school on the Continent, and at present was spending her vacation in England with friends.

There was nothing very different from other young ladies to be noted in Miss Winthrop's appearance. She was a tall and graceful blonde, a charming girl, with a bright, intelligent face, a cheery voice and winning manners; and her large, laughing eyes, fringed by long, dark lashes, and a smile of indescribable sweetness with which she welcomed or entertained you, denoted qualities of uncommon gentleness, while in other respects you were impressed as if in the presence of one whose character would develop unusual strength.

She was not "shy," as Mrs. Conant had described her—or, perhaps, we should say she was not timid. By nature she seemed to be equal to great things; but, at the first meeting, neither Tom nor the young lady was free from embarrassment.

Are these young people thus *distrait* and self-conscious because, though strangers, they have dreamed of each other? Who shall fix the metes and bounds of common sense, beyond which the extravagance of romance shall not wander, or make plain the mysteries which regulate the dreams of young and inexperienced hearts?

Mrs. Conant was an English gentlewoman, and seemed more like the sister than the mother of Tom, who was her only son. She had followed three children, a son and two daughters, to the grave. Perhaps this experience had cast a tinge of sadness over her earnest and expressive face, which was more comely than beautiful, but, when lighted by the glow of sympathy, was full of charm. There are those whose whole character is expressed by a look or a smile, who seem to invite your confidence at first sight, and promise you the interest and friendship which might fitly have been born of years. You see the soul in the eyes, and you know its gentleness and purity by a magnetic intuition which you can feel but cannot explain. You wonder how, all these years, you have lived without knowing these people; and life seems warmer and richer when you have met them. Bound by the tenderest ties, they have room in their hearts for a sympathy which is universal. If one is wrong, their very greeting is a protection; if right, their simple presence is an encouragement. They are environed by an atmosphere of unconscious worth, and their good influences work quiet results, to which they are strangers.

There are many such people, though they do not abound in the world; but good Mrs. Conant was one of their number, and people said Tom was his mother's son. His little sister completed the family circle, but she is in the nursery now, listening to the hoary mysteries of Santa Claus and the enchantment of Mother Goose's melodies.

At table, Dr. Elmwood was beginning to lead the conversation in a quiet way. He was the rector of a fashionable church in New York, the metropolis of the Great West. The Church of England had left her eldest daughter to the occupancy of America. There was little to distinguish the mother from the child. Both had nominally preserved an austere orthodoxy, which the members of each had modified and mollified in practice. The Church was wise enough to look upon diversities without seeing them, and broad enough to embrace the believers of all degrees. If restless spirits sometimes invoked controversy and challenged declarations of faith, the members were generally willing to leave mysteries to the spiritual heads, and were content, for themselves, with seeking the wisdom to love God supremely, and their neighbors as themselves. Dr. Elmwood was a Broad Churchman and a devout man. He was the idol of his people, who listened to him with rapt attention, and lavishly put money in his purse. Perhaps, after the weary excitement of the week, there were vivacious passages with which the Doctor sometimes interlarded his discourses—there was a tinge of exaggeration and hyperbole, an imagery, drawn from familiar things, just a *soupçon* of quaint humor, or even wit, which, though it had disturbed the unaccustomed ear of Tom, was a grateful stimulant to the Doctor's Western hearers.

He was scholarly and logical; his elocution was faultless, and his oratory masterly. Nobody went to sleep when he preached. If, within such limits, there was scope to practise two styles of expression, who should say when the manner of the preacher, or the taste of the hearer was at fault? If you have no accepted standard, who is to decide between Tom and Dr. Elmwood's people?

"I suppose you have often seen the pretty town where my niece is at school," said the Doctor, addressing Tom for the first time. Tom replied that he had not, but should be more interested in seeing it now than ever.

Mrs. Conant remembered sadly her last visit to Heidelberg. Her little daughter had contracted the cold there, which finally carried her off.

Tom ventured to ask if Miss Winthrop liked her school, and was answered "yes," with the slightest foreign accent.

Mr. Holt, who is a stranger to us, as yet, though one of Mrs. Conant's guests, attacked the system of female education altogether.

Tom curtly disposed of the whole subject in a single word, whereat Mr. Holt looked flushed and mortified.

Dr. Elmwood admitted its importance, and kind Mrs. Conant felt sure that Mr. Holt was right, for the whole system required revision.

This smoothed Mr. Holt's ruffled feathers, and, somewhat to the disgust of Tom, set him on his legs again.

Mr. Holt was inveterate, if one may apply that word to a good talker. The famous Doctor was his *vis-à-vis* and he wanted to bring him out.

"Capt. Conant thinks, perhaps, one should not introduce such a subject in the presence of so distinguished a devotee," said Mr. Holt, smiling grimly.

"If you refer to me," said the young lady, "don't mind me at all; I am neither the adjective nor the noun you have mentioned, sir."

Tom winced, but was silent, and after a pause, Dr. Elmwood said:

"Without regard to any system, I have serious doubts as to the propriety of educating young Americans in Europe at all. Of course, I do not refer to the higher work of the universities."

"Not to go further, sir," said Tom, "such ideas would have deprived us of a great pleasure to-day. Miss Winthrop would not have been spending her Continental vacation in England, and Dr. Elmwood would not have been visiting us with his niece. Seriously, however, if no scholastic advantages are thus acquired, are not such studies pursued with the happy result of making the student a cosmopolitan?"

"That's what I object to," said the Doctor; "the schools may be more efficient, and pupils may get on faster when away from home, but our schools are improving rapidly, and one of our boys educated here, at Rugby or Harrow, or at any public school in England, may become denationalized by going abroad for his education. He will be trained with a class of boys, who belong to an order of society unknown in his own country. He goes home unsettled, unfitted, perhaps, for the pursuits which fortune has assigned him. No doubt, an American boy may be trained at school with the young bloods of this aristocratic land, and go home satisfied to his yard-stick and his counting room, but for every one such there will be another to sigh for the blue blood and heraldic trappings of his school dreams."

"Dear me, uncle," said Miss Winthrop, "do you not think they would be improved by the superior associations that would surround them?"

"Ah!" said Dr. Elmwood, "I should think so."

"I should think so too," she continued, "and they might acquire a polish and refinement to last them all their days."

"And learn to discount the polish and refinement of their homes!" broke in the Doctor.

"I quite seize your point, Doctor," said Tom, "but if you will pardon me, I think it more plausible than exact. Take English boys; Lords and Commoners are educated in the same class. Yet, in the great world, the middle classes never bow down before nobility."

"You are young, Tom," said Mr. Holt, "and may change your views as you extend your observation."

"Besides," added Dr. Elmwood, "here both classes are English, and there is no question of denationalization. But a young American who apes the English upper classes——have you seen a dude?"

"I am not quite sure," said Tom, "but I have seen what the comic papers say about him. He is to be pitied."

"He is the ideal American dandy at home," said Dr. Elmwood, "striving to imitate English high-life."

"But he is not the offspring of English schools," said Miss Winthrop, with animation.

"I do not know," replied Dr. Elmwood, "but I would not lead the boys into temptation."

"There is another difference between English and American boys," said Mr. Holt, "*apropos* of the middle classes not bowing the knee to the nobles, if they do not, indeed. An English boy is satisfied to hold the position his father held before him. He neither expects nor is ambitious, to surpass him. All young Americans, on the contrary, hope to become President some day in their own country, and many of them would like to become Dukes and Lords over here. There is a great deal to be proud of, though much to improve, in our schools. But I doubt whether all the benefits Tom Brown derived from his school-days would be compensation to an American boy for that love of his country, and that pride in her development, which inhere in every American at home. Just now, after many years of experience, and after all nations, including England, have come to acknowledge that the world is better for what the thirteen colonies did, you don't want to build up a sickly class of tuft-hunters in America, who, for the sake of social chances, would sigh for the old days of dependence."

As the ladies withdrew, Mrs. Conant politely regretted that she should lose the pleasure of listening further to the conversation; and we take credit for having reported it, or it might have been lost to the world.

"My uncle and I rarely disagree; perhaps I ought to make it a duty that we should never do so," said Miss Winthrop, in the drawing-room, to the elder lady; "he is so good and wise that I always feel condemned if I have contradicted him. And, indeed, I love my own country and am proud of my own people; but I would willingly see more of the grace and culture I see here engrafted upon our popular manners. We have done a great deal in a few years, and, in our hurry to reach results, we are sometimes unmindful of the forms which might add to their grace, without impairing their substance. Speaking of schools, I know a dozen well-educated boys and girls who constantly speak, though they would never write, ungrammatically. And this remark applies to many of our best people in America. From what I have seen, I should think this seldom happens in England."

"I have observed something of the kind, but it is a venial sin," said Mrs. Conant, kindly; "a mere education could not correct it. Theoretically, society is on a common level in America. Our manner of speech is the result of our associations. We speak a language as we are accustomed to hear it spoken. The ear is the educator. Speech is extemporaneous and leaves us no time to apply grammatical rules. The fault that disturbs you must be common to all new countries. No doubt the prevalence of education in America is marvellous; and if there is the need, there are also the facilities for improvement. But I see the gentlemen are coming, and we must take them for a stroll in the garden."

Tom was devoted to Mr. Holt, as if he wanted to make amends for something, and that gentleman received his attentions with the lofty grace of one who had not been offended.

Dr. Elmwood delighted Mrs. Conant with his knowledge of flowers, and his ready interpretation of their delicate beauties. Miss Winthrop, who had wandered from the others, and stood alone, regarded with rapt and absent gaze the placid waters beyond. Tom had not been unobservant, and rather timidly joined her.

"Miss Winthrop!" She started. "Oh, I was dreaming," she said, "and I had travelled far over the waters."

"And do you so long for distant scenes?" was Tom's answer.

"Yes, and no. I always long for home, though I do not at present wish to go there."

"I would like to see your home," said Tom, simply. "I hope before long to see America."

"Oh! I hope you will visit my country, and I wish I could be there to greet you."

"It would not seem to me like your home and you not there," rejoined Tom.

"But you would have a warm welcome from those who love me, and who will know before then that you and yours have been kind to me."

"They ought to love you. Tell me about them," said Tom, eagerly.

"Not now; I must know better how you like Americans first. I am full of my countrymen's sensitiveness about English opinions. But, perhaps, you don't feel much interest, yet ——"

"Yes, more than I should dare tell you."

"Isn't it curious," she continued, interrupting him, "how we wince under the sarcasms of an English book, magazine, or newspaper article? And we have had many such inflictions to bear. My Lord goes across, and then he writes a book about what he saw when he was there. It is a funny book, written from strange points of observation. It is not a friendly book, though it says kind things; but it displays a *hauteur* which chills, and assumes a superiority which affronts us. Have you never seen such works?"

"Yes," said Tom, "but they are not always unfriendly."

"No, they are patronizing," she continued. "I want you to read these books and see if you can verify their statements in your travels. I suppose I am too young to understand such things, but I am always wondering why Englishmen are unjust to us."

Tom made a deprecatory shrug, and was about to speak, but Miss Winthrop added, "I mean in their books, you know."

"Why," said Tom, in a conciliatory tone, "I hope you

exaggerate, Miss Winthrop. I suppose it may be because we are jealous of your wonderful growth, and are a little on the lookout for our laurels; but, I am sure there is not much public sentiment to justify them, if they are published."

"Such books are written to sell," was the quiet reply, and the subject was dropped for lighter topics.

Tea was served in the arbor, but Tom did not leave the young lady to Mr. Holt, or to anybody else; and later on, when the two separated, each felt that the other was a friend, without having been told so. Will the feeling grow and ripen as years roll on? or will their paths diverge till it fades into a memory?

How little we know of the mysteries of life, except as, one by one, they are unfolded to us!

As Mrs. Conant's guests were taking their leave, Mr. Holt lingered, hat in hand, for a last word with his hostess.

"It was very good of you to take so much trouble, Robert," she said; "but your love of charity and your kind action will be their own reward."

"Don't give me too much credit, Aunt," he answered, sadly. "If I have rendered you a little service, in aiding your good work, leave me to the lesson it teaches, of improving neglected opportunities of doing good. Oh, how slow I was in the work, and how your mission and your instructions have quickened me in it. Men speak truly of charity as a virtue, and of the Golden Rule, as if some sacrifice were entailed in the observance of it. What human pleasure can equal that of having wiped a tear and assuaged a grief? What can Dives buy with all his wealth, that may equal the satisfaction of him who has ministered according to his means to the wants of the poor? What music can equal in harmony the widow's thanks for the food which has fed her starvelings? What reward of any kind open to human effort, can compare with the consciousness of good deeds, well done, which have removed the disabilities and aroused the gratitude of the unfortunate? Human gratitude! The evidence of acts of kindness, great and small—what a witness that will be for us, in the day when we shall need a cloud of witnesses!"

"You are magnifying a trifle, Robert," said the lady, modestly.

"If you had heard the messages I brought you, it would not have seemed a trifle! I *felt* that it was more blessed to give than to receive, and I almost envied you. It may seem a trifle to you, an incident in your life work; but to me it was an experience, and I shall cherish it. And I hope, in some small way, to cultivate the spirit of your act. What men we might become with such angels of mercy to lead us!" he continued, musingly. "What misery and sin we might alleviate or even turn to joy!"

"Thank God," she said, "if your little plan has really relieved misery and made the stricken heart light again. We must not lose sight of these poor people. It is your work more than mine. But there is more to do. That woman is not the mother of the little girl, I think, and when they are all well again, we shall have a mystery to unravel."

"You will command me when you want me," said Robert Holt. "I can wear Heaven's livery in your service, Mrs. Conant, and never tire of the work you may set me to do."

"Thank you," she answered, softly, "I shall see them in London soon. In the meantime our experience must be secret till we know more."

That night, in his lodgings, Robert Holt wondered that the appearance of these strange people had not suggested more even to him. "But the man and woman were sick with fever," he said. "There was little to denote the condition of life to which they belonged; and I only noticed the child's wonderful eyes, and thought of the quickest means to rescue her from danger. She is safe with the old nurse at the hospital. She is too young to tell her story, if she has one, but if there is a mystery it may transpire. What a wonderful woman is Mrs. Conant, with all her social and domestic cares, to find time for so much love and good-will for strangers! I wish Tom knew more of his mother's work. He might aid her, and he is equal to great things. But she is afraid to cloud his young spirit with dark pictures, and she trusts me. Well, I am proud of the mother's confidence, and, if I can be worthy of it, I am sure to be led into noble work."

Robert Holt was the son of Scotch parents, and was related to Mrs. Conant on his mother's side. He had won high honors at Edinburgh, and had left the university with the reputation of being a clever polemic and a democrat. Everybody liked him, though everybody would not have copied his ways. He was brusque and aggressive in dispute, and toward his equals he was exacting; but toward his inferiors, and those who would need his aid, he was generous to a fault: he had the soul of a prince and the heart of a woman. He was, moreover, a man of wealth and leisure; he held political opinions which were considered advanced, and he was too straightforward and outspoken to tolerate the diplomat or the temporizer. He was earnest and sincere before all things.

Such a character might have fallen little short of petulance; and he was exacting at times, but he was too full of loving kindness to persist unduly in any course that might wound the feelings of others.

He has fallen asleep as we have discussed him.

Robert Holt, idealist and disputant, *au revoir*.

CHAPTER IV.

THE PLOT THICKENS.

A FEW afternoons later, Tom attended a reception at Lady D.'s at Bloomington House, and found her Ladyship exceedingly gracious.

"Here is Col. Lyons, Mr. Conant," she said, "who tells me that you spent Sunday at Brighton with your good mother, who ought to be here. The Professor has just left me, and I have some American friends whom you must meet. Oh! here they are."

Tom greeted Dr. Elmwood and Miss Winthrop; he had not met the young lady since Sunday, and, as if by common consent, they selfishly strolled away together.

"I was afraid I should lose you," said Tom, "I wanted to see you so much."

"Then I suppose you have something to tell me," was the rejoinder; "so many things may have happened since we met."

"No, I did not want to see you on business," was the laughing response. "But I have volunteered to guard you from the crush here. Will you permit me?"

"If it please you," answered the young lady, seeming at a loss for words.

Tom observed her embarrassed manner, and said, "You see I may be my own master for a few moments only. Lord Lester, the Governor-General of Canada, is here, and my father has set his heart on my paying my humble respects to him; but if I have to leave you, I hope I may be able to find you again."

"I see Mr. Marshall, our minister, and his daughters by the alcove yonder," observed Miss Winthrop; "let us join them."

Tom gave a reluctant assent, but he did not hurry forward, and, indeed, for the moment, Miss Winthrop did not press him to do so. Their conversation flowed freely enough now; but, need we relate, it interested them more than it would have done other people.

Later in the evening, several gentlemen were conversing together, and among them were Lord Lester and Mr. Marshall. The Professor, with Tom, joined them.

"Tom tells me you are coming to America," said Lord Lester, addressing the Professor. "I shall return within the month delighted, if I may welcome you to Canada."

"Our trip is as yet uncertain," said Dr. Conant, "and, though we shall not exactly be the guests, we are to be the companions of Lord Bolton, who goes to New York. I do not think it has been arranged to include Canada in our route, though I should like it much, if that is possible."

"Ah, that won't do," said his Lordship; "England can't afford to send out her best men for journeys of observation through America, which do not even include her own possessions. Canada has the most convenient steamboat and railroad services, and you are altogether without the excuses which did duty in former years for neglecting us."

"Oh, it is not neglect," interposed Tom.

"We are so sure of Canadian loyalty," remarked Mr. Holt, with a laugh.

"Yet, there was a good deal said about a separation of the colonies a few years ago," Mr. Marshall observed, somewhat mischievously.

"More on this side than in Canada," rejoined the Professor, " but Canadian independence was boldly and ably discussed, and found many sympathizers, even there."

"Oh, that was before the Washington Treaty," said Mr. Holt, "and while the Alabama claims were pending. There was a dangerous controversy between us and the States. At that time the peace which ruled was not likely to be lasting. A feeling prevailed largely in England that our North American possessions were not worth fighting for. The Irish Fenians hovered all along the Canadian border, and the question was asked in Canada with some trepidation, Can the Empire defend us? It was added, If England wants us to go we are ready."

"It was a very sickly feeling in Canada," said Lord Lester.

"At least, one Governor-General commended it," remarked Mr. Holt, significantly.

"But the Washington Treaty changed all that in both countries," said the Professor. "That was a great experiment, the resort to arbitration instead of to battle; to reason instead of to the blind rage of war and carnage. If the controversies, thus happily settled, had been allowed to drift, they would have culminated in war, and the two nations might have reduced each other to a third rate power."

"We had a good deal to swallow," said Lord Lester.

"There were concessions on both sides," observed Mr. Marshall.

"And the best evidence that, on the whole, the settlement was a wise one, is to be found in the conciliatory and satisfied mood, in which we discuss the whole subject to-day," interjected Dr. Elmwood, with spirit.

"All this history was made a little before your time, Tom," said Lord Lester, with good humor.

"I hope its good consequences may be lasting," rejoined Tom. "The thought of going to America incites me to become familiar with these topics."

"My dear Tom," urged Col. Lyons, "begin your work, by taking your first lesson, which so few Englishmen have learned, that going to Canada is a voyage to America, as well as going to New York. Canada is a fine country, with five millions of hardy and enterprising people, and after the States, is a land of magnificent promise. You should act upon the hint of Lord Lester, and visit it. No loyal Englishman having done so once will ever be disposed to throw the country off."

"And let me add," said Mr. Marshall, "that whether as a dependency of yours, or as an independent state, my countrymen will always rejoice in her progress towards wealth and power. She has a mission of freedom to fulfill by solving in her own way, and on American soil, the problem of British Parliamentary government."

When Tom joined the ladies, he was full of funny conceits as to the dangers he had escaped while among the politicians; but Lady D. told him he was only trying his 'prentice hand, and Miss Winthrop declared he had been so absorbed that she had found it impossible to attract his attention. Tom denied, however, having any political ambition, and in the best of spirits he took his leave.

We will not weary the reader with details of the adventure, which for the moment rescued from the jaws of death a man, a woman, and a child, and thus gratified the kindliness of Mrs. Conant, and whetted the appetite of Robert Holt for good works. Mrs. Conant, on her return from Brighton, found these people, of whom we have already spoken, at a private hospital, where they were supported by the beneficence of Holt. The man was deadly ill of fever; the woman, though stricken, was still able to aid in nursing him, and the child had been removed to a place of safety.

"The fever is malignant," the Doctor had said to Mrs. Conant; "you must not remain here nor come again, and the woman herself must be removed. The man is well cared for, and the presence of neither of you will do him good. He is quite unconscious."

The woman was inconsolable, but the Doctor's orders were obeyed. "Oh," she said, "it is a punishment for our sin." And she moaned like one in deep suffering. "You angel!" she would say to Mrs. Conant, "Why have you sheltered a wretch like me?" And then she would give herself up to sobs and lamentations. "He did it," she moaned with a convulsive shudder; "it was not in my heart to wrong the child. *Pauvre enfant*, I will tell the good lady before I die." She would continue her ravings and say, "Hush, I will not speak! he will hang if I betray him. He is so sick perhaps he will die, and then —— God have mercy!"

Mrs. Conant went to the parlor and saw the child—a sweet little girl of two years, who could not speak nor give any sign to aid in her identification. It had escaped the plague, it had been dressed in neat clothes, and was beautiful. Such eyes! though an infant's, full of sweetness and expression. The child clung to Mrs. Conant as if it had known her.

"The child has been wronged," said the nurse. "Do you think she belongs to those people?"

"Hush," said Mrs. Conant, "we must not say such things. But she *is* lovely," she added, "and we will try to protect her."

"It may be a mere superstition," said the nurse, "but I think the child inherits those eyes from her mother, who must have been a beautiful woman."

"You are silly," said Mrs. Conant, musingly, and she went back to the woman, who still talked and wandered.

"Will he die?" she asked.

"I hope not," was the gentle response.

"Ah, I knew it," continued the woman, "our path led to this in my dream. He was with me, but he had horns and a cloven foot, and he scoffed at my doubts and scruples. He said there was no rule of right and wrong for such as we, and that we should follow our inclinations and desires. That fearful night! The heavens were overcast with blackness. The lightnings blazed anon, and peal after peal the thunder rolled over the mountains. We climbed the crags, and were pricked by the thorns and terrified by the howling of the wild beasts. It was a dreadful dream. But we reached the summit, and beheld the deep cañon below, livid with heat and alive with groans, and yawning to receive us. The wages of sin is death," she continued, after a silence. "I was taught but did not heed that. Do I dream now? Do I rave?" she added, fixing her large dark eyes on Mrs. Conant, who stood, tearful, by her side; "my heart is heavy, but my mind is clear. Before it may be too late I must tell you, not the story of my life, which must be buried in shame, but the story of another life which mine has clouded. I did not mean it all," she said, sobbing hysterically; and after a pause, "no, no, not now! why do you press me? His eyes are upon me. He stands in the door. Oh! send him away. How he frightens me! Not now," she repeated, "but I will tell you all to-morrow."

With a few soothing words, Mrs. Conant took her leave, wearied and disappointed. She surmised that the proffered confidence related to the child, and she was not sure in what state the woman might be on the morrow. There were things to be done, but she knew Mr. Holt would attend to them. In the meantime, she would see the chaplain herself and then return to her home.

Mrs. Conant was reticent, and the Professor was too busy to be made the confidant of her charitable labors; but he interposed no obstacles, if he afforded her little aid. He was, nevertheless, proud to have given her a well-filled purse, and gratified at the fact that she went about doing good.

That night there came a note from the chaplain to say that the child was well, the woman delirious, and the man past all hope.

"How unfortunate," thought Mrs. Conant, "should the woman die without telling the story of the child! I felt sure from the first, of what I have never dared to say, that both the man and the woman are adventurers, and that the child has been spirited away from respectable parents. The woman's ravings suggest as much, and perhaps even other and darker crimes. Who can tell whence they have come? If they die without giving a sign, what means would be left of identification? Oh, what havoc vice makes with happiness! Somewhere in the wide world there are a frantic mother and a broken household mourning for this little innocent; and, perhaps, even the wrong-doers are the greatest sufferers, while sinking under their load of infamy and self-reproach into a miserable grave."

CHAPTER V.

THE AMERICAN COUSIN DAZZLES MY LORD.

Lord Bolton had just returned after a sojourn of two months in Paris. He had telegraphed a few friends to meet him that night in his rooms, in Piccadilly, and among them were Tom Conant and Robert Holt. His Lordship loved Tom's sprightly good nature and intelligence, and he admired Robert's varied accomplishments; while that gentleman's advanced views, and his readiness to maintain them, made him always an object of interest to the eccentric nobleman. His rooms were lighted by electric jets, the glare of which was softened by the fantastic ornaments of various and unique designs which served as lamps and decorations. Everything bespoke luxurious comfort and refinement.

A number of gentlemen were assembled, and as Tom entered, he found Lord Bolton in earnest conversation with Holt and Fred Cuthbert.

"I was saying to his Lordship," said Fred, with a drawl, "that he must have wasted his time in Paris. To have left London, in the height of the season for those frog-eating Frenchmen, was bad enough, but he has learned nothing—he can't tell us the name of the reigning *belle*, or recount the latest scandal."

"Perhaps he is reticent," remarked Tom, with a laugh. "He may prefer making his confession to the *confidante* of his choice."

"No," said Lord Bolton, with simulated irritation, "I did not follow the traditions of my young countrymen in the French capital, and I avoided society and dissipation. I was interested, but only as a spectator."

"Well, tell us what you saw, please," said the first speaker. "*Imprimis*, no doubt, that missing link, the American tourist, for whom there is never room enough and the price is never high enough."

"They are a queer lot, some of those travellers," said Lord Bolton, "and in the invasion of Paris by these people I have thought at times that the gay capital would altogether lose her identity."

"No doubt, some of those Americans who have just struck 'bonanzas' are queer folk," said Robert. "They suddenly acquire boundless wealth by some accident —and accidents of that kind are abundant in their country—and they have no judgment as to its use. They are like the *nouveaux riches* everywhere. Sudden wealth does not relieve vulgarity. I know a city where a few men grew fabulously rich in a night. They were equal to their fortunes, to the extent of taking care of them. They secured control of the enormous industry by which they had prospered. They controlled the agencies which manufacture opinion, and they created a speculative mania which engulfed alike the highest and the lowest. The whole community—the cautious lawyer, the pious parson, the prudent merchant, as well as the most thrifty and the most impoverished sons and daughters of toil, strained their credit, denied themselves necessaries, borrowed, or even begged, the means to buy what rose or fell at the beck of these newly-made millionaires; till that community, from the cellar to the garret, was ruined; and these men counted by hundreds of millions the spoils which their neighbors had lost. Soon some of them commenced to flaunt their vast acquisitions in the faces of the poor. They vied with each other, at home and abroad, in the vulgar display of money; they bought high offices, which they neglected and disgraced; they chartered special trains; built royal palaces, and corrupted for their purposes such influence as they could not crush or otherwise control. Is it strange that though their wealth was kingly their manners were boorish? If they were vulgar, there was excuse for them. Do we not, sometimes, see rich and educated men of our own country playing, according to their means, the same rôle? These men are not the outcome of democratic institutions. They are only possible among such extraordinary material developments as one sees in that wonderful country. *Ab uno disce omnes.*"

"Put a pin there, Bob," said his Lordship; "I have been thinking of all this, but I could not have said it. I want to hear the rest. I must stroll among my guests for a little while, but I will rejoin you."

"Now that he has gone," said Fred, "you may refresh yourself, and, during recess, tell us quietly, who these nabobs were, Holt?"

Tom, willing to rescue him, recited slowly,

> "Once in the flight of ages past,
> There lived a man, and who was he?
> Mortal! Howe'er thy lot be cast,
> That man resembled thee."

"If your muse sings of me," said Fred, "I would risk that my 'lot be cast' in the very midst of those frightful millions. And *apropos* of Americans, Holt," he continued, "as I don't worship those democratic people at home or abroad, you may be glad to know that I recognize exceptions to my rule. I met at a friend's last night some charming people, who called themselves Americans. But I fancy they owe a good deal to the education of schools and to travel, which they did not acquire at home. I always liked old Marshall and his daughters; but then, you know, they have lived mostly in England. The people I refer to are a Dr. Elmwood, of New York, and his charming niece, Miss Winthrop, of Boston. Winthrop, you know, is a good old English name, and, I believe, in America, it is the cognomen of a fine family."

Tom was intently reading an illustrated book, and Holt was amused to notice his apparent abstraction.

"The uncle is a thorough gentleman," Fred went on, "and Lawson, of our Embassy at Washington, told me that his grandfather was General Somebody, of the rebellion or revolution, or something of that sort, which Washington made after the apple-tree failed him. I had never heard of the apple-tree, and I had never supposed that Americans had grandfathers. But the young lady was charming. I cannot say that she is beautiful, but her sweetness and grace and a *je ne sais quoi* of good sense and good breeding quite won me. I did not ask the Parson, but I suppose there is no end to her wealth, and you know in regard to *that* I am not insured against the weakness which has so often befallen my sex."

"The American nation will be profoundly moved," said Holt, "when this news is wired across the water."

"Fancy the flaring headings," said Tom; "'An Aristocrat Caught!' 'Flirtation in High Life!' 'Another American Triumph!'"

"Oh, she's not an American," said Fred. "The Winthrops were English, and she has been educated on this side of the water."

"Nonsense!" growled Holt; "how many of the people are of English descent, with a British parentage as good as ours, whom you misrepresent and deride because you fear that, following their example, the masses in this country may become as powerful as their brethren in that? If you would give them here the blessings they enjoy there, the masses of England, imitating the masses in America, would multiply vastly the power and prestige of their country."

"I shall leave you, gentlemen," said Tom, "till his Lordship returns. It is not fair to waste so much eloquence in his absence."

At that moment they were handed a message from Lord Bolton, asking them to join him in the library at ten, at which hour he would be free to receive them.

"That means business," said Cuthbert; "you must dilute your splendid oration for the simplest digestion to assimilate, Bob."

"Bah!" said Tom, turning away; "why must you say disagreeable things?"

The guests were dispersed in little knots about the room. Some were discussing the latest novel, others the latest play. A young author, who had just electrified London, was in the middle of a distinguished group, and wit and repartee, if we may so distinguish, were holding high holiday. On his right, under an alcove, mellow with shaded lights, stood the great monarch of the English stage; and his *vis-à-vis* was the eldest son of the legitimate drama in America. Lord Lester and Mr. Marshall were on the right, and the Professor and Dr. Elmwood, who had come late, were on the left; and the question was, how to arrest the downfall of Shakespeare, which seemed imminent, and restore the ballet and the sensuous stage to their proper place after the legitimate drama. It was admitted that much depends on the actor's conception of his work and upon his genius in the interpretation of it.

"The world is running mad after display," the Professor had said. "The beautiful thoughts of the olden time are supplanted by the beautiful ankles and the realistic scenes which the stage puts on exhibition to-day. Once the stage roused men to great deeds by the presentation of great thoughts. Virtue found an ally in the drama, and a private life that fell short was only condoned by great gifts. To-day the popular favorite wins if she is graceful or beautiful, or, above all, if she is known to be a professional beauty, or to have transfixed a royal heart. The world must be amused, but amusements that are not instructive have no place among the agencies of good works."

"There is force in what you say, Professor," said the great English actor, "but the evil is not local. My American friend will tell you that in his country the legitimate drama struggles and wanes, and that scenic display is the goddess of the hour."

"The stage cannot tread the higher paths if the people will not sustain it there," said the American. "The tendency of all amusements is the same. The old-fashioned ballads and their sweet airs have fallen into neglect, though more heavenly music was never rendered; and now our favorites are snatches from Patience and Iolanthe."

"All this decadence," said Lord Lester, "may be traced to the upheavals of modern social life—to the democratic sub-soiling which is constantly raising the lowest *stratum* and imparting its clammy chill to the surface. You can only maintain the standard of refinement in communities that are not over-weighted with the elements of degradation. You must not elevate ignorance too rapidly, or you drag intelligence down to its level. You may vitiate popular taste exactly as you degrade popular opinion, by giving vulgarity a jurisdiction which, in the nature of things, it cannot comprehend."

"I fear your position is more plausible than defensible," said Mr. Marshall. "I do not know how far the stage is supported by the lower stratum. There are multitudes who have not, as yet, been raised to the surface; and as to this question of vitiated taste, it remains to be proved that it is not inherent in the upper classes. We are all living in great haste. Men are absorbed in the bustle of affairs. They patronize the amusements for rest and relaxation. The day's excitement has wearied them. They are in no mood to study serious things, and they go rather where they are invited to laugh than to think."

"Nero was a cultivated man, but Rome was profligate. Complaints against the popular taste are not new to history," said Dr. Elmwood; "only a sound education can really elevate it or maintain the standard when once it is established. There is great need of reform and vast room for individual effort. We shall have gained much when we have agreed upon what we want, and can then clear the deck for action. In the meantime, the stage itself might do much of the work; it should labor to create good taste, instead of catering to a bad one."

A pleasant evening was far spent, and most of the guests had departed. The old-fashioned library was aglow with light and warmth, and Lord Bolton had gathered a few choice spirits about him. Wine and the fragrant cigar were there doing duty, and Tom was chiding Mr. Cuthbert, who had grown impulsive and loquacious, and who felt moved to sing

"We won't go home till morning."

Holt had not forgotten his theme, and had more to say if the hint had been given him, but his Lordship "took the word," as the French say.

"I don't think your picture would have been overdrawn, Holt, if I had allowed you to finish it," he said; "you always startle me a little with your strong words and your radical views. You can't expect me to be a democrat, though, thanks to you, no doubt, I can't help leaning that way."

"No, no, let me go on," he exclaimed, as Holt seemed about to interrupt him. "I know what it would mean for me and my class. But it may be a fair question, why should we be pampered? Why should the poor delve and we idle in affluence? If it were my clear duty, I could lay down my rank. Conscious of what is duty, there are many of my class who would follow suit. But would the State profit by this? And how would our degradation exalt the poor?"

"My dear Lord Bolton," ejaculated Holt, with warmth, "I have not proposed such a thing!"

"Oh, you are very kind, no doubt, and would do nobody harm; but your doctrines lead up to that or they mean nothing. That is a grand doctrine—the equality of man. But hereditary distinctions must go when that comes." He paused, and then exclaimed: "How many men are my superiors but for the maintenance of these class distinctions? The ennobled class must think of these things. We are not called to act now, but we ought to form intelligent and defensible opinions. You are young yet, Holt, and have no titles to throw away, but how wouldst thou like to sell all that thou hast and give to the poor? What a strange *mélange* is the French Republic! How the old traditions bear against the democratic faith. '*Egalité*,' but the noble confronts the citizen at every turn. '*Liberté*,' yet old restrictions are not yet removed. '*Fraternité!*'—look at the virulence of the press and the deadly malice that pervades discussions. Are they better or worse for the new *régime*? I don't know, though I am trying to study them. Has the Revolution, that great reaction against centuries of abuse, done its work? In '30 and '48 and '71 had it ended? Pardon me, gentlemen, but these things weigh upon me, and to whom should I speak but to my friends? In Paris, there was no devotion to equality, in the ostentatious display of wealth among the favored sons of the model American Republic. They had not come over as propagandists, to teach the world that all men were born free and equal. They outstripped the Shah in extravagance, and their diamonds outshone the stars of the firmament in splendor. They counted their wealth by millions. They must have hoarded the gold of the people—the hard earnings of the poor—and there must be some startling wrong that makes such exactions possible! If wealth is to be hoarded in a few hands, are these *nouveaux riches* better than an ancient nobility?"

"Much learning hath made thee mad," said Cuthbert, interrupting; but he continued:

"Gentlemen, do I surprise you? Did you fancy I only thought of revels and sports? I have been taught the maxim, *noblesse oblige*, and have been thinking over grave questions, though I have not solved them. I see difficulties both ways."

"Holt shall help you," said Cuthbert.

"Yes, but not to-night," said his Lordship, gravely. "I turn to a brighter side of my Paris picture. There is an inner circle of American life in Paris into which I have never penetrated. I have met delightful Americans here, but I thought their associations had been English. A dozen of my friends married lovely American wives, but they had for the most part been educated here. And when I met these noisy, showy people in France I instinctively avoided the whole race. How much I have lost has only now been revealed to me. One night, I met a gentleman at the American Minister's, whose conversation entertained and delighted me. He told me he was in Europe for the first time; his wife and sister were in Paris with him, and the next day he asked me to dine with them. I met a large party, and was sumptuously entertained. I never enjoyed myself more thoroughly; my host excelled; his wife was a perfect hostess, and the sister was the finest woman I had ever seen. The whole evening was to me a social and intellectual treat and I have rarely enjoyed myself more. In the course of conversation, I acknowledged bluntly that I was glad to find myself at an exclusively American entertainment.

"Had I never been in America? the hostess asked me, and had I never known Americans?

'Yes,' I answered, 'I had a few American friends in London.'

'Oh, they are really English, I suppose,' she said.

'They are generally residents with us,' I admitted.

'But you must come to America,' said both my host and hostess.

"I admitted that it was my wish and my intention to do so. There was a shout of welcome for me, in advance, from the whole delightful party. They promised me no end of attention, for myself and my friends, and they would all be at home next month to receive us. I said I could not speak for my friends, but I would myself try and arrange to go over soon. May I depend upon you, Tom, to hasten the expedition? The Professor will be responsible for us. We must have Holt for spokesman, and Cuthbert to do the disagreeable without which Englishmen in a foreign country would not be recognized."

Tom thought things might be arranged. Fred was asleep by this time, and Robert vouchsafed no remark.

"But to return to my dinner," said Lord Bolton; "my hostess asked me if I had seen many Americans in Paris." I answered, 'yes, but mostly in the streets and Boulevards.' 'They make some show and perhaps some noise,' she said, apologetically. But a great deal that is unfair is said of these people. They are sometimes vulgar, but they are not unkind, and if they are ostentatious, they are generous. They are not all millionaires, but they have been blessed with thrift; they can't stay at home in the hot cities, and it is as easy to spend the summer in Europe as at the extravagant watering places of their own country. They measure blessings by what they cost, because they have not a better standard. They know, for example, that pictures are evidences of refinement; but how should they know the difference between a mere daub and a work of genius? Many of them have grown suddenly rich without any refined ideas of the use of money. And after all, they are only a fraction of the Americans who travel. They attract attention, and you judge us all by their ostentation. Americans generally here are polite and cultivated people. But of course this noisy class provokes prejudice. You have examples of the same fortunates in England, but they don't occur in swarms as with us. American vulgarity, indeed! What do you think a Shoreditch cabman would do, going to bed poor at night and awaking the master of millions? He would build a castle, first—rival Buckingham Palace, or Marlboro' House, that he might be master of a mansion—in the like of which, and in its humbler rooms, he had waited for charity crusts in his boyhood. You will find vulgar Englishmen enough here, but they are gentlemen at home; that's only their traditional character in a foreign country; but you do not find Englishmen of the same class as our tourists with the same fortunes.

'Far from being ashamed of my countrymen, because they are vulgar, I am inclined to pity yours, who are tied to poverty and have not the means to air their vulgarity at foreign courts."

"That was an eye-opener," said Fred, who was awake now, "and, my Lord, you recite with wonderful precision; you were born for the stage."

"Thank you," said my Lord in good humor, "I half think I have surpassed myself. Well, these excellent people will go to America with us, and you will see if I have been too cheaply charmed."

All London, for a week, had been chanting the praises of Professor Conant's first speech in Parliament. It had displayed great power in the House, and had struck the popular key-note in the country. It was a masterly arraignment of his opponents on the dangers of their policy and the shortcomings of their latest administration. It was what ought to have been said before, and just what the popular ear had been longing for. The friendly newspapers recognized its worth, though they had not been prepared for its oratorical completeness. They saw in Dr. Conant the coming man, and it was time to see a firmer hand grasp public affairs, for all interests, at home and abroad. Economy must be rigorously enforced, and the British lion must growl, if the British people would be respected by foreign nations. Not that Dr. Conant had spoken in this strain, but the leaders of opinion used hackneyed battle cries, and rode over country with a loose reign when popular enthusiasm was to be aroused. But the adversary was on the alert, and feared the speech had been imprudent and dangerous. Great learning, eloquence of diction, oratorical power—all these were conceded; but nations were ruled by concession and compromise, and not by rhetoric, however polished, or logic, however exact. But these deprecations fell upon unwilling ears. The people still heard the graceful periods, the pathetic appeals, and the wise admonitions of the orator, and from that moment he became their idol. He had won his spurs in the House and the nation claimed him as a leader.

While all this was going on in the city, a very warm and pardonable interest was felt in the Conant mansion. Mrs. Conant had never been too well reconciled to her husband's entering public life. She knew that political and parliamentary duties would sadly encroach on the Professor's home-life, and Tom had thought that his father's studious habits and quiet tastes would be sadly broken in upon by the exactions and excitements of active political duties. But the die was cast, the prize was won, and doubts and regrets were forgotten. Mrs. Conant confessed that she received congratulations upon her husband's success with *assumed* indifference, though her heart was full of interest and pride; but Tom was outspoken at all times, and declared without reserve that he would rather be the son of his father than heir to the proudest earldom in the Kingdom.

The Doctor himself was worn with the great labor of preparation and the exhaustion of long speech, and, as he said, was "laid up a few days for repairs." He had gained a great success, to which, however, he always felt himself equal; and he was thankful. If he was destined to higher honors, he would strive to bear them meekly and well; but if he knew himself, his highest ambitions were not personal; he would be gratified by successful service to his country and his kind. He had been overwhelmed by congratulations, which were grateful to him, and by hints of higher work to which he must shortly be called. He was ready for greater burdens, but he knew they would detain him still more from his favorite studies and his sweet domestic life. The soft strains of "Home, Sweet Home," were heard in an adjoining room, and he knew that his wife was recalling the melody.

"Yes, darling," he said, and the tears filled his eyes, "let it ever be 'Home, Sweet Home!' What are these huzzas and plaudits but the changing breath of an hour? Love and rest abide only by one's hearthstone."

CHAPTER VI.

A VOICE FROM THE TROSSACHS.

AT breakfast, one morning, Tom received a dainty little note, addressed "Capt. Thomas Conant, —— Guards, Belmont House, May Fair." And that gentleman read aloud the words following:

Cox's Hotel,
Jermyn St., ——, 18—

My Dear Capt. Conant:

We have just returned from Scotland, where we have been visiting friends, and where everybody is wild about your father's great speech in the House of Commons last week. My uncle says it recalls the days of Burke and Sheridan, and would you mind if I tell you that he added Webster, too?

I read every word of it by a Trossachs' lamp light, and though I am only a girl, and I dare say did not understand it all, I thought it magnificent, like Macaulay. I could not sleep for hours, and I did not wonder that the people were roused and electrified. I wish I could have heard the rich tones as they fell upon the enchanted ears of the listeners. What a God-given gift is speech! And except that their work remains, how inferior is the painter or the sculptor to the great masters of eloquence! My uncle is calling out that my letter will be too long. But you won't misunderstand me, Capt. Conant. You will forgive my enthusiasm over the great event which has electrified a nation, but in which I am chiefly concerned with what it brings to my friends. Surely Dr. Conant is pleased with his great triumph, and Mrs. Conant will regard hers as the lot which only falls to few women—while her devoted son will not misinterpret the interest and the friendship which move me to write this.

With kindest love to your father and mother, and regards to yourself,

     Yours sincerely,
       AGNES WINTHROP.

"Oh, she is a good girl," said Mrs. Conant; "I wish you could have seen more of Dr. Elmwood, dear; I think them charming people."

The Professor said he had met Dr. Elmwood several times, and had found him a man of good breeding and of enlightened views. "It was no surprise to me, as it seems to have been with some of our friends, to meet an accomplished gentleman from America, because I knew he was as likely to be found there as in the most polished European society. The prevalence of sudden wealth in the large American cities, to an extent not known in other countries, brings the rough class to the surface, and it will require a generation to refine them; but there is a charming and necessarily exclusive society in America, equal in all the essentials of good breeding to anything you will find on this side of the water, and it bears as large a proportion to the whole population as does refined society here; while you see influences disturbing the lower strata, the masses, and setting before them the incentives to improve themselves and elevate their children, in a degree unknown to us."

"Miss Winthrop is a lovely girl," said Mrs. Conant. "She is a child yet, but she has the tact of a woman and the information and culture of mature years. This is a noble little letter she has written, and we must waive ceremony and call upon them this very morning."

"I am disengaged," said the Professor. Tom said nothing, but perhaps he thought, they had forgotten that the dear little note had been written to him. So they paid a morning call at the dingy old English Hotel, to find their friends at home, and delighted to receive them. The Professor was the hero, and the young lady was full of kindness and compliments. Mrs. Conant, too, was remembered with the gentlest and most undemonstrative flattery. And Tom, who might have been forgotten but for little Miss Winthrop's ready tact, was made the happiest of the morning callers.

"I like this dingy old hotel," said Dr. Elmwood to the Professor, looking round at the capacious and well-furnished rooms.

"You generally find the best people here," said the Professor. "The late proprietor was a remarkable man and an advanced spiritualist. He used to tell strange stories of his experiences. In his time, Wilson, the great apostle of Spiritualism, made his home here. It was in this room that Lord Brougham and Sir David Brewster held their memorable investigations. It was said that Brougham was staggered at first by what he saw, but Sir David was consistently orthodox. I think they both agreed at last to report in a sense adverse to the pretensions of Wilson."

Dr. Elmwood, who was greatly interested in what he had seen in London, called it the survival of the seven wonders of the world. And, manifestly, he wanted to talk about it. To him, it was the great centre of thought, of boundless wealth and fabulous development. There was want of taste, there were November fogs and smoke; but where else do you encounter the traditions, the antiquities, Dick Whittington, Prince Hal, Queen Bess, Charles the First, and Cromwell? It was with a strange emotion, he said, that an American descendant of Englishmen trod for the first time the old soil. In all the busy throng about him there might not be one of his kith or kin: but, for the nonce, he had gone back to the musty ages when his fathers occupied where he was now a reverent stranger. He had stood at the tomb of Napoleon in the *Hotel des Invalides*, in Paris, and while a thoughtless multitude chattered around, he was over awed in the great presence. He heard the clangor of arms, the shouts of battle from Austerlitz, Marengo, and Waterloo, and, as if to recall still earlier conflicts, there seemed to fall upon his ear the echoes of that voice, "Soldiers! from these pyramids the deeds of forty centuries look down upon you!" So to him, in Westminster, the dead past was animate with the living memory of deeds. His imagination peopled the chambers of death, and re-enacted the historical activities of the past. A Londoner is open to the misfortune of regarding all such thoughts with the familiarity that breeds contempt; but they are sacredly enshrined in the heart of the American, who is capable of reverent emotions, and who knows the history of England and understands his own.

As Mrs. Conant rose to go, Tom proposed a drive in the park; but the Professor pleaded an engagement, and finally it was arranged that, as Miss Winthrop preferred to walk, she and Tom should stroll together. "I like to be self-reliant," she said to Tom's mother. "Some of my English young lady friends are half-scandalized at my original views; but I never took kindly to a chaperon."

"You can't come to harm with my Tom to guard you," said Mrs. Conant, proudly; and the young people sauntered toward an aimless destination, each conscious only of the other's presence, and both caring only, if the truth must be told, to be left to themselves. To that extent, it was a natural, but not of necessity a very serious feeling, and might have been shared by dozens of their young friends, who only occupied a half-interested, and half-indifferent relation to each other.

"You received my note this morning?" she asked. "Was it in bad taste for a little girl to feel so much interested in a great man? Uncle was doubtful if I should write it, because he was not sure of the customs here. But I felt an irresistible desire to share my joy with you all, and I said, What is the difference between telling him what I would say if I saw him, and writing the same thing in a note? I hope I did not shock you, Capt. Conant."

"You delighted us all, Miss Winthrop, with your great kindness, and you honored me most by addressing me."

"Then let it pass for the right thing," said Miss Winthrop; "one does not know always where to 'draw the line' among the customs of a strange country."

"We were pleased for my father's sake," said Tom, "but we had as much faith in him before the great speech, as we had afterwards. We loved him neither more nor less; and, as to his distinctions, he had won honors in other fields before he entered Parliament."

"I have a great veneration for the English House of Commons," said his fair companion, "the first body of gentlemen in the world. I was taught that at school in my own country, and I hope I am not the less an American, because I learned that the British Parliament affords one of the broadest fields for the exercise of a noble human effort. To have excelled in the ancient halls, that have echoed with the eloquence of Pitt, and Fox, and Burke, and Sheridan, seems wonderful to me, in these degenerate days, when eloquence is so rare a gift, and popular fervor is so slow to kindle; but I see you laugh, and I know I am beyond my depth; my uncle says young girls are such talkers."

"Pray don't excuse yourself," said Tom, "for talking well. I often feel it would be a great boon to know what to say. I should envy your gifts if I were not so proud to see you exercise them, and only second to graceful speech is a facile pen. Your note was charming."

"Do you remember where Falstaff says 'No more o' that Hal, an' thou lovest me?'" She had not intended to make the occasion for him, but what man would not have thought of it? And yet he was not precipitate, but let it pass, and, looking earnestly into her face, said: "I hope you have not written me your last note, and I also hope that I may be permitted to write you when I cannot see you. May I?" he asked in a low voice; and after a long pause, during which she returned his earnest look, she answered: "Great occasions may excuse some divergence, but we must observe the rules in steady weather."

"How much I wish you could be in America when I am there," he said; "it would be so jolly to meet such a friend in a strange country."

"What is your object in going?" she asked abruptly; "Is it fun, or information? Is Mr. Cuthbert a friend of yours? He told me he was to be one of your party. I do not think he will lead you to deep study. Would you heed a real friend, who would love to serve you? The son of Professor Conant will have great opportunities in America. Fashion will open wide her doors, but literature, art, science, all the rational agencies and economies of life will gladly contribute to your store if you find time to encourage them. You are startled at such views from me, but I have been a little trained in these matters. I must tell you more of my people before you go. They all know you now, and I have a darling brother, who will be eager to meet and welcome you when you arrive. Boston, you will find like an English city; it abounds in wealth and culture, but society is quiet there. New York is more mercurial and versatile; but you will see for yourself. It is worth your while to make America a study. I know this from my brother. He says young Englishmen go over for 'a spree,' and neglect their opportunities of observation. Avoid that, for your own sake. I want you, and you ought, to understand my country as well as your own."

"You shall teach me," said Tom, "now and here."

"Are you candid?" was her response, "or do you trifle with me? I have heard, though I do not believe it, that a rational confidence is impossible between a man and a woman. Is that true? Are you to verify it this morning?"

"Upon my word," said Tom, "I listen, with the deepest interest to all you say, and I will follow your advice, but you amaze me with the breadth of your views, and the apparent maturity of your thought."

"Are you candid, again? Oh, perhaps I am precocious," she said, "or it may be that unusual interest has developed unusual powers."

"Are you interested in me, Miss Winthrop?" Tom awkwardly rejoined.

"Why ask me a question which my actions have answered?" said the young lady, archly.

"Your interest is reciprocated, my dear Miss Winthrop."

"Ah, now we are approaching forbidden ground," said the lady, as she pointed to an impassable barrier in front of them, which they were nearing. "The poor Heidelberg school-girl may need a chaperon after all, unless you promise to be very good, and only say such things as a school-girl ought to hear. I am going back to Germany in a few days, and when we have to say 'good-bye' there should be no blush, or pang, born of imprudent confidences, or premature avowals. Another year at school! And in that time the world must be a sealed book to me!"

"But may I not hope?" said Tom passionately.

"We will return," said Miss Winthrop, "wiser and better for the experiences of the morning." And so, at the door of the old hotel, they parted as they had met, in good spirits—Tom to seek his rooms, and to be engrossed in his meditations, and little Miss Winthrop to hide her emotions as she stood with pretended unconcern at the door.

On her return from the hotel that morning, Mrs. Conant found a note from Robert Holt, which agitated and alarmed her. It related to her *protegés* at the hospital. The man, as Mrs. Conant knew, had died some days before of the fever. The unfortunate woman had breathed her last the previous night. Both had remained unconscious or delirious to the last. The woman sometimes had raved about a crime and a confession, but all attempts to obtain information from her had failed, and she died with her secret, such as it was, locked in her poor, stricken heart. Holt was himself ill, but he had provided for such service as remained to be rendered. The child was well, and would be further cared for. Mr. Holt begged his aunt not to trouble herself, as there was nothing she could do. Above all things, she must not go to the hospital, nor visit him, as his physician entertained fears that he might have contracted the fever there; but to provide against the worst, he must put his house in order, and would make ample provision for the wants of the child.

"There is nothing to show," the letter said, "that this child was not born of these parents. The woman spoke French as well as English. Did they come from France? I believe the child is of gentle blood, but where are her friends, and how can we find them? The child's life will be blighted if it grows up as the acknowledged offspring of vulgarity and vice. Can we keep her secret? Or ought we not to advertise her story in hope of tracing her friends? I am irritable, and these things worry me. In a day or two, when I am well again, you will let me call and talk to you. It all seems to me of so much importance, that I want to take the Professor into my confidence."

"Robert is right," mused Mrs. Conant, "my husband must advise us. But in the meantime, the poor boy is ill, and I must go to him. Is it safe? I have found myself a hundred times impervious to contagion, and I don't believe Robert is stricken with any contagious disease. It may be only a simple fever, or more likely it may be a false alarm. Even if there were danger, I must go. And yet, perhaps, that would mean danger to our little daughter, my husband's darling and my own. But this letter was written in the early morning. Hours have intervened. The conditions may have changed— he may be better or worse. I must see." In the afternoon there came a message from Robert again. He was better and apprehended no further trouble. He would pay his respects on the morrow. At that moment there arose a great noise as of an earthquake from the dining-room below. "That is a frolic, indeed," thought Mrs. Conant; "that's Tom's way of entertaining his little sister," and the child, who had escaped from both Tom and the nurse, ran wildly to her mother for protection.

"Oh, Tom," said his mother, "how can you tease her so?" The child from the shelter of its mother's arms, regarded him with defiance, and cried out, "Do it again, Tom."

"You see," he said, "she has not been teased against her will, mother. She is father's child. How little she resembles you! It follows that she is not a beauty in the esthetic sense; but to me her strong, lithe little form, with its romping grace and poetry of motion, is superior to all conventional beauty, and then her boundless good nature and joyous spirits make her the jolliest of little girls with whom to kick up a row. Then look at her face, the red pouting lips, made on purpose to kiss, the honest gray eyes, with arched brows—that nose is father's own—and the whole likeness, except that it is a smaller type, is so exact, that I often laugh over it."

"Oh yes, she is like her father in looks, in disposition, in everything," said Mrs. Conant; "but, sometimes, I think her side face is like yours, and, you know, they used to say you resembled me, Tom. It was a poor compliment to you, perhaps, but do you know, I used to be proud of it. I don't know that I wouldn't be so to this day. She is as mischievous as you used to be, at any rate, and in your most boisterous moods you were more noisy than your mother, and she is like you there again; and I may say for you both, that when your attention is arrested, by anything touching, or pathetic, you are full of self-denial, and as gentle and sympathetic as a nun. But I suppose the more aggressive and masculine traits, would be a tower of strength in more trying times, and when rougher work is to be done. You will soon go away from me, Tom, and it will be a great trial to part with you, though I know it will be in the way of duty as well as of pleasure; but a mother's love is selfish, let the poets sing as they may."

"Oh, I shall not be gone long, and I shall come back to you laden with tales of the unknown land,—and it is a land of mystery, of great resources, of vast possibilities, and of a future that may some day outshine the splendors of all climes and countries. I hope I may have time, as I am sure I have the inclination, to make myself acquainted with all I see. You, my dear little mother, will miss me, I know, but you will always feel sure of my love and my prayers. What a home I leave, and what a mother! What have I ever done to be worthy of them? But I have an ambition so to labor in the days to come, that honors may befall me in my country's service; that some day it may be fairly said of me, that I left the world not unworthy of my family and its fame."

Holt called the next morning, and found Mrs. Conant

with the Professor, waiting for him. He said he had been ill the morning before, and the doctor's fears added to his discomfort, but he had grown speedily better, and a good night's sleep had restored him to his wonted good health. He had been worried lately and had naturally felt the wear and tear.

"Well, you seem to be all right now," said the Professor. "After what your aunt told me, I waited for you. Indiscriminate charity often leads to embarrassment, and your poor *protégés* did not gain much by your benevolence, I am sure. If they had been relieved through the recognized channels, something might have been got from the woman, to shed light on your present darkness. It might have been found out that the poor child was hers, or the story of its abduction might have been told."

"I don't think so," said Mrs. Conant. "The vagaries of the woman were the result of disease and would have displayed themselves all the same, to whatever influence she had been subjected. But it is a sad story we have to tell, and there is a fearful darkness all around us."

"There is left us only the child," said Robert, "and that is so innocent and sprightly in the midst of its misfortunes, that it nestles strangely into my heart. It would be a sad blight on its life, to grow up as the acknowledged offspring of these unknown outcasts. Secrecy is the only safeguard, and the sad story is known only to us three. My faith is strong in the idea that they abducted the child from respectable parents, who, probably, were expected to pay a ransom; but I have no proof. The child itself is evidence to me that it was born to better things. It has nothing in common with those vagrants. But there is not a shred of evidence to speak of better days. The woman let fall enough to suggest that the child had been abducted, though she fell short of any statement. She raved of a crime, she promised a confession, and once, in her wanderings, she declared that she had never intended to do the child harm. She spoke of him, who had misled her, as a monster, and she seemed to have a conscience, and, at times, some refined feeling. But if the child has friends, we should hear of them. The newspapers ought to be full of the outrage; if it has been stolen, the crime must have occurred within a few weeks. If this were a romance, a clever novelist would find some family mark, locket, or needlework, or a convenient scar to serve as a means of identification. But we are absolutely in the dark, and the child is too young to aid us. The woman spoke French like a native. It is not likely that she learned the language in London. Had they come from a foreign country, Belgium or France perhaps? Might the abduction have occurred in one of the provinces, and the news not have reached the metropolitan journals? Suppose, first, that the parents had been travelling, and that the child had been left with this woman, as nurse, and then that the man had seduced the woman from her duty, and the parents had not yet returned——. Ah me! how could they? all that is absurd. They must have left friends, who would have noticed the child's disappearance, and the alarm would have been given. I speculate upon all this night and day. While the woman lived there was still hope, but now the darkness grows thicker, hour by hour. I am weary and disheartened, and I brood over the calamity as if it were, as it really is, my own."

"The misfortunes of life are distributed among millions of sufferers," said the Professor, "and the duty of the charitable is to alleviate want and woe; but while our benevolence is God-like, and our sympathies heaven-born, we cannot personally take upon ourselves the load of suffering of all these poor multitudes. That has only been done once; unaided human nature is not equal to it."

"Oh, I know what you mean, and you are right," said Holt, "but my sympathies are exceptional, and irresistible. I have tried to be reasonable, but I am the helpless creature of uncontrollable impulse. Sometimes when I am alone, in the shadows of the wee sma' hours, I seem to hear a sublime voice urging me on, as if some great work were underlying all this mystery. I am not superstitious, and I know better, yet, in my calmest moments, I would not dare withdraw a hair's breadth from the line I have laid down for myself. You may think me demented, but you must deal with me as I am, and who knows but that child, and these events, are in some way connected with my destiny."

"This is dreadful, Robert," said Mrs. Conant. "You suffer from a strange prostration; perhaps change of scene would restore you."

"Well, no," said Holt, "I do not act an unwilling part. When once I have settled upon my course it will be easy enough. *Aunt, I must adopt that child as my own!*"

"Nonsense," said the Professor; "that course would expose you to ridicule and possibly to scandal. But we have talked enough about this to-day. The riddle will some day solve itself, and perhaps unexpectedly. Meantime, you are right, the affair should be kept as quiet as possible; and, perhaps, in a few days, we shall find ourselves guided as to the course you should pursue. So off, now, with your aunt, for a drive and recreation, and I will go to an engagement for which, I fear, I am late."

CHAPTER VII.

"THE JOLLIEST TRIP EVER PROJECTED."

AFTER a sojourn of two or three days in London, Lord Bolton had returned to Paris, and had spent the week in the society of his American friends. His interest in them had increased as he knew them better, and they——, how could they be indifferent to the attentions of a man of Lord Bolton's parts and station? He had written Tom to get his leave, and to muster friends for an early voyage. His Lordship spoke kindly of the Professor, and of his late distinction, and expressed the belief that he would be speedily called to higher duties; but he hoped that they would not interfere with this American trip, upon which he had set his heart. "The Professor must go," he wrote; "who more than he, after this harassing session, needs change of scene and relaxation? I know there will be strong pressure brought to detain him by some of his friends, as well as by the agents of party; but I leave you to plead our cause as best you may, and I am sure not vainly. We shall have the addition of this charming party of Americans, if we are ready to go by the same steamer. I think I told you who they are, but they have been recruited by a young couple who were in Switzerland when I was here before. The lady is from the States, and is of remarkable beauty and refinement; the gentleman is of

Canadian birth, but of French descent, and is the head of a family of the old *noblesse*, of which there are still some scions in Canada. They are people of large wealth, I believe, and they reside in Quebec, the classic scene of Wolfe's conquest, and the only walled town in America. The lady wears an expression of sadness, which, to my mind, is not complimentary to her handsome lord, whom, nevertheless, her large blue eyes seem always to follow with nervous adoration, which she does not disguise. He met her, while he was 'sowing his wild oats,' in the capital of his fatherland. I am told that these young French provincials of rank and fortune are both wicked and extravagant in the world of fashion here, and are much in request in some circles. At all events, these people married here, only a few years ago, and they will be our *compagnons de voyage*. Could we not catch the fine steamer *Alaric*, and sail on the fifteenth proximo, from Liverpool, with our friends for New York? You will, I am sure, forgive this trouble, as you are the only friend who has leisure, whom I could trust with a delicate mission."

"It never rains, but it pours," thought Tom; which wise and original observation was explained by the fact that he had just met Dr. Elmwood in the Strand, who had told him that Miss Winthrop would probably go home with him by the same steamer, on account of recent occurrences in her family. That night Tom telegraphed to Lord Bolton, that Col. Lyons, Fred Cuthbert, and himself were ready; but, that his father and Robert Holt could not answer for a day or two.

"Tell them not to spoil the jolliest trip ever projected," was wired back, in reply, and Tom, weary with his day's work, retired early. But it was not decreed that the trip should be spoiled, or that my Lord should be disappointed. The Professor had managed it by promising to return early, and Robert, by the assurance of Mrs. Conant that she would look after the baby. As to that very young lady, it had been agreed that for the present her secret should be kept, although the necessity was apparent that the nurse should be more or less trusted. Robert had confidence in her, and kept her in his service. Cautious advertisements addressed to "the parents of a lost child," were inserted in the French and English metropolitan journals, and we may as well anticipate the future by avowing that they led to no results; nobody thought of America as a possible field of inquiry. Meantime, the infant grew and prospered, and was not even interested in the photographs which its foster-father insisted on taking with him across the water, or conscious of the emotion with which, on the eve of his journey, he bade her a tender farewell.

Tom took Dr. Elmwood to the House of Commons one night, where they heard the veteran Prime Minister summing up the work of the session. Everything, but the conduct of the opposition, which he mildly regretted, was painted *couleur de rose*. The administration of the year had apparently paved the way for the millennium to be rung in; abroad, peace prevailed, where war had threatened; at home, except that there was some obstruction in the House, and some turbulence outside of it, contentment and prosperity prevailed. "A loyal Englishman may safely leave the country in such hands," said the Doctor. "The House will be dull after this. You shall first point out to me a few of the distinguished men in the House, whom I have not met, and then we will repair to my rooms, where we shall find friends, who will be glad to welcome us."

"Do you see the benignant face of that old gentleman," said Tom, "who is speaking to my father just now? He is the great leader of the Peace party, and the finest orator in England."

"Oh, I know him well," said the Doctor, "his name is a household word in America."

"Well, he has a difficult path to tread, sometimes, and one could not subscribe to all his teaching; but I would rather enjoy his reputation than sit with the peers of the realm. And that nervous young man who sits opposite him, near the table, is Lord North, a cousin of Bolton's. He leads a Tory faction of the House. He has been making rather a fiery record here, but his industry and pluck, and above all, his long and noble lineage, will bring him to the front, when his time comes. That tall, graceful member standing on the right of the speaker's chair, is Mr. O'Halloran, the leader of the Irish Home Rulers. He and his party have been the 'obstructives' of the session, claiming that the way to get concessions from John Bull is to bully and annoy him. It is our national calamity, this Irish question, and Ireland is the avenging Nemesis of England, as you well know. But, I believe, there are few Englishmen who would not be glad to do her justice, if they could see their way without pulling the temple about their heads."

"After all, I know these men by appearance and reputation," said the Doctor, "but I had not recognized them in the distant gaslight."

"Heigho," said Tom, "I am tired and prosy. Let

us go;" and the two gentlemen walked rapidly in the direction of Jermyn Street, to find Miss Winthrop entertaining Fred Cuthbert and half a dozen young friends. "Oh, Capt. Conant," she said, "I do hope you are coming by the *Alaric*, so that we may all go home together. Mr. Cuthbert speaks doubtfully of the time you are likely to sail, but I think it would be wicked if you do not come with us."

"Oh, Fred teases everybody with his uncertain ways," said his sister, Miss Alice Cuthbert, saucily; "and if he had been the good brother he pretends, he might have induced Capt. Conant to persuade his mother to accompany the Professor, and I might go under her protection."

"At first we did not propose," said Tom, ——

"To burden yourself with ladies," chimed in Miss Alice, with assumed petulance; "but a party, now in Paris, is likely to join us, and when I found Miss Winthrop would also do us that honor, I did try to persuade my mother to come; but she pleaded inconvenience, and finally said she had absolute engagements, which must detain her here for the next few weeks. You know she has a colony of poor people under her charge; she has to distribute to some, and provide for others, and I do believe she is fast becoming one of the hardest worked women in England."

"It is a noble work," said Dr. Elmwood.

"Yes, I would rather be a successful dispenser of charities; I would rather devote my life to elevate the poor, or to feed them—to bind up the wounds of those who have fallen by the way, to wipe the tears and assuage the grief of the broken hearted, than to reign as Queen of England."

"Yes, Agnes!" said several young ladies in concert. But Miss Cuthbert, nothing daunted, returned to the charge.

"Mrs. Conant might surely be just as good, and at the same time enjoy recreation and pleasure. The poor she will always have with her, but she can't always go to America with me."

"Oh, Alice," said her brother, "you should think before you speak; your pug would die of sea-sickness on the voyage, and surely you could not think of leaving it behind."

"My husband shall punish your impertinence some day, sir," she retorted. Further discussion showed what the company thought, and the current opinion convinced Tom that his mother ought to go; but he was not able to persuade her. He did not know of her engagements to Robert Holt's child.

CHAPTER VIII.

"GOING DOWN TO THE SEA IN SHIPS."

TIME sped, and our travellers were busy with their adieux to friends, and with their preparations for the voyage. Lord Bolton, whose confidence in the Captain and his good ship did not extend to what he called her library, her larder, or her cellar, had furnished choice books, rare delicacies, and old wines; and every one provided necessaries which were never again seen during the voyage. Fred gathered prescriptions, given him by anxious friends, at the clubs and the street corners, against that terrible ailment—*mal de mer*. The Professor, overwhelmed with work, was still doubtful whether he could go or not, and when Tom took an affectionate leave of his family, it was an open question whether his father would or would not be able to join them at Queenstown, by a Sunday flight through Ireland, by rail. He dreaded to start. He half dreaded, he told Mrs. Conant, lest some calamity should befall her while he was gone. But she who had committed her darling son to the merciless deep, felt that all would be safer if her husband bore him company. Besides, the Professor needed rest. She would persuade him gently, by-and-bye, she said to Tom; for the present, she did not doubt he would go. Fred tenderly embraced his family, and had been overwhelmed with mock reproaches from his sister, who still complained.

The time of the ship's departure depends upon the tide, and it was by a night journey to Liverpool that our tourists reached the sea. That sprightly town was shrouded in fog, and drenched in its accustomed rains, on the eventful morning. The hotels were thronged with passengers, bound for the *Alaric*, and for other steamers; and the piles of baggage, from the tiny valise to the huge "Saratoga" of fashion, that blocked the streets, had rather the appearance of a military expedition than the peaceful outfit of quiet travellers.

The fine steamer lay, a majestic sight, in the distant waters; a dingy tug was the only means of approaching her. The shop-keepers are on the alert, the hack-men are reaping fortunes, everybody hurries, as if the first on the tug would be the first at home. The crowds on the little tug can find no rest or comfort, except in the hope that they may soon be able to leave her; and, when Tom had climbed up the side of the great steamer, and went to the state-room that had been allotted him, he found two or three excited people claiming it, and the purser explaining that their own quarters were this way or that, and they themselves declaring that the geography of the ship was an impenetrable puzzle. It would all be plain enough in a day or two, but one could not master the magnificent distances at first sight. Tom sought the deck, and was crushed by the crowd of jostling and excited passengers. On the one hand, was the broad expanse of the sea around him; on the other, lay the great city in the distance, with its magnificent wharves and its far-stretching environs. The fresh breeze, freighted with briny odors, fanned his cheeks, and the fleecy clouds, far away, assumed the fantastic shapes of antique men and women, who beckoned him out to the deep waters. It was the beginning of a new life. What had it in store for him? Would the peaceful wave befriend him, or was he to be lashed and overwhelmed with the dangers which had made seafaring perilous since the earliest days, when men "went down to the sea in ships?" From the times of Jonah and Ulysses, no skill guaranteed immunity from the dangers of angry waters. He did not fear; he only pondered, as the bravest and most experienced mariners had done in all time before. What was his life compared with the vast waste of ages, which could only be computed when the "sea should give up her dead?" But he would rouse and reassure himself, and look after the comfort of his friends.

"Have you seen Mr. Holt?" he asked of his servant.

"No, sir; but Col. Lyons is in his cabin, and Mr. Cuthbert is beyond the wheel-house yonder."

"What are you doing there, Fred?"

"Oh, I'm rehearsing," said the other, as he leaned over the ship's rail; "I dare say I shall get used to it, and I am learning to go it alone."

"Are you sick in these still waters, and the ship not in motion?"

"I am discounting the future," said Fred, slowly, "after the manner of the Jews. I am practising attitudes in my hour of strength, and against the day of need; I am drawing on my imagination at about two hours sight. I expect to attract attention. I shall become the distinguished passenger. Don't you see the advantage of my studying my *pose?*"

Tom, with an ejaculation of "nonsense," turned away;

he was in no mood for *badinage*, and he would see if he could be useful to others.

"Why, Holt," he said, "you look desolate. Are you really forlorn at leaving home? Well, I am sad myself; and yet we English are notorious wanderers. Perhaps the race is running out."

"I am not cheerful I confess," said Robert, "and yet I don't know why, for nothing would have deterred me from taking this voyage. It is an event in my life. I am not going half willingly, for I seem drawn by unseen hands. There is some mystery for me in this journey. You will see, perhaps, when it is solved."

"You are out of sorts, Robert," said Tom; "the sea air will restore you."

Lord Bolton sauntered into the saloon with Tom, to note the long tables groaning with delf and crystal, and to watch the ample preparations for dinner.

"Can I have a private table for my party?" he asked.

The steward looked puzzled. "Have you made no arrangements, sir?"

"None," said his Lordship. "James should have seen to this."

"They do not know his rank," said Tom, aside.

"We are crowded, sir," said the steward; "your friends will be safer to take the seats first, as they want them."

"Oh, I'll see the captain," said Tom.

"No, stay," said my Lord; "we will take our chances. Things will regulate themselves in a day or two, and we will commence the practice of equality in our own waters."

The great ship steamed slowly out to sea, and by the

time she was fairly under way dinner was served at a table which could accommodate three hundred, in a ship numbering five hundred first-class passengers. There was ill-concealed irritation from the unfortunates left to wait, and whose keen relish of the savory odors did not improve their tempers; while, as in the outer world, the well provided classes paid little heed to the tempted and famished.

After dinner, Lord Bolton had been unremitting in his endeavors to bring his friends together at the earliest moment; and they had indulged in the cordial commonplaces of strangers. But, in the evening, when they were all ensconced on the broad deck, *en famille*, and the waves gently washed the ship, and the pale moon looked wistfully down upon them, they forgot the restraints of their first meeting, and their conversation sparkled with wit, and abounded in good nature.

How often has the friendship of a life-time been kindled at sea? Social intercourse is more unrestrained, and there is an unconscious search for novelty and adventure on shipboard; each has the same restricted amusements and common interests, the feelings are more easily touched, and there is less distracting competition and variety than are found in the great world of society, with the fixed rules that govern it. Some may cavil at this solution, and we do not insist upon it; but these pages will bear witness to the fact that friendships grow rapidly at sea.

Mr. and Mrs. Roberts and Miss Roberts, of Washington, and M. and Madame De Luynes, of Quebec, Lord Bolton's friends in Paris, were what he had described them, "charming people;" and Fred Cuthbert, aside to Miss Winthrop, had maliciously whispered, that there would shortly be another case of a great Lord prostrate before an American beauty.

Our travellers were spending a pleasant evening, and were already on the footing of friends. Fred was in unusual spirits, and had forgotten his sea-sickness and his cynicism. Tom and Miss Winthrop were rather selfishly absorbed in each other; and Robert Holt was full of fun and anecdotes. The latter seemed to have forgotten the mysteries of his destiny, toward which he had dreamed the ship was bearing him.

M. De Luynes, Robert thought, was an excitable and impetuous talker, intolerant, but witty and clever; and Robert observed that his wife was ill at ease when he spoke, as if she feared an extravagance of some sort, perhaps only an imprudence of expression. De Luynes was tall, handsome and intellectual; but his eyes were restless, and his manner unassured. His fine young face wore a weary look of care, beyond his years, and might have denoted one not unfamiliar with "revelry by night."

Madame De Luynes' great beauty was not marred by the tinge of melancholy which had touched her face; and when her expression was animated by sympathy or by thought, Robert felt that he had never seen anything so lovely. Her sweet voice and gentle manner had at first touched him as indescribably charming; and as the evening wore on, he wondered, could it be that this rollicking husband was indifferent to such unusual fascinations.

She, on her part, had not been unobservant of the young man's interest; and her husband had spoken to her in terms of admiration for him. "He is a scholar and a thinker, and I shall be deceived if you do not find him a Christian gentleman," De Luynes said; and she had answered that his quiet dignity inspired a feeling of restfulness and confidence, as if he were equal to great occasions—one who might defy dangers and rescue the unfortunate from perils.

In the midst of these conversations, the heavens were suddenly overcast, and the wind freshened, to be succeeded by mists and fogs, as so often happens in these weary nights along the coast of Ireland. The ladies, therefore, heeded the warning to retire.

Fred Cuthbert, who had felt a little *de trop*, upbraided Tom for his dulness all the evening. "Where have you been, and what have you done for the welfare of my fellow travellers and myself?" said Fred. "I wish I had brought Alice, who would at least have scolded me, and that would have been better than to be left without attention." Looking at Lord Bolton, he added, "Why could you not follow an illustrious example, Tom, and give initial lessons in the only art which is not in danger of being lost? Why, you've been sitting alone the whole evening."

"Don't be disagreeable, Fred," said Robert, half alarmed.

"Impertinence is not wit, Mr. Cuthbert," said Lord Bolton, with assumed severity; "but that I love your father I should be tempted to throw you overboard."

"I am my father's debtor in many ways," said Fred; "but this great forbearance of my Lord I shall credit to his own prudent kindness."

There was a laugh, and with cordial "good-nights," the party separated.

Half an hour later, Robert found himself discussing

sardines on toast, among other things, with M. Maurice De Luynes, in the saloon.

"The Canadian trip to Liverpool is lovely in summer," De Luynes said; "you descend the river to the Gulf, and the Straits, and you are three days in sight of land before reaching the sea. The ships are fine, the service reasonable, and the voyage out from our Canadian shores is much patronized by people from the States."

"I have heard that it is beset with dangers," said Robert.

"Oh, the navigation of the whole Northern Atlantic is somewhat perilous," replied De Luynes. "In earlier days the St. Lawrence route was not well-known, and there were many terrible disasters; but for years there has been apparent safety. I would not care to return by these boats, they are so crowded with steerage passengers. In the event of serious accident, the number on board would greatly diminish the chances of escape. I always go out from home and return by New York in the Saturday boats for this reason. You have never been in Quebec? The old city will interest one of your taste and acquirements. It is not a commercial city, though its harbor is magnificent, and its railway facilities are, and will be, ample for any trade; but we are slow to take advantage of our opportunities, and have been over-matched, and often outstripped by more enterprising commercial rivals. A great man once slandered us by saying that no one had as yet been born in Quebec who could see beyond her walls. But I love the old city, though I wish that, in many things, I had the power to reform her. She has many historical landmarks, and is full of interesting reminiscences. Quebec, moreover, was the theatre upon which those great Apostles, who sought to create French empire on this continent, labored, and if they failed, their successors have maintained a supremacy under foreign rule, which if it had been foreseen a hundred years ago, would have shocked her conquerors. These influences have entrenched themselves in their own little province, and are preparing the machinery of a propagandism which nobody understands, and against which nobody provides, but which will make itself felt by-and-bye, in the controversies of the New World. These people have not learned the lessons of liberty, and they are dangerous to her; but, beyond their own small jurisdiction, their methods are not understood, and no one is preparing to withstand their aggressions when the time comes. It seems a small affair by the light of the moment; but a great contest is brewing between those who love freedom and those who have been its traditional enemies; and Englishmen will repent in sack-cloth and ashes the hostile forces they have been unconsciously fostering, in territories they once wrenched from old France in America."

"You surprise me," said Robert, with deep interest.

"It is a long, sad story," added De Luynes, slowly; "but if it interests you, we will talk more about it by-and-bye."

CHAPTER IX.

"ALL WENT MERRY AS A MARRIAGE BELL."

It was a beautiful Sunday morning as they neared the lovely harbor of Queenstown, and dropped anchor to await the arrival of the Saturday night's mails and the passengers from London. The Professor, bright and cheery, was the first to put foot upon the ship, and was hilariously welcomed by the friends who had expected him. Tom was eager for news from home. But, beyond a private, and it seemed reassuring, word to Robert, the Professor had nothing to tell.

"I am afraid Tom was hoping you would not come," said Fred Cuthbert in a low tone; "his attentions to us all have been so extravagantly general that you might not approve."

"What a tease you are, Fred," said Holt, who had caught enough to guess at the drift; "Is nobody to escape you?"

"At any rate, you are safe till we reach deep water," was the reply.

The Professor laughingly observed that Fred was a better fellow than he wanted the world to believe. And Tom advised his father to reserve his judgment till he had experience of the young man's life on the "ocean wave."

Miss Roberts offered to champion him at any time, when he found himself hard pressed by his rough companions, and Fred declared that with such a prospect, he should invite assaults from all the ill-conditioned passengers.

"Oh! the blarney stone!" cried Miss Roberts; "Did you find it this morning, or have you been here before?"

"I am glad to say I never embraced it," replied Fred, "and I am sure no Irishman whose privilege it is to cross with us will ever kiss it again."

"What a national revulsion," said Lord Bolton. "Pray, Fred, could you trace it to its cause?"

"I might, if my station were such that nobody would dare resent what I say," was the retort.

"Oh, you are ambitious for the cap and bells," laughingly observed his Lordship.

"Mr. Cuthbert, come with me," said Miss Winthrop.

"Can you find me a harbor of refuge near by?" rejoined Fred, as he obeyed the summons and sauntered down the deck by her side.

Col. Lyons, who was a sailor, pointed out the objects of interest, as the *Alaric* steamed away through the placid waters, and, as every one on his last look is observant, there were few talkers and the conversation flagged.

Lord Bolton was the exception; his accustomed reticence in the society of ladies had given way to a strain of loquacious mirth, which surprised his friends and amused everybody, and he was so persistently at Miss Roberts's side, that she seemed at first disposed to avoid him. "But the besieged must always surrender," Fred was saying to Miss Winthrop, "if he is short of rations, and the enemy is equipped with titles and no end of thousands a year."

"Is she not a lovely brunette of the Southern type, graceful as a queen and beautiful as a houri? I have been struck by the apparent gentleness and sweetness of her disposition. No wonder Lord Bolton is charmed. If he wins her, it must be through her heart. If she is mercenary I shall despair of my sex, and never attempt to read character again. If I were a man, I should fall in love with that girl myself," said the young lady.

"Oh, then there would be bloodshed between you and my Lord," remarked her companion. "He was never in love in his life, and he won't be easy to tame."

"How absurd," she rejoined. "I see nothing to justify these jokes."

"Oh, if you don't see," said Fred, "with all your experience,——"

"Have a care!" she said, "Mr. Cynic!"

"Then, of course, I am blind!" he added, without heeding the interruption.

"Do you like Lord Bolton?" she asked with a young girl's directness.

"Do you think that it is impossible because I sometimes laugh at his expense?"

"Please answer my question," she persisted.

"Miss Winthrop," he said, with a drawl; "do you think a cockney could be sensible, or a cynic serious? I am going to surprise you. I do more than like Lord Bolton, I love him. He is never the great Lord, but always the dear friend, to me. Sometimes I mimic his aristocratic lisp, and laugh at his eccentric idiosyncrasies, because it suits my humor, and this as often before his face as behind his back. I really believe it amuses him more than others. He is a great Lord, but he is a good man. He has a clumsy manner but a kind heart. And what to him are the little graces which he might display in common with his tailor? As he grows older, higher hereditary honors will fall to him, and he will become a great man in England. He will be better known for his benevolence than for his exalted honors; and to enjoy his friendship will be abundant pleasure for those who deserve it. His love for man or woman will be a precious gift. He is earnest and honest before all things; Miss Roberts must not trifle with him."

"I believe every word you say," said Miss Winthrop. "I knew you were not really a cynic all the time."

Lord Bolton and Miss Roberts approached. "We came to remind you of something you had forgotten, Fred," he said gaily.

"What? My Lord!"

"Your prescriptions; you need not have gone to Epps of Piccadilly, if you had known what antidotes were to be found here."

"Your cheerful face saved me," replied Fred, with a polite bow to Miss Roberts. "As a faithful retainer, I must give precedence to you."

"Are you not a good sailor?" asked Miss Winthrop.

"Oh, I don't know," he answered "everybody told me of the terrible ordeal, and everybody gave me a remedy; of course I imparted my secret to my friends, and they became cognizant of my tremors when I first came on board; but I have not thought of them since. His Lordship's unusual spirits remind me I can think of something that would give him a more terrible shock than I dreaded. It seems to me Miss Roberts is reserved and coy. Miss Winthrop, do you think it possible for an American girl to be indifferent to a great Lord who loves her?"

"Why, yes, I should think so of any girl who did not reciprocate his affection. Why do you distinguish American girls? Are they more wicked than others?"

"I am afraid I should have said, yes, a month ago, as to this particular sin; but I don't believe it now," said Fred. Cuthbert. "We live to learn———"

They saw Robert and Mme. De Luynes promenading the deck, and Miss Winthrop motioned Tom to join her.

"She is a charming person," remarked Miss Winthrop.

"I did not observe her much," said Tom, "but Robert says she is most interesting and accomplished."

"Her husband is a dry stick," added Fred, shrugging his shoulders.

"Not at all," Tom replied. "Robert says he is a man of brilliant parts. At first Robert thought he had a dissolute look, though he is handsome and *distingué*, but he says he has met no man on board ship from whom we are likely to derive so much useful information. He was educated in Paris, and I believe he sowed his wild oats there. At any rate, in his young days, he won his beautiful wife in that fashionable city; but Robert says he has the whole history of America at his tongue's end and that we may expect pleasure from intercourse with him."

"I dare say he will be my fate," said Fred, "but Robert seems to prefer Madame."

"You don't think he expects to marry her," rejoined Tom, in tones of disgust.

"Not in this world," remarked Fred.

"Well, in the next world, they neither marry nor are given in marriage," said Miss Winthrop.

"So you have been reading up that subject, my young friend," replied the cynic. "That rule was needed to meet the case of the seven brothers in the old days; but now it would be more imperative under the jurisdiction of the divorce courts."

"As we are all unmarried," said Tom, "let us leave these things to the benedicts!" and he led Miss Winthrop to a seat which his father had reserved for her.

"Do you know," said the Professor, "I feel like a school-boy off for his holidays? No letters, no telegrams for ten days."

"It might be nine," remarked Tom.

"Or eight," said Miss Winthrop; "I believe the *Alaska* has made the voyage in seven days, some odd hours."

"It has been, and will be greatly shortened," said the Professor. "There is already direct railway communication to Halifax, and it is proposed to traverse Newfoundland by rail. Four to five days will be the extent of the ocean trip before we are much older."

"I should rather go all the way by sea," said Miss Winthrop. "It is such a trouble to change."

"Oh, yes, if you are a good sailor," interposed Dr. Elmwood. "But if you were ill, from the moment you took the ship till you left it, I think you would tolerate the proposed new route. Five days instead of ten would be a relief incalculable to a bad sailor."

Robert was busy in conversation with Madame De Luynes. She was telling him that she was born in a Connecticut village, had been educated in Paris, and, on the Continent and while still a school-girl, had met her

LITTLE ETHEL AS CARLOTTA LEFT HER.

"Dear old Quebec," she continued, musingly, * * * "I left my baby, a dear little girl of two years, there."—*Page* 83.

husband in Paris and married him, and had become a resident of Quebec. She loved the old city. There was a respectable English contingent there, but the people were chiefly French, and they had been devoted to her, as they always were to an American speaking their language. She loved the French people. She was a protestant, but they made her faith no reproach to her, as they would to a pervert from their own faith; and she thought the *mélange* of French and English in society charming. The *brusquerie* of the English manners was softened by the *politesse* of the French, and gave an inimitable charm to the society of the old capital. She hoped to welcome him there, and, that as he had so much impressed her husband, he would accept the hospitalities of their house when he came to Canada.

Robert was not slow to reciprocate these kind sentiments, and declared that he had been charmed by her husband's knowledge of affairs, his sound political views, and the ready tact with which he expressed them.

She remarked that her husband had not been a fortunate politician, as he would have been in Connecticut or in Paris; for Lower Canada was peculiar, and nobody came to distinction without the confidence of the priests. "Dear old Quebec," she continued, musingly, "I never longed to see the place so much as I do now. I left my baby, a dear little girl of two years there. She is well, and with a faithful old nurse in a quiet village by the sea; but of late I have rarely heard of her. I have worried incessantly about this. We ought not to have left the child; and we are returning a month before my husband was ready to come. He is not alarmed, of course; he is a man, and says I am cherishing imaginary fears; but I cannot rest until I see my child. Are you married, Mr. Holt?" she asked abruptly.

Robert answered "No." And he thought tenderly of the little girl he, too, had left behind. Should he see her again? Would she become an influence in his life, this little waif who had drifted to him?

"Oh, I thought if you had children," Mme. De Luynes remarked, "you might feel an interest in my story."

Robert avowed his interest, but said nothing of the child he was himself interested in, and they joined the others who were basking in the warm rays of the setting sun, by the door of the captain's cabin.

Capt. Graham was a short, stout man, with a ruddy sunburnt face, and a cheery, kind expression. "Ladies," he said, with the rich brogue which comes only from the north of the Tweed, "we are fortunate to have a cloudless sky, and the sunset is peerless. You could not match it on land. Many travellers have tried, but always in vain, to portray the beauties of a brilliant sunset at sea."

"But there *are* clouds," interposed Miss Roberts; "and oh, how magnificent!"

"They are only the illuminated background of this great picture," remarked De Luynes absently. "What a wealth of golden lights and fleecy shades enlivens the heavenly canvas!"

"What animated coloring!" said one. "And what blending!" "And what variegations!" said the others. And they stood there enraptured with the scene till the sun went down, and the twilight deepened into night.

In the old days, when the passenger list was smaller,

everybody came to know everybody else, during the passage, and indeed, the captain, as head of the ship's family, was accustomed to present the notables to each other, early in the voyage. But modern passengers herd in such numbers on the great ships, that, except in small circles, they generally remain indifferent strangers to their fellows; and this isolation amid a crowd promotes a warmer sympathy in the narrow circle of one's friends. The resources of each are unconsciously taxed for the general amusement. If a fourth is wanted at whist you are ready for the sacrifice, though you neither love the game, nor understand it; and if you are asked to sing, you seat yourself at the piano, without any of the coyness which might be excused in a country house ashore.

There was a pretty little parlor, just off the saloon, which Lord Bolton and his friends had already appropriated. There were an organ, a harp, and a guitar, with soiled sheets of music; a church hymnal and the Moody and Sankey hymns, waiting to be made use of; and De Luynes, seating himself at the organ, called his wife, saying, "Come, Carlotta, let us set these young people an example." He ran his fingers along the keys as if testing the qualities of the instrument, and then with the self-absorbed air of an enthusiast brought forth strains so pathetic and full of harmony that one wondered at the skill that could summon at will such melodies.

"It is Sunday night, Maurice," said his wife gently. "There may be those who prefer a hymn to your weird improvisations."

"To me, those chords were beautiful," he said. "I expect some day to hear them with you, in heaven."

The instrument gave out "The sweet by-and-bye," with exquisite variations, and the De Luynes accompanied the music with their fine voices through a sweet rendering of the words. By this time, the room and the approaches were crowded with passengers, whom the music had attracted, but De Luynes was lost to all but the strains he was producing. As these died away and they commenced to sing "Nearer my God to Thee," the strains were taken up by the throng, and carried along the ship till it seemed that the inspiration was general, and as if a thousand voices were singing with a marvellous harmony the touching and beautiful hymn. Women wept and strong men sought to hide their emotion.

After a little, De Luynes arose composedly and said, "We Catholics do not practise these hymns as a religious duty; but I love to sing them with my wife, and sometimes in this way we entertain our neighbors." Politely excusing themselves, M. and Mme. De Luynes retired.

"They are charming people," said the Professor, a remark which was warmly seconded by Dr. Elmwood.

"I knew De Luynes' father," said Col. Lyons, "when I was in Canada some years ago. He was a clever man, and at one time, wielded great political power, but he was not in accord with the clergy on the question of the tithes and some other things, and, notwithstanding his lineage and his wealth, his high character and the distinguished services he had rendered the people, his public life was soon at an end. Maurice was then in France pursuing his studies, but I always heard him spoken of as a young man of great promise; it is said he has cultivated his father's independence and is not a favorite with the church, which means a good deal in the way of trouble for him in Canada, if he looks to politics as an occupation."

"How sadly one may misjudge at first," said Tom. "We all looked askance at him, and traced his lovely wife's melancholy to his neglect and persecution. Now we find him a model domestic man, of rare acquirements and virtues."

"We certainly did misjudge them," remarked Robert. "Even the wife's melancholy has found a solution which fully exonerates the husband, and accounts in the most positive way for her nervous and anxious manner."

"Let us give up reading character and take to reading books," said Fred.

"You may do both things profitably, by devoting to each a little care," interpolated the Professor; "half the misunderstandings of life are precipitated by jumping to conclusions."

"It is a rule of polite society to avoid hurting the feelings of others," said Col. Lyons, "and it would be as good a rule, perhaps, to avoid speaking against them."

"Yes," said Dr. Elmwood, "or you might copy the newspapers and only speak ill of your neighbors, when the public interest demands it."

"That would be a *pressing* alternative," said Fred; "the sea is rough," he added, looking out, "and the ship is lurching. Let us woo tired nature's sweet restorer———"

CHAPTER X.

"COMING INTO THE TRACK OF A STORM."

The orthodox occupation of a passenger at sea is killing time. At first this is easy, for everything is new and fresh at the outset; but there is no "infinite variety" at one's service. He treads the same measure day after day, and by-and-bye the time "hangs heavy on his hands." He begins to count the days, and anon, the hours. He has seen the whale and the porpoise, and perhaps, the iceberg. He has watched the ship speed in her spiritless race, from day to day, against her own time. The Captain on the bridge and the sailors in the rigging cease to amuse him. All this, unless he can enjoy good books, or that better resource at sea, good company.

Our own travellers were among the fortunate few. They were good sailors, good talkers, and good listeners; and they were, moreover, interested in each other. Their first day had been a delightful experience to each, and even at this early hour if a requisition had been circulated to prolong the voyage, they would all (if we except Madame De Luynes and Dr. Elmwood), have signed it.

All were early astir on that bright Monday morning; they had been refreshed and were happy; and their greetings were as cheery and affectionate as if they had known each other for years. The decks and saloons were less crowded than they were yesterday, for many had yielded to the discomforts of the sea. And the jolly Captain, who knew the misfortune had its limits, was willing to have his joke about it.

"Your sympathy with sea-sickness does you credit, ladies," he said, "but sea-sickness is not always an unmixed evil. I was sailing from New York once in October with a long passenger list; room was a sacred trust everywhere. Two rather distinguished New York ladies, not acquainted with each other, had been placed in my charge for the voyage. Their husbands had been detained at the last moment, but were to follow them next month. Neither of the ladies knew me. They had each two children, and they all had seats at my left, or rather, they should have had; but, as it turned out, the steward had only reserved two seats instead of four. As we steamed out of the harbor late in the afternoon, I was engaged, and asked a friend to take my place at the dinner-table. He was a good lawyer, but he didn't know the difference between a jib-boom and a rudder. The day was beautiful, and nobody who enjoyed it could have thought there was anything but happiness in store. The ladies came to the table without the children, and each claimed the two seats. They spoke with the frigid politeness of people who did not intend to yield an inch. 'These seats belong to my little girl and boy,' said Number One. 'You are mistaken, madame, they were reserved for my two children,' said Number Two. 'The captain shall decide between us,' they both said, appealing to my friend. He was, however, 'wise in his generation,' and, without nautical skill, settled a delicate nautical matter.

"'Ladies,' he said, 'Rome was not built in a day; it is a rule of this service to take twenty-four hours for consideration, when embarrassing questions are submitted. It has happened that in this way such questions settled themselves.' Each, confident of victory, was satisfied. Would you believe it, those ladies were not at the table again till we sighted land, ten days afterwards. So you see, *le mal de mer* is not an unmixed evil."

"You are cruel, captain," said the ladies.

"I am practical, ladies," he replied, with a loud laugh, which bespoke the measure of his good humor.

"Do you like to answer questions, captain?" said Miss Roberts.

"Yes, when I know how," he rejoined.

"I have heard that some captains regard curiosity with ill-favor."

"Well, yes, and no," he said. "It depends upon the man and the circumstances. But if we are crusty we sometimes get the worst of it. The commodore of our line, in the midst of a storm, was asked by a lady some simple question. 'Do you take me for the steward, Madame?' he said gruffly. 'I mistook you for a gentleman, sir,' was the quiet reply."

The day was beautiful but uneventful to the ordinary passenger, and, unheeded by our friends, some of whom discussed books, finance, and politics, according to their tastes; others were engaged in gentler and perhaps more engrossing studies.

Mr. and Mrs. Roberts sought to shield their young charge from the too pronounced attentions of Lord Bolton, who seemed to have forgotten the rest of the party, and could not understand why he should be shunned. He had even complained to Mr. Roberts, and protested his sincerity; but that gentleman had only met him with mysterious and conventional assurances. Finally, he told him frankly, that his sister had a high sense of the honor he intended her, but that he would explain later a reason why she could only receive him on the footing of a friend, and that there must be no thought of any more serious relations.

His Lordship had accepted the situation, and the young lady was once more cheerful and reassured.

Tom and Miss Winthrop were still engaged in a sort of old-fashioned flirtation, which did not threaten to be serious, and seemed to include Fred Cuthbert in their confidence. The De Luynes and Robert were inseparable, and the lively and sparkling conversation of these interesting and accomplished people was a treat to the Professor and to Dr. Elmwood. The captain, as an old friend of Col. Lyons, rather monopolized that gentleman, and so all were delightfully occupied, and the time sped and they did not heed it till another day had been reeled off their voyage.

That night there was heavy weather, and a rougher sea, and an old sailor said they were coming into the track of a storm.

The next morning at breakfast the tables were ornamented with the traditional "racks." The passengers were thinly represented in the saloon, and these seemed serious and apprehensive; but, though the wind was growing fresher, and the sea boiled with agitation, the sky was clear and the sun was bright. There were but few ladies visible, and these threaded their unaccustomed way with difficulty in the ship's uncertain motion. The dishes rattled, the *Alaric* groaned, and now and then as the vessel plunged, some luckless promenader was caught, and hurled against chairs and tables to the opposite corner. At last, the general gloom was lifted and a hearty laugh ran "along the line" while the victims looked silly and crestfallen.

Our travellers were on deck, clinging to the ropes and rails, with supreme indifference to their sufferings. Poor Madame De Luynes had not reported, though Maurice said she was not ill, but only a little disquieted. The other ladies were with difficulty dissuaded from going at once in search of her, but her husband thought she would be better if left to such repose as, in the circumstances, was possible. He promised to bring her to them as good as new, in an hour or two.

The Captain had just left the bridge and was making cautiously for his cabin, and the young ladies began to ply him with jokes and questions. He was polite, but stern and reserved, another man altogether than him they had left the night before, full of fun and anecdote. He was responsible for a large property, and a thousand lives, and the sea was giving signs that troubled him. From stem to stern the ship was playing pitch and toss in the liveliest manner, and the great waves were pounding her sides like battering-rams, now and then drenching her decks with spray. The Captain half listened as if he were expecting something, and dreaded it. Our observers watched his anxious face and were silent. Then, as the ship plunged her nose under the waters, there was a slight scraping sound like the friction of timbers, and momently she halted and trembled; women screamed and men held their breath.

"Port your helm!" shouted an unknown voice. The

man at the wheel obeyed, and the ship rocked and groaned under the awkward pressure.

"Steady your wheel!" roared the Captain, rushing forward. The scraping was repeated tenfold, and there was a terrible bump! bump! bump!! as if they were rushing at full speed over boulders, and the ship leaped above the waters as if she were being hurled out of the sea. Men and women were thrown indiscriminately athwart the vessel, which seemed to hang hesitatingly between the air and ocean, and writhed and quivered as if in bodily pain. The ship righted herself quickly, and stood still during two awful minutes of suspense before the engine resumed work.

"Look yonder!" shouted the first officer, pointing to her wake behind the stern. The water was black with the *débris*, which consisted of spars and timbers that were leaping from the depths to the surface.

"Is the danger past, Captain?" inquired a passenger, who had recovered himself, and was eager for an explanation, for which he would have to wait.

"That was a queer snag," remarked the Captain.

"We ran into a wreck, sir," said the first officer.

"Its rebound was tremendous against the bottom of the *Alaric*," observed the Captain. "It is a mercy we are not disabled."

"We must examine her first," was the reply.

The Captain explained to Lord Bolton what had happened, and asked him to reassure his friends. Then he proceeded to find out to what extent the ship had suffered; meantime, the usual word was passed along among those of the crew and servants who were likely to encounter inquisitive passengers, to respond to all questions with the answer, "all is right." The noble ship, nevertheless, continued to speed on her usual course, across the rough waters, and quiet and confidence were slowly restored.

"I always feel that I have taken my life in my hands when I go to sea," said Madame De Luynes.

"Oh, I think that in a computation of chances it would be found the accidents are not in greater proportion at sea than by other means of travel," her husband replied. "But the imagination has much to do with our impressions. Look at the fatalities by rail; and yet, we are so accustomed to that mode of travel, that a journey does not terrify us. We take steamer voyages so seldom that we do not get used to them, as in the other case. And yet, now-a-days, with first-class ships there are fewer casualties."

"Do you not think we have just escaped a great calamity?" inquired Miss Winthrop.

"Oh, a miss is as good as a mile," Fred Cuthbert answered.

"How very original," said Tom. "Why don't you give us something familiar?"

"Because familiarity breeds contempt," rejoined Fred.

"All this is too serious to make fun of," mildly suggested Robert Holt. "How fearful are the perils of the deep! It is not that shipwreck means death, or that one is afraid to die. But we are surrounded by such majesty of power, that our own puny helplessness is made plainer to us. Where does nature marshal more awful strength and grandeur than surround us here? And yet there is a relief to our humiliation in the thought that if the hand of man cannot control, we may utilize and enjoy them. What changeful scenes!

The quiet sea is a symbol of tranquillity, but who does not tremble, as he commits himself to the awful forces of the storm?"

"They say drowning is a peaceful death," remarked Miss Roberts; "but they must be speaking of the calm waters, and the heavenly view which one beholds, yielding his life in the watery depths, from which he may gaze upward to the broad heavens radiant in the bright sunshine."

"From battle and murder, and from sudden death, good Lord, deliver us," said Mrs. Roberts.

"Amen," said Lord Bolton, solemnly.

"What we need is constant preparation for death," interposed Dr. Elmwood.

"And these startling adventures are intended to prepare us," said the Professor. "Let us all thank God for his mercies," and there was an acquiescence of silent meditation and prayer, which lasted several minutes. Throughout the steamer the merciful deliverance had disposed many hearts to thankfulness; and for the moment, at least, it had awakened many to a sense of the uncertainty of human life.

Prayer is not always a sign of piety. A reverent man, from a sense of duty, may offer up petitions which are formal and without fervor; while the man without any sense of duty may pray earnestly for help, when he feels that he has need and is dependent. We put aside the theory that the skeptic has no care, nor wish for Divine aid; not doubting that he unconsciously leans on a higher power, and that in severe stress of weather he would be one of the first to cry out, "God be merciful;" and so, we doubt not, great perils dispose the human heart, good or bad, to hope in God, and to turn to him. The feeling is not the less real because it is fitful and undisciplined. That was a sudden conversion of the thief on the cross; yet, had he lived he might have back-slidden. No doubt, a great and common terror rouses the emotions of men, and reverence may be religious and is often emotional. The passengers of the *Alaric* were no exception; they felt that they had an almost miraculous escape, and they thanked God for it. It may be, they would soon forget, but such gratitude inspired them to prayer, and brought them nearer Divine things. They had asked Dr. Elmwood to conduct a religious service in the evening, and almost to a man and a woman the passengers assembled to join with him. There were appropriate devotions and a short address, followed by a generous collection for that noble charity, the "Seamen's Fund." The Professor had been surprised at the large amount collected; and the Captain said to him, with grateful tears, that " the Americans are always liberal givers."

CHAPTER XI.

DE LUYNES DISCUSSES BURNING QUESTIONS.

The night was dark, the sea was rough, and after such a day the ladies wisely retired early. The smoking-room was almost deserted when De Luynes and Robert took possession of it; but other friends dropped in, and general conversation was in progress. Robert reminded Maurice that he had promised another chapter of his observations, begun a few nights before. Col. Lyons knew how to interest him, and asked if he had taken part in the politics of his country.

"Not a distinguished part," he replied, "and yet I am not an indifferent observer. Like my father, I have the misfortune to quarrel with a powerful influence among us on some questions, and that shuts the door of public life against me. I have been in Parliament twice, but only sat a few months and was beaten, ostensibly because my people were told that I was a Freemason which was false; though they did not know what it meant. The real reason, however, was that an unseen influence, which controlled them, was hostile to me. In my youth, the clergy of my district offered me their support in an election then pending for my county, but by my father's advice I refused it, because it would involve a bondage to which no man of spirit could submit. I bore my father's name; I had followed his advice against theirs, and they never forgave me. I am a Catholic, and I want to be a true son of the Church; but to me there is a difference between the spiritual and the temporal. I accept her teachings as to matters of faith and morals, but as to the franchise, the taxation, the public administration of affairs, I cannot allow her to dictate my course. Other young men have held the same views, and have suffered the same disabilities. In England and France you see gentlemen of wealth preferred to positions of great political distinction on both sides. If you do not obey these men, there is an iron heel always waiting to crush you. Kind gentlemen in religious and private life, they are intolerant above all things in that which relates to political freedom of speech or action. Their influence is enormous; some of my friends have often said to me: 'Why not go with the tide? Why slam the door of preferment forever in your face? Your name, your rank, the loyalty of your people, would maintain you in influence and honor, if you would conciliate this hostile power.' It, however, is not always absolutely dominant; thanks to influences beyond its control, its party has been sometimes beaten, though it has formed such strange alliances that its influence seems as great among its traditional enemies as among its own people. When the Liberals are in power, it happens, of course, that independent French Canadians who do not follow it are appointed to office. But this happens only when they cannot help it. When their own party rules, they are absolute masters of Lower Canada; and as to patronage and toleration, they rule with a rod of iron."

"I suppose," said the Professor, "it is a revival of the old controversies we have known so well in England."

"That is not altogether true of modern controversy," rejoined Maurice. "With you, the Catholics, if they were British subjects, fought for emancipation; that cause was plausible and just. But these men fight for power, for the education of the young, for the control of the franchise, and of the avenues which lead to the preferment of their own people. There was once a great controversy between the Gallicans and the Ultramontanes in France. You know its history, and how the former kept faith with the nation; substitute Canada for France, and we could work with the Gallican Churchmen. But these men would practically set the Church over the State, giving to the latter only the power to register the decrees of the former; if you chide them for this, you will be denounced from a hundred pulpits. The more intelligent revolt against these extreme views. Did I say revolt? But I spoke of their intelligence; they do not want to 'kick against the pricks,' and so they drift along with the current, and reap the easy rewards of complaisance. An Englishman thrown casually into our society would see little and hear less of these troubles. He would meet men of letters and men of the world at the head of these influences, and they would charm him with their manners. The mailed hand is shown when there is resistance to be crushed among their own people. Thirty years ago my father and a dozen young men of culture, formed an association, founded a newspaper, and published a political programme. Their platform embraced nearly all the measures of reform which have been enacted since that time; but the projectors were denounced and vilified by men who, ever since, have maintained their hostility, but have taken credit for the work. But why do I speak of these things to comparative strangers? It is because you are Englishmen of rank, statesmen, soldiers, and men of affairs; you are studying the forces which in coming years are to guide opinion in the wide British Empire. You have a dependency across this water, weak it may be in numbers, but in territory, and in possibilities, large like the United States, and larger than Europe with her family of nations. It is a self-governing country, and you do not wish to interfere with it. But you should study the forces which at least control one-fourth of its population, forces which hold the balance of power and control it. You will find the bulk of your own race there careless and lukewarm, singing to the air that Nero must have played, *Après moi le Déluge.* Do I appeal to strangers against my race? God forbid! I love my countrymen. They belong to liberty and I would save them. I tell their sad tale to strong men who have loved and upheld freedom, not that you could coerce or restrain them; but while you might do something to open their eyes, you would render a service to your own race, as well as mine, in dispelling clouds that to-day may seem to you no bigger than a man's hand, but which are fraught with storm and peril."

He ceased, his fine face aglow with the excitement of his earnest pleadings; all were in sympathy with his burning words, and no one seemed willing to break the silence.

After De Luynes retired there was another pause, which was finally broken by Col. Lyons, who observed, "He is a superior but disappointed man. He has meditated upon his wrongs till they have colored his life."

"His is a blighted career, I fear," said Dr. Elmwood. "But he seems to have been a philosopher, and to have acted as well as he speaks."

"It might have been better taste not to pronounce that harangue in mixed company," observed a stranger, who had been listening. "It is calculated to wound some, and to produce a false impression upon others."

"Were the clergy to stand idly by, and permit a lot of hair-brained youths to paralyze the Church and sever British connection? These Liberals are irreligious and disloyal." The speaker was a middle-aged man of easy speech and dignified bearing.

Robert had noticed the interest with which the latter had followed De Luynes; and his slightly foreign accent suggested that perhaps he was a countryman of De Luynes, and probably a political opponent.

"Oh, these are charges easy to make," he said. "I have not studied their teachings, but I suspect they are not new; no doubt, under altered conditions, the same controversies are current in Europe as well as in Canada. But what have these Liberals done?"

"Nothing," said the stranger, "but disturb and agitate the people."

"They have held office," persisted Robert. "Did they undermine society? or legislate against the interests of the Church? or the Crown?"

"They never administered long, because their policy was distrusted by our people."

"I should like to hear this discussion," said the Professor, "but I propose we adjourn it. Our time is far spent, and the night is stormy."

A wave broke over the deck, which crushed the door of the room like a piece of brittle glass, and washed its way among the unfortunate occupants, who were deluged for a moment and thrown hither and thither with the advancing and receding element. A deck steward had fractured a rib against one of the arms of the long seat, and our friends had been shaken and drenched; but they speedily gathered themselves up and made for their berths, thankful for another almost miraculous escape. In the morning the storm had abated, the weather was bright, and the waters more tranquil. The deck was alive with passengers, who seemed to have forgotten the discomforts of yesterday, and completely to have regained their spirits. The spar-deck was lined with chairs which the ladies, covered with wraps, chiefly occupied; and, ere long, the amusements and hilarities were resumed.

"Sail, ho!" cried the lookout from forward.

"Where away?" said the officer of the deck.

"Dead ahead, sir."

"Give me the long glass, Quartermaster," shouted the officer.

"Aye, aye, sir," he responded.

The officer took the glass and made an observation. "Report to the Captain a steamer ahead, Quartermaster."

"Tell the officer to hoist an ensign, and set our numbers, and when he makes out the ship, report to me," said the Captain, turning again to the passengers with whom he had been conversing.

By this time the passengers were on the alert; trifles create an excitement at sea. The vessel proved to be the homeward-bound steamer of the same line. It was a beautiful sight as the ships passed each other, dipping their flags and saluting. Everybody felt as if they had been calling at a station in mid-ocean and meeting friends who formed a link with home. Our friends were not the only distinguished people on board, and there had already been pleasant recognitions and presentations. The Governor of Connecticut, with his family, was returning after a three months' absence; so were a distinguished Senator from Michigan and the Attorney-General of the United States. Notwithstanding the untowardness so far of the voyage, the two parties had mingled and grown intimate. There were also half a dozen young English travellers going out to "do" America, whom Lord Bolton had welcomed and presented to his friends. One of them had just been saying to Miss Roberts, "If the winds had been propitious our journey would have been awfully jolly."

"Oh, there is plenty of time for fine weather," was her reply. "Do you remain long in America?"

"Only the few weeks of my vacation," he answered. "All the fellows will return then. To see the States has now become the rage, and we have just snatched a chance open to us."

The Professor was answering questions of the American statesman regarding Civil Service Reform in England. Fred Cuthbert was amusing the American ladies with his drolleries, and De Luynes was explaining to the young men the mysteries of such Canadian winter sports as flourish in the deep snow with a low thermometer. Tom and Miss Winthrop had ensconced themselves in a cosy corner; and the others were all taking good care of themselves.

"Oh, you may laugh," said Miss Winthrop; "but I think enthusiasm about Boston is a very common and very venial sin among Bostonians. But I shall leave you to study the place for yourself and form your own conclusions. My own egotism will be satisfied by talking a little about myself. My poor mother's younger brother is Dr. Elmwood. My father's only brother is Horace Winthrop, of Boston. He is a lawyer at home, and a United States Senator at Washington; his time is divided between the two cities. My brother George and myself are his adopted children; and," she added, her eyes filling with tears, "we are orphans. To you, who have always felt the strength of a father's arm, and the warmth and tenderness of a mother's love, I cannot explain the loneliness, the isolation, which that means. George was graduated at Harvard. He has always lived with my uncle in Boston, and is a lawyer. I have been much with Dr. Elmwood, but both uncles have been our tender and generous protectors. I know of no love stronger than I bear them both; but I dream of a deeper, tenderer feeling I might have cherished toward her I could have called my mother."

"I can understand it all, Miss Winthrop," said Tom, with emotion. "Experience is not the only teacher."

"My experience has been confined to the want of a mother's love, which I have never known," she said. "It is harder for a girl than for a boy to bear. It is the elixir of her life, transfused through her whole being. With that love she is exalted, beatified; her place is little lower than the angels; without it the most cherished delights are cold, and the first place in her heart is vacant. But why speak of what I have lost, since my life is so full of compensations? You must know my brother, and then you will understand what I enjoy in his affection."

"He is no doubt a good brother," said Tom, "but

no one should claim credit for loving you. I have striven in vain myself to avoid that." Noticing that she was disturbed, he added, "I will remember my promise, but why bind me to it?"

"I will tell you by-and-bye," rejoined Miss Winthrop, "but at present I am to speak of myself. I was sent to Germany with an aunt, whom you did not see, though she was with us in London. This was my last year, but we had spent the vacation in the British Isles, and the time was approaching for my return to school, when my uncle announced that I must go home with him, on the plea that family matters required it, though he declined, for the present, to explain. He merely assured me that everyone was well, but said further confidence would be unwise till we reached home. You can fancy my disquietude and apprehension. Here is a secret which I cannot fathom. It was of sufficient importance to call me home. George does not know it, for I have weekly letters from him; it is a mystery. Is it a romance? Both my uncles are unmarried; Dr. Elmwood buried his wife years ago, and my uncle Horace is a bachelor. Do you think me only curious when I feel myself a prey to these anxieties? But why seek to explain the impenetrable? I long to see my brother, and other dear friends await me. I have a score or so of relations in the country round about. They may lack the fashionable refinements, but they love me, and they are very dear to me."

"Of course they love you," said Tom. "I *must* speak! Why do you smother my words, when you know my heart?"

"I must insist upon your promise, my dear friend," she said firmly. "You know nothing of me, and little of my family, or of my position in life. You ought not to be compromised: Is there no middle course for a man and a woman between indifference and infatuation? Be just to yourself and do not embarrass me. I am only a school-girl, though I may seem older than my years. I give you my friendship, and am grateful for your preference. Let us stop here and leave the rest to time."

"I am silenced but not convinced," said Tom, "but I will not press you. Miss Winthrop, there are voices in life, which, if one heed not, become silent—such a voice in your inmost heart, I still hope is pleading for me."

Miss Winthrop's emotion was apparent, but she stifled it.

"Let me join my uncle," she said.

"I only ask for a hope, Miss Roberts," said Lord Bolton; "for permission to renew, at another time, the suit which you deny me now; perhaps I have been too vehement, but forgive me, for my heart has inspired every word I have uttered."

"What you ask is impossible," replied Miss Roberts. "Your attentions honor me, and I cannot say what might happen, were I in a position to receive them, but there is an impassable gulf between us."

"Can you not tell me this mystery? Am I unworthy of your confidence?" he interrupted. "It is dreadful that you should have a secret locked against me in your heart."

"My secret belongs to another. If it were mine to tell, it should be yours; and in that case you would not esteem me less, but you would pity me more."

Tom and Miss Winthrop caught only these words as

they strolled along, and the voices died away in the distance. "How he loves her," said Miss Winthrop, looking with tearful eyes into Tom's face. "She has refused him. Does she love him?"

"Yes," said Miss Winthrop, after a pause.

"What can be her secret?" asked Tom. "She spoke of a gulf that separates them; I wonder if she would really cross it, if her own inclinations were alone consulted."

"I think so," replied Miss Winthrop; "and yet she did not plead for delay."

"Would there have been hope in that?" Tom asked. "What a strange coincidence!" she continued, but her uncle was waiting for her, and Tom politely took his leave. He found De Luynes, with other gentlemen, in earnest conversation. He was in no mood to be interested, but he could not refuse to hear.

"I have always believed," said Mr. Burrows, the Attorney-General, "that the destiny of your country is annexation to mine."

"She would thus become part of a glorious Republic," observed De Luynes, "and it may be that such a change is in store for us. Might not the interests of the Continent be better served if Canada grew to be a great and friendly neighbor? No doubt annexation would solve great commercial and political questions. Canada is growing too rapidly to remain forever as she is. In local matters she is only a nominal dependency, enjoying, practically, control of her own affairs. But the day will come, though perhaps not soon, when she will outgrow this tutelage which sits lightly on her now. Then why should she turn to you? Her children are the offspring of the two foremost nations of the world; they both know how to govern. Canadians have had experience in the methods of constitutional reform; as to her local jurisdiction Canada is a free country; she is working out the problem of British Parliamentary government. There are, indeed, enemies within her borders, but, if the people are wise, they will overcome them. She has verge and scope enough to satisfy the wildest hopes of an ambitious people. Why not encourage her to set up for herself, that there may be wrought out on this Continent two systems of constitutional liberty, so much akin as to create friendship among both peoples, and divergent enough to form a contrast and enable us to compare the two systems?"

"But why maintain the two systems?" interposed Mr. Burrows, "with the expense and annoyance of two long lines of custom-houses, and the general administration of two governments? Why not let us welcome you to our markets, and to the protection and the *prestige* of our power? These are not myths; they have been founded in blood and treasure. I honor your attachment to the Old Country that has served you so well, but which would not hold you a moment after it was manifestly your interest to go. We, too, are your kinsmen, and United North America would be to us all a guarantee of prosperity and peace."

"Oh, why do you covet more?" said De Luynes, "with your boundless territories and your varieties of climate, soil and production? If we were safely intrenched against foreign foes, might there not grow up greater dangers in the way of domestic discord? This question will be settled by the generation which has to solve it, and possibly by lights that are obscure to us now; but, do you not think greed of territory grows like love of accumulation? If you had Canada, how long would Mexico remain out in the cold? and which of the mongrel Spanish-American States could resist, after that, your powerful fascination? All this might increase commerce, but where would remain that sheet-anchor of freedom, intelligent popular opinion? If my thought suggests danger, the peril would threaten us all."

"I had never regarded it in that light," said Mr. Burrows, "and yours is a plausible view."

"I admire your great republic," De Luynes remarked, "and have been rebuked among my own people for my out-spoken opinions. There is a class with us who regard friendship for the 'States' as incompatible with loyalty to the Empire. But if I could return here in a hundred years, I should like to find in North America two great countries which had been true to their traditions, and had promoted the enjoyment of liberty under those two systems among hundreds of millions of prosperous freemen. To have achieved such results would have required wisdom and forbearance, for there are evils now, which, if not suppressed, will insure the destruction of both countries. I have always advocated an extended franchise, but it is a source of danger where the people are mercenary, or where they do not understand their rights. The demagogue is a perpetual menace to free governments. The mere politician looks only to the moment. What we need are statesmen of honor and worth, to lead the people to look beyond for ulterior results. Despotism, with all its hatefulness, moves in a narrow circle, and, controlling few influences, may be comparatively pure. The worst forms of corruption are found where a corrupt people govern. And you have but one safeguard—a healthy public opinion. We must treat as an enemy of the state the man who would debauch it. Thus protected, our free peoples, separate or united, will have before them a glorious future."

"These are noble sentiments," said the Professor, "the stateman's work would be easy where such principles prevailed."

"Utopia!" exclaimed our stranger of the night before.

"We cannot always realize in practice our theories of excellence," remarked the Professor. "But we can set before us a high standard and strive to reach it, and our efforts will improve if they do not perfect us."

The conversation was continued, but Tom was too preoccupied to listen further.

CHAPTER XII.

AVE SANCTISSIMA.

We left Dr. Elmwood and Miss Winthrop together. "My darling, you seem agitated," said the Doctor, addressing her tenderly. "Are you troubled?"

"You shall judge when you know all, my dear uncle," and she told him the story of her relations with Tom.

"Bless me," said the uncle, "I might have suspected this, but you both seemed so old-fashioned that I thought you the most prudent of friends."

Then there was a long silence, broken at intervals by the girl's stifled sobs. At length he took her hand affectionately: "Poor child," he said, "are you really distressed?" She did not answer, and he continued, "You have done right; you are both too young, and you have acted nobly; and the poor young man—was he greatly disappointed by your refusal?"

"Oh, uncle," she sobbed, "I only meant to say that I asked him to wait."

"Cheer up, little one," said the Doctor, "I will tell you a secret. You always like to think of others, and now it will do you good. I only kept the news from you to please George, who wanted to tell you himself. You are going home at his request, and he is shortly to be married."

The young lady clutched his arm nervously. "To whom? Tell me all," she said with a changed and imperious manner. "George has wronged me! What does it mean?"

"Compose yourself, my dear," said her uncle, "George has intended no wrong. He was undergoing a new experience, and his course has been eccentric toward us all. He besought me to help him in his own way, and how could I refuse the boy? He formed a sudden attachment for a young lady in Washington last winter. They were in every way worthy of each other, and she returned his love, but persisted in postponing the engagement. George and her friends remonstrated, but she was going abroad in the spring and desired to be free till her return. Finally, she yielded, but only to the extent that their plighted troth should not be announced till the autumn."

"Who is she?" interrupted the young lady passionately. "Has she been in Europe this summer?"

"Yes, but you did not see her," said he. "George must have pressed her with letters, for she has consented to return and marry him. By his invitation we are going home to the wedding."

"The naughty boy! I ought to refuse my consent, but how can I while the bride is a stranger. I know George would make a wise choice. But this terrible mystery!"

"It was foolish," said the Doctor; "but it will soon be solved, and I shall have betrayed my trust."

"George will forgive you," she whispered. "Tell me all."

"By a strange coincidence," he continued, "the young lady is on board this ship."

"Here, uncle!" she cried excitedly, "lead me to my sister."

"Hush, child," urged the Doctor; "you will need all your prudence and composure. From what I have seen here, there may be trouble in store for poor George. The young lady is Miss Roberts!"

"Then I will answer for her with my life, uncle," she added.

"How can you tell that George may not find a dangerous rival in Lord Bolton?" asked the uncle.

"Never!" she said with emphasis; "I know it." And she told him of the conversation to which she had involuntarily been a listener.

But it did not altogether reassure either of them. Miss Roberts was true, but was her heart engaged in her refusal of Lord Bolton's suit?

"She is a noble girl," observed the Doctor, "and she has resisted a great temptation."

"Not if she loves George," said his companion.

"All the same," he continued, "I wish this *contretemps* could have been avoided."

"I wish I might tell Capt. Conant this strange story," said Miss Winthrop musingly.

"I see no objection, but it should be in confidence," remarked the uncle. "I will send him to you."

"No, *bring* him to me, please; we will consult him together."

"He must be a dull scholar if he does not understand what it means that she needs to confide in him," mused the Doctor, and, almost momently, he returned with Tom on his arm.

"I sent for you, Capt. Conant," she began with a constrained manner, "to tell you a family secret and a strange story."

"I shall be proud of your confidence, Miss Winthop,"

he replied with polite reserve, "and if in any way I can serve you———"

"Wait a little," remarked Miss Winthrop, "till you have heard my story." And she related the particulars as her uncle had told them.

"That *is* a strange story," said Tom; "has it distressed you very much, Miss Winthrop?"

"Oh, I have not thought of myself," she replied. "Do you think I ought to be troubled? My uncle and I wanted the opinion of a third person and we could only trust our secret to you."

"The position is delicate," observed the Doctor, "and suggests thoughts which one dares not express. Have the conditions changed since Miss Roberts accepted my nephew?"

"I think not," Tom replied, "except that I don't believe she is indifferent to Bolton's attentions. He is madly in love with her, at any rate. Many a girl would be fascinated by his wealth and station."

"In our country, George's position is as good as his," said Miss Winthrop curtly. "Oh, I am speaking from an English point of view, some girls regard titles as an unusual distinction," Tom rejoined.

"And they are universally so regarded," remarked Dr. Elmwood.

"But she has refused Lord Bolton, though we have no right to know it," said Tom.

"Was it because she loved George, or that she is in honor bound to him?" inquired his sister. "Something makes me feel that it was an unwilling refusal. George shall know this."

"But she will tell him herself, if it is true," said Tom. "For I believe she *is* a noble woman." "At any rate, it is a matter they must settle themselves, and an affair about which no one should speak to either of them till they have had the opportunity."

"It is strange," said the young lady, musingly, "but I have felt that Miss Roberts avoids me. Can it be that they know who I am? They must have known I was in Europe, and, probably, that I was returning for the wedding."

"One would think," said Tom, "that finding Miss Winthrop of Boston here would suggest your brother."

"One thing seems clear," remarked Dr. Elmwood, "we must avoid embarrassing recognitions."

"If I knew she loved George still, I would throw myself upon her neck; but how awkward, if she should really be struggling to smother another passion," said George's sister.

"Yes, you ought to preserve an incognito toward her. Things have gone so far that it is your wiser course," remarked Tom. "It is a pity you came out in the same steamer; but she must know that Bolton's attentions have been remarked, and it would be embarrassing to discuss them with the sister of her *fiancé*."

"And they ought to have been embarrassing in the presence of that sister," observed Miss Winthrop.

"True," said Tom, "but I don't believe she knows you after all; your name is not uncommon. It may have suggested nothing to her."

It was agreed that Miss Winthrop should be reticent, and for the rest of the voyage maintain the *status quo*. The conversation was interrupted by the announcement of dinner.

In the evening, our friends again assembled in the small parlor off the saloon. The social atmosphere was dull and enervating; for the buoyancy of spirit was lacking which had distinguished their former reunions. Miss Winthrop in one corner and Miss Roberts in another, each with book in hand, and in no mood for reading, appeared taciturn and melancholy. Lord Bolton looked like one in the depths of despair. It was easy for Tom to follow suit. Fred Cuthbert said he was gloomy, because it was the fashion, and one might as well be out of the world as out of the fashion, you know.

"Our friends are out of sorts," said Robert to De Luynes. "You must pour sweet music into their souls."

"Carlotta," he whispered to his wife, "are you, too, under the spell that prevails here?" He ran his fingers over the keys, and, striking a few chords, they sang together that touching invocation:

> Ave Sanctissima
> We lift our souls to thee,
> Ora pro nobis,
> 'Tis nightfall on the sea.
>
> Watch us while shadows lie,
> Far o'er the water spread,
> Hear the heart's lonely sigh,
> Thine too hath bled.
>
> Thou that hast looked on death,
> Aid us when death is near;
> Whisper of heaven to faith,
> Sweet Mother, hear!
>
> Ora pro nobis,
> The wave must rock our sleep,
> Ora, Mater, Ora,
> Star of the deep.

"Something sparkling," said his wife, leaning over De Luynes' shoulder. And the instrument gave forth one of Strauss' inspiriting airs. The mercurial audience was once more all smiles. Such charms hath music to sadden or delight the heart.

"Where is Miss Roberts," inquired Fred Cuthbert of Lord Bolton. "She sings divinely."

"She would have need to do so to follow the music we have heard," replied his Lordship.

"There is a magnetism about the De Luynes that strangely affects me. Husband and wife are alike fascinating," said Robert Holt.

"And they are so accomplished," Fred added.

"Nobody will sing to-night after what has gone before," remarked Lord Bolton. "It is stifling here; I must seek the fresh air."

As he ascended the stairs, Lord Bolton met a lady emerging from the companion-way. "Will you join me in a promenade, Miss Roberts?" he asked.

She assented, and they walked slowly up and down the deck, in the moonlight.

"'Ave Sanctissima,' the heavenly hymn," said Lord Bolton.

"And with what sweetness they rendered it," was the rejoinder; "it touched me as so appropriate at sea."

"I could hardly master my emotion," observed his Lordship. "Its pathos vibrated into the recesses of my soul. I wanted to thank them, but I shrank from trusting myself with words."

"Were you indeed so overpowered?" inquired his companion. "I thought I alone had been weak."

"Oh, emotion is not weakness," Lord Bolton replied. "It springs from the noblest hearts," and the most generous impulse. If I dared I would say a word more."

"Go on," was the reply.

"Miss Roberts," he continued, " you and I have been prepared for such emotions by our interview, which was the most important event of my life, and I know you were not indifferent. Am I unkind to speak to you again? You would forgive me if you could realize how my hopes have centered in you. You are the light of my life. With you I could welcome death and defy misfortune; without you who shall be my deliverer?"

"God," she answered; "we must trust in Him."

"Oh! if we could trust in each other, too.

> 'Yes—loving is a painful thrill,
> And not to love more painful still;
> But surely 'tis the worst of pain
> To love and not be loved again.'"

"Lord Bolton," she said, "Why wring my heart? It pains me if you suffer, but you do not suffer alone. More than this I ought not, must not, tell you; you must spare me and forget me. My troth is plighted to another. It was his secret, and your persistent suit wrung it from me."

"This is a cruel fate," said Lord Bolton, like one stunned. "You are my first love, and I shall never forget you, but I will speak no more of it."

"Great trials are not everlasting," she answered; " they mellow into tender memories as time passes. Let us find my sister."

Meantime, the others had quietly taken their leave, and De Luynes and Robert found themselves alone.

LITTLE ETHEL AS ROBERT LEFT HER.

"A few weeks ago," said Holt, "I found at a police station in London, a man and a woman, with this child."—*Page* 119.

Robert invited his companion to a quiet smoke in his room, where they could talk without molestation.

"I always give myself this little recreation, here, before retiring," he said, "and it delights me to have you share it."

"Thanks, very much," said De Luynes, as he absently examined some books on a shelf against the wall. "May I look at these pictures, Holt?" he asked, as he picked up some photographs that were lying there. "Good heavens! this is the likeness of my child; my little Ethel! where did you get this?"

"Nonsense," said Holt, "I left that child the other day in my own house in London."

"The likeness is unmistakable," persisted De Luynes; "of course it is impossible. Let me show it to my wife;" and he started to go.

"Stay," said Holt, "you must not take it."

"Is there a mystery?" inquired the other.

"I can tell you nothing," was the reply; "but it would be unwise to excite your wife."

"It seems more serious than I thought," said De Luynes. "Is there a secret involved that you cannot confide to me?"

"Compose yourself," said Holt. "Give me time to think," and after a moment's pause, he added, "I will tell you all I know."

"It cannot be," mused Maurice; "the child looks younger."

"A few weeks ago," said Holt, "I found at a police station in London a man and a woman with this child. They had been picked up destitute in the street. The man was silent and morose, but the woman was comely and had an air of patient resignation that attracted me.

They had been without food for two days, the woman said, except what she had begged for the child. They had seen better days but were reduced by misfortune. The child was pale and wan, but her beautiful eyes seemed to appeal to me. An irresistible impulse bade me shield her. The man and woman seemed ill, and not knowing what else to do, I sent them to a private hospital and provided a favorite nurse for the little girl."

"Those eyes *are* Ethel's," interrupted De Luynes, absently regarding the picture. "Describe the child."

"No, let me go on in my own way."

"Pardon me, but I am so impatient," added De Luynes.

"My aunt, who devotes her life to charity, visited these people often afterward, and ministered to the comfort of the child. It was shortly removed because the man and woman were stricken with what seemed a deadly illness. In a few days they both died of a malignant fever. The man was unconscious to the last; the woman raved of some great crime, and her desire to confess it. She continued delirious, however. Once only she alluded to the child, which she averred she had not intended to wrong. It is my aunt's belief that the poor little thing had been abducted from respectable parents; but we had no proof. We advertised but without result in the London and Paris journals for *the parents of a lost child.*' Nothing was left us but to provide for it. I placed it, with its nurse, in my own house and under the direct supervision of my aunt. It was obvious that, if the child lived, what we knew of its origin ought to be kept secret. I must depend upon your discretion. You are the second person only to whom the story has been told."

"It *is* Ethel!" said De Luynes, as if dreaming; and rousing himself, he added, "describe the nurse to me."

Robert endeavored to do so.

"It seems like Nora, the dear old nurse, whom we have so trusted," said De Luynes; "but who was the man?"

"He may have been the father of the child," Holt replied; "but we believe and hope not."

"My God!" ejaculated Maurice, "it is all plain to me now. What if he persuaded the weak woman to elope with him; she loved the child and would not have abandoned it. Moreover, he may have had hope of a ransom. It might have all happened; my poor old mother is an invalid at home. The child was not expected back for the season. There is more than one way they might have managed to deceive her. Holy Virgin! Was Carlotta's disquietude a miraculous warning! Oh! no, I am raving. Yet, for the moment, it all seemed so real." Then, looking at the likeness again, he pursued, "It is the child; if I could return to England by an inward bound vessel———but Carlotta would know all and it would madden her."

"If the child is yours, she is safe," said Robert, soothingly. "So Madame De Luynes' ignorance is bliss, and the child does not suffer. A few days, more or less, will solve the mystery; after all, your Ethel is probably safe at home."

"Poor Nora!" murmured Maurice.

"Compose yourself," pleaded Holt.

"Is it such a tale as would inspire me with composure? My home robbed, my child lost, the treachery of my servants———Heavens! and you would have me tranquil over it?"

6

"My poor friend!" said Robert, "your child is safe at the worst, either in your home or in mine. There would be room for frenzy if she were lost to you altogether. As a strong man it is your duty to be composed. There must be no outward sign of agitation; remember your wife, and save her from the terrible ordeal."

"You are right, Holt," said Maurice, giving him his hand. "I must seek the fresh air and solitude. Let me keep the picture. *Au revoir.*" And he was gone.

"Poor fellow!" said Robert, "I honor his emotions, but he was made for a romantic life. Madame De Luynes need never know that the child was lost till it has again been found." The next morning Robert told the Professor of his interview with Maurice the night before, but that gentleman saw nothing remarkable in what he had to relate, and did not sympathize with Robert's impressions that the parents of the lost child had been found. "A romance of this sort must be reserved for the novels," he said; "such coincidences rarely happen in real life. The child is as likely to have been abducted in London as in Canada, and if you admit this, your fabric falls to the ground."

Tom enjoyed a *tête-à-tête* with Madame De Luynes, and Fred Cuthbert was indefatigable in his attention to Miss Winthrop. Neither Lord Bolton nor Miss Roberts was yet visible; Maurice was absent and pre-occupied, and parried the attempts of his American friends to draw him into further conversation. Mr. and Mrs. Roberts and Dr. Elmwood were watching the sports of the passengers; and thus the day passed from one thing to another without excitement or adventure.

There was an attempt to renew the previous evening's entertainment, but the De Luynes did not sing, and the music languished for want of inspiration. Thus it happens at sea that our feelings are alternately depressed and excited, and the jokes which arouse hilarity to-day will to-morrow fall upon listless and unwilling ears. With our friends the rule had no exception; and if there was cause for want of spirits, it was apparent only to those who knew it.

The next day, and the next, except that the weather was beautiful and that the *Alaric* was making good speed, witnessed nothing of great interest. But on the following morning a ship was sighted which signalled a desire to communicate. The ship "hove to," and the stranger lowered a boat with a single passenger, which quickly made for the *Alaric*. There was great excitement on board at this unusual proceeding, and, as the boat neared the ship, De Luynes, recognizing some one, motioned to his wife and shouted, "Gustave!" To climb up the side of the vessel was the work of a moment.

The greeting between Maurice and his friend was most cordial.

"Gustave, my cousin, you bring bad news," said Madame De Luynes.

"No, no," he answered, embracing her tenderly. "I have but a moment, let me speak to Maurice alone."

"Is Ethel alive? Only tell me that," she persisted.

"Oh! Carlotta, she was quite well when last I saw her. I wanted to save you, but my bad news is that Madame De Luynes is dead."

Carlotta dropped passively into her chair, and Maurice stepped aside with his cousin.

"My poor friend, prepare yourself for worse news; I knew you were coming on the *Alaric*. Your little Ethel is lost. Nora cannot be found and the country is being searched for them."

"I know it," said Maurice, motioning to Holt to join them. "Give me my child's address in London."

Holt wrote it with a puzzled air; Maurice continued, "Gustave, Nora ran away with the child, and died the other day in London; this good friend rescued my darling, and she is now safe in his house. Carlotta knows nothing, but she has been wild with imaginary fears; she has had a supernatural prescience that something was wrong, though she knew not what. Look at that likeness!" handing him the portrait.

"Great heaven! that *is* Ethel," said Gustave.

"It is the likeness of the child my friend rescued," continued Maurice. "You are bound for Paris, but go at once to London, identify the child and cable me."

Holt, who had divined his motive in calling him, had scribbled a hasty note which he handed to Gustave. "Present this," he said, "and if you recognize the baby your course will be easy."

"Good-bye," cried Gustave. "I must go. Salute Carlotta for me. It was this shock that killed your poor mother. Trust me." And bowing to the Captain he re-entered the boat and returned to the ship in waiting.

"I should have gone with him," said Maurice to Holt, "if I could have left my wife. Oh God! my poor mother."

The De Luynes retired, and the lively curiosity of the inquiring passengers was not gratified.

"This has been an unusual incident," remarked the

Captain, as he watched Gustave going off; "the De Luynes must be people of some influence."

In the evening, the Professor and Dr. Elmwood sat alone in a quiet corner of the saloon discussing a toddy before retiring. Right or wrong, this was a custom they both enjoyed and never abused. They did not approach excess; perhaps, as they lingered over the generous glass, where others would have become hilarious, they might have been convivial, reaching just a faint tinge of exaggeration, just a little mellowing of their confidences in and to each other; but never transcending the orthodox limits. They had been speaking of various subjects, of theories of navigation, of the economies of the ship, of its log, its record as to speed, and the manner in which adverse winds had delayed her, the events of the past day, of the way in which Gustave had boarded her, which they thought extraordinary, De Luynes being a mystery to them both. They thought him clever, versatile, and possessed of remarkable qualities. The Professor felt that he might safely confide in his friend, and he told him all we know of poor De Luynes' distractions, including an account of the interview with Robert and the revelations of Gustave.

The Doctor was profoundly impressed; he was, moreover, proud of the confidence, and of the fact that he was in some measure in a position to return it. He told the Professor what he knew of the story of Tom and his niece.

The Professor thanked him, but he already knew it. His boy, he said tenderly, had no secrets from him. The young people he hoped would come to understand each other, but he thought the best way to deal with such matters was to leave them to themselves.

With increasing confidence, Dr. Elmwood then related the story of Miss Roberts and Lord Bolton. There again Tom had forestalled him, but this only left them in a better position to discuss the subject, which seemed full of interest to both. The voyage was not uneventful, they both said, and they agreed that it was better to look on than to interfere; but they expressed their opinions freely, as if nobody could ever know what each had said to the other. So, calmly, do men of middle-age look down upon the tumults that agitate the young. They have had their trials and overcome them; they know that life is full of sorrow, and that time is the great healer; they have learned, also, that one door of enjoyment opens as another closes. They do not expect to enjoy happiness unalloyed, and they know that every cloud has a silver lining. After a while, both retired, sympathetic, but confident that all would come right in the end.

CHAPTER XIII.

"WHO COULD FORESEE PERILS?"

The night was beautiful; and there was only a gentle motion of the waters, and

> 'Every wave with dimpled face,
>   That leaped up in the air,
> Had caught a star in its embrace,
>   And held it trembling there.'

There was silence in the haunts of the passengers, and the great ship moved majestically all the long night over the quiet sea. Who could foresee perils or dream that her strength would fail?

Towards morning the fog-horn, that terror of passengers, began to send forth unearthly sounds. These were warnings to approaching vessels of danger ahead, and they also warned the experienced passenger that a thick fog was prevailing. The sharp eye of the "look-out" could scarcely penetrate the mist, and the chances of collision with vessels in the track were imminent. No position is more calculated to arouse the anxiety of travellers at sea.

"The *Alaric* is a fine ship," said De Luynes, "and well manned; as things go, she is considered to be finely equipped, but she is on a fast line and there is the danger. No human eye could descry a ship in this thick mist, making towards her in time to arrest an inevitable crash; and yet she will rush on at full speed in order to make time, when she ought to go slowly and cautiously. In case of accident, what provision have we for saving life? The boats, if they could be safely lowered, would not accommodate two hundred passengers, and, including cabin and steerage, we have on board well nigh a thousand souls. The life-preservers would be useless to most of us, because we have not been taught how to wear them, and, awkwardly adjusted, they would create more danger than they would avoid. All is delightful in smooth sailing, but who shall say that disasters may not occur which would put human life in unnecessary jeopardy?"

"Let us count the boats," said the Professor; they did so and found there were but ten; each could carry safely but twenty people. "This is fearful," he added; "what can we do?"

"Oh, we must take our chances, accidents are the exception; the ships generally make prosperous voyages, and so these defects are not exposed. They are neither noticed nor remedied."

"I hope the fog will lift soon," said Robert Holt. "This darkness is becoming intolerable."

But all day long it enveloped them, and the dreadful whistle continued to herald the fact. The passengers became gloomy and apprehensive as the night closed in, and there seemed on every countenance a common dread of danger. The decks and the saloons were early deserted; the anxieties of some were forgotten in sleep, but most people wooed it in vain.

There was a timid rap at Dr. Elmwood's door. "May I come in, dear uncle? I am distracted with this terrible whistle and with these gloomy surroundings. May I sit with you?"

"Sit down, child," he responded; "we are making splendid time, and I see no cause for alarm; yet life is uncertain and apprehensions are natural. We must look above for strength.

"What a field of thought is open to one who watches at midnight in such a sea, feeling that the next moment may precipitate a crash which might engulf every one in the deep waters. How the far-off past returns to one with forgotten scenes which are now made familiar again; one's boyhood, one's school days, the companions of one's youth—and how the minutest details of one's life are lived over again. Home and friends are with him, and it seems as if their presence were real; the good he has done, the wrongs he has suffered, and been guilty of, how all are reviewed and re-enacted, and how he thinks he would undo this and do that could he live his life over again. Clearly he sees now the path of duty, and feels that it would have been easy to follow it; in such a mood, the triumphs of his life are trifles light as air and his trials not worth remembering. He will make amends if he is spared by becoming the almoner of God's bounties to the poor. He wonders at his own indifference in the past, and as for the future he piously pledges himself to do unto others as he would they should do unto him.

"Of all the hundreds in this great ship, how many are realizing this description? How many, being fearful would amend their lives? How many, once safe again, would renew them? But thank God we are in no such extremity; we are sailing over a smooth sea, in a strong ship, which has weathered the voyage these fifty times, and not always in fine weather. Humanly speaking, the conditions are all in our favor, and whatever happens will be under the eye of Him without whose knowledge 'not a sparrow falls.'

"You are weary and excited, and you need repose," continued the Doctor. "The morning will bring relief and further evidences of God's mercies. We are rapidly nearing home now, and in a few days you will be recounting these trials with a smile, to your friends. You may have great need of strength when you reach them. Summon courage and seek rest."

"Pray with me, uncle," she said; and they joined in a fervent prayer of thanksgiving, petitioning the Almighty Father for protection and peace.

"I feel better, uncle; you have soothed and comforted me; I can sleep now; good night."

"Poor girl!" said Dr. Elmwood, musingly, after she left. "I wish I could comfort myself with the confidence which I tried to impart to her. She will have a fearful burden to carry when she reaches home. I wonder, would she not have been better able to meet it had she accepted Tom's suit?"

It was late at night, but De Luynes and the young men were still on deck. "I cannot sleep," said De Luynes; "this fog is so dense and our speed is so great, that I am afraid; we are within the chapter of accidents, and a collision would sink us; beyond the whistle, the ship can take no precautions. The sea is alive with steamships and coasters. I have been trying in vain to persuade the Captain to slacken speed; he was not rude, but he gave me to understand that he was in command of the vessel. Heavens! that light!" There was a cry of "ship ahead!"

"Port your helm!" shouted the officer; it was too late; a brig had struck them, and a terrible crash followed; everybody was hurled prostrate. In two minutes the deck was covered with half-dressed and terrified passengers. The confusion was fearful; the excitement had no bounds; women and children rushed aimlessly about uttering piteous cries and supplications; and, with few exceptions, the men were equally frantic.

Above all the tumult was heard the clear, ringing voice of De Luynes shouting, "Silence! We are all safe; let us have order and all may yet be well."

Courage always inspires hope, and there was a lull, as if men waited to see what he would do next. The ship had righted herself, but the engine and machinery had stopped. There were cries of distress from the neighboring brig. She was disabled and sinking. Her crew had taken to the water. To lower the boats of the *Alaric* was but the work of a few minutes; they moved toward the wreck cautiously in the darkness, that they might avoid the suction of the sinking ship while they sought to rescue her people. The lanterns could not penetrate the thick fog, and the sailors, who could not see, shouted that help was at hand, and thus encouraged the desperate swimmers. Some were pulled into the boats; some having made for the ship's signal lights, were assisted to climb up her side, while others, alas! less fortunate, were lost.

The passengers of the *Alaric* had, momently, forgotten their own troubles in striving to watch the struggles for life going on around them. Of course, they could see nothing, but they heard the cries of distress with, now and again, a word of encouragement. At length all was silent, except the voices of the men as the boats were returning. Meantime, the Captain had been examining the ship and had found her sadly damaged. Her bow had been crushed in; some of the rigging of the lost vessel had been entangled with the screw, and had stopped the engine, leaving no motive power, except the canvas, which, under the most favorable circumstances could only propel the steamer a few miles an hour.

The rescued sailors reported their vessel as the Spanish brig *Isabella*, bound from the West Indies to Liverpool. She had been struck amidships and cut in two. The Captain, his wife and children were among the lost.

"Poor sufferers," said our Captain, "only with this brief record do their lives come into ours; perhaps he was a brave seaman and his wife a lovely help-meet; was it not after all a mercy that when they were called they might tread together the shoreless depths of the sea of death? They were not like the two women grinding at the mill; the one taken and the other left; they died as they had lived, united."

The passengers began slowly to withdraw from the deck, and thus quiet was restored; for notwithstanding all their misfortunes, there was as yet no actual discomfort. They had now to depend on the sails, and might be days longer at sea; but if they could avoid a storm, the good ship would weather it out.

What a day was that which followed! the presence of death, the sense of danger escaped; the reaction from intense excitement and fear, was like the bruised sensation that follows extreme tension of the muscles. Each had lived a life-time in a few hours, and yet all felt that their sufferings had been rewarded, because comparative safety had succeeded the hour of trial.

Our travellers were not so prostrated, for they possessed more than the average of courage and self-reliance; but they were thoughtful and disquieted. Perhaps all this strain had been a mercy to those who had suffered. At any rate, it had brought the lovers together again, and for the moment they had forgotten the cause of their recent separation. Was it because they were dear that they were again near to each other? The distraction was a positive relief to the De Luynes, who had been so much oppressed by their own troubles.

"Carlotta," De Luynes said to his wife, "I felt at one time that the hope you have so often expressed would be realized—that we should die together."

"Oh! Maurice," she answered, "if it had come to that, I could not have borne that you should go alone." She spoke of home, which they were nearing, of their poor old mother, whom they should meet no more.

"What a sweet, pure life she led, Maurice! Oh that my life could be such a blessing to others! How calmly I am sure she went to her reward. But she loves us still. Do you not think she watches over us now in our perils?"

"She loves us still, dear Carlotta," he said to her, as the eyes of both filled with tears. "She sent Gustave with that message," he added aside. "It is all clear to me now. Is this an inspiration? Are hidden things revealed to us as we grow older?"

"Good morning, Holt," he said aloud, as that gentleman with a polite bow to Carlotta joined them. They spoke of the accident; Holt was hopeful, nay, confident.

The machinery was disabled, Holt remarked; but apart from that, the ship as good as new. The sailing would be slow, but it was not dangerous.

All had words of sympathy for the poor fellows who had been lost from the unfortunate vessel.

"Sister Ethel will be waiting for us with our dear little one," said Madame De Luynes abruptly. "God grant that we may reach them safely; my sister would start for Quebec yesterday; you must see my sister Ethel, Mr. Holt; she is a dear girl, and they flatter me by saying that she resembles me."

"Yes," said Maurice, "Sister Ethel is among the loveliest of women, and in appearance and disposition she is like my wife."

Robert responded politely.

"Oh, my baby," resumed Madame De Luynes; "how I long to embrace her! I wonder if she has changed much, and will she know me, Maurice? Of course, you don't care for babies, Mr. Holt, but you would be struck with the child's great, lustrous eyes."

"They are like her mother's," said Maurice.

"Dear old Nora, her nurse, has been so faithful," continued the child's mother; "I am glad we brought her presents from Paris. I don't mean that she is 'old' in years; one uses the word as a term of endearment;" and so the fond mother continued to speak of her darling, till her husband and friend persuaded her to seek rest and composure.

It was mid-day; the ship was doing poor work and the sky was overcast and lowering. The wind had freshened and the fog was lifting; but the most powerful glass showed no signs of the lost vessel; all hope was abandoned for the safety of those who had not been rescued in the morning.

"I fear that our troubles are not over," Dr. Elmwood observed to the Professor; "there is a storm gathering, and in a storm we should navigate poorly with a disabled ship."

"I have great confidence in the Captain," was the answer. "These ships maintain the discipline of a man-of-war; our position is not unprecedented, and we can depend upon the best of human skill to bring us safely into port."

"Yet we owe our misfortune to a palpable blunder, or worse," remarked the Doctor; "running at full speed through a dense fog. It might have saved us a day, if there had been no accident, but it multiplied our chances of disaster. Do you believe the collision would have occurred if we had been running at half speed? De Luynes was frantic about it all last evening, and, I am told, had sharp words with the Captain,——"

"Who, I suppose, was simply obeying his orders," interrupted the Professor.

"Oh, as to that, the criticism is just the same, whether the responsibility rests with the Company or with the officers of the ship; already, lives have been lost and more are in jeopardy. It would be a poor compensation to say that the *Alaric* tried to make better time than vessels of another line."

"There is truth in what you say," said the Professor. "When we commit ourselves to the mercies of the deep we are entitled to every protection from those who are amply paid for transporting us safely."

"Yes," rejoined the Doctor, "and if we are lost, there will be censure and, perhaps for a time, more caution; but if we come safely into port our adventures will be forgotten, and the abuse will go on till others, less fortunate, are lost by the blunders which threatened us.

Men are slow to prevent mishaps, even when the danger is plain enough; we are apt to move against them, with a strong hand, after they have occurred."

"Cheer up," said the Professor; "you are morbid, my dear friend."

"We are in God's hands," remarked the Doctor, as he walked leisurely away.

Knots of passengers were talking earnestly here and there. There were now none of the amusements and hilarities of the early days of the voyage. During the afternoon the storm continued to threaten, and a stiff north-easterly wind set in. The sea, which had been tranquil, became agitated, and the ship drifted at its mercy. Her bow had been stove in, and the forward compartment was filled with water.

"If this should increase to a gale we shall have a rough night," the captain said to the first officer. "We are prepared for the worst, sir; the side lights have been screwed up, and everything about the deck is securely lashed." "She seems to lie easy now, with the help of this aft-sail, but I am afraid, with a heavy sea, she might fall off into the trough of it."

"That's so, sir," responded the first officer. "And, in that case, we might lose our boats and start the bulkhead." "We must do our best; though the chances are against us."

Toward the night the wind blew a gale, and the outlook was gloomy and threatening. The terrors of the morning were reviving among the passengers. De Luynes, calm and resolute, his wife leaning on his arm, was everywhere seeking to encourage them. The ship tumbled and rolled on the agitated waters; a heavy sea washed the deck and bore two unfortunate sailors to destruction. A third clung to the lee-rigging and was rescued in a state of exhaustion.

De Luynes summoned his friends to his cabin and instructed them as to the use of the life-preservers.

"Our danger is," he said, "that our ship may be swamped in a trough of the sea and founder. That risk may be remote, but it is well to prepare for it."

"The danger is not imminent," remarked Lord Bolton, "but it is right to adopt precautions."

All this time the ship was pitching and lurching, as if each strain might be her last; everywhere children were crying, women were moaning and screaming, and men and women, more composed, were kneeling; some in silent, others in audible, prayer. It was a scene which few have witnessed, and, once witnessed, no one can forget. There was a universal bidding adieu to life and a supplication for mercy.

At length the storm burst, the wind blew a gale, and the waves became rolling mountains of water; yet, up to this time, the ship had kept her course, and the sails had assisted to steady her. The wind suddenly shifted and blew a hurricane, which made a cross-sea. She reeled and tumbled, under the strange pressure, like one who was becoming weary in an unequal fight, and was attacked by fresh enemies; twisting and turning, in the fierce conflict, she was at length caught in a trough of the sea. It was a peril from which it seemed she could never be rescued. The commotion on board was frightful. Passengers clung to whatever was strong enough to support them, or were hurled, helpless and bruised, along the deck. Some shrieked with pain from their hurts; others from the terror of the surroundings. This state of things continued all night, but in the morning the wind had moderated, and there was a lull.

"Captain," said Lord Bolton, clinging to a life-line, "will you lower a boat and allow me with my companions to put to sea in her?"

"Impossible," was the reply. "No boat could live in this sea, and we have neither men nor officers to spare."

"We want no help," urged Lord Bolton. "Half a dozen of us have been in the navy and can manage a boat in a storm. I would risk one in the open sea sooner than this."

The captain always said in excuse afterward that he had been magnetized by Lord Bolton's vehement manner. His lordship had already gathered his friends. One of the boats, that had done service yesternight, was lowered. His friends at first assented and then refused to accompany him. "There is no time to be lost," he said; "it is a choice of evils." He had trusty companions to aid in managing the boat, and the majesty of his manner persuaded them. The passengers looked on, but nobody would have taken the risk. The difficulty of boarding her seemed insurmountable.

"Come with us, De Luynes, you will be safer," said he. "The boat will be well manned and the chances are a hundred to one in our favor."

"Shall we go, Carlotta?"

"As you like," she responded.

After many attempts, they were finally successful, and Lord Bolton's boat, manned by his friends and laden with his party, was launched upon the turbulent waters.

"Now, boys, keep her before the wind," he cried; "we are all safe if you obey me;" and they sailed away, and were soon out of sight of the ship. There was no panic, such was the magnetic influence of their brave pilot; and there was even little apprehension.

On board the ship things went from bad to worse, with no prospect, except of that final relief, which, at first, they had all so much dreaded. The sails were blown away, the sea had been breaking over the ship, and the water, rushing down the sky-lights and companion-ways, was slowly filling her. At this moment a steamer was reported coming toward them. Signals of distress were hoisted, and, to their intense relief, were promptly answered. The reaction aboard ship was instantaneous; despair was replaced by hope and even confidence, and the emotions of the passengers were scarcely less manifest under the latter conditions than they had been in the former.

The captain of the sinking steamer signalled his condition, and asked the stranger for aid. She approached and promised by signals to send out boats. The boats of the *Alaric*, except two on the lee-quarter, were washed away, as were also her life-rafts, and the decks had been swept of everything movable; but torn shreds of sail hung from the broken yards, and the whistling of the winds over the deck, and through the cordage, was like a concert of fiends in the ears of the imprisoned passengers. The gale exhausted itself in fitful squalls and copious showers, which the sailors knew would shortly smooth the waters. On board the succoring ship strong and willing hands were at work swinging out the boats preparatory to lowering them for the rescue of the doomed ship's passengers. Within three hours, so skilfully had the work been managed, every man, woman and child had been transferred to the stranger vessel, and not too soon; for scarcely had an hour elapsed before the ill-fated *Alaric*, dipping and plunging, sank beneath the sea.

It was night now, and darkness prevailed. The rescued passengers were safe on board the good steamer *Thiers*, bound for Havre. At the suggestion of the Captain of the *Alaric*, the *Thiers* passed the night and a great part of the next day in a fruitless search for the missing life-boat. There would be many discomforts in a crowded ship, but the most fastidious would bear them for the sake of security and rest. But where were Lord Bolton and his friends? The most callous would have been glad to know, and wished them kindly. Would they be all lost? Would they not have been safer to have remained with the ship?

CHAPTER XIV.

"THE KING OF TERRORS."

THE next morning was bright, but there was a reminiscence of the storm in the agitation of the waters. A life-boat was lying to, and a single glass was seeking to descry a sail. It was Lord Bolton's. The night had been stormy and perilous to his frail craft. Precious lives had been lost; and the survivors were in mourning. Early the night before, a dip of the boat had thrown Miss Roberts into the sea; half a dozen bold swimmers had leaped after her, but she had not been rescued, and only half of those who had gone to her aid returned. Lord Bolton, Tom, Cuthbert, and Holt were saved, but two of the young men, and alas! De Luynes, who had almost saved the young girl, and had performed prodigies of daring, had finally succumbed and been drowned. Overwhelmed by this calamity, Madame De Luynes had swooned and was still unconscious. Such restoratives as they had, were applied without effect, and the greatest anxiety was entertained. Mrs. Roberts was scarcely less overcome. Lord Bolton, mindful of his responsibilities, exercised a wonderful self-command, and did everything to give his friends comfort and confidence. In his management of the boat he had displayed the skill of a sailor and the courage of a hero; they were well provided with rations, but all were anxious to sight a ship, and had been watching for a sail the whole morning. The ranks of the crew had been sadly thinned, and those who were left were mourners; but they had stout hearts and brawny arms; and they made for the west, the sun and the stars guiding them, and as the waves would permit. Their invalids for some time did not improve. Mrs. Roberts had regained consciousness, but was still suffering from nervous prostration. Madame De Luynes remained in an unconscious state and without much sign of vitality. Taken all in all, it was a lamentable outlook, and stronger hearts, if one could have found them, might have quailed. But the sea grew quieter as the day wore on, and they hoisted a sail and sped onward as best they could.

Miss Winthrop was unceasing in her attentions to Madame De Luynes. Lord Bolton thought it better to let her rest; but Miss Winthrop feared that the prolonged swoon would endanger her chances of resuscitation. They all expressed hopes or fears, but no one could give advice as to treatment; and so it happened that nature was left to herself, and sometimes she is the best physician. At all events, while the intellect was obscured, her deadly misfortunes did not haunt her, and returning consciousness might set her faculties on edge and render grief more wearing than prostration. She remained thus till toward evening, when a deep sigh denoted returning animation. She spoke, but her voice was hoarse and unnatural; opening her eyes, she regarded them with the vacant stare of one dazed and trying to remember.

"Papa will meet us at the station, darling," she said; "he has been waiting long for us, and, oh, how his little Ethel and mamma will love him!" There was not a dry eye among them. "Dear Maurice," she continued, "how cruelly he has been misunderstood by his enemies; he only wanted to do good, but they painted him black to his own dear people whom he loved, and they thwarted him at every turn. But he was patient, he never cursed them. 'I must render good for evil,' he said to me. Maurice, darling, did I chide you sometimes? Well, it's all over now; I was exacting, perhaps; my love was selfish. Come, let us embrace and forgive each other." Then she would seem to fondle her child and address her dear friends, and finally she lapsed into stupor again.

"This is dreadful," said Lord Bolton; and so they passed the long night, some of them between waking and sleeping, others on the watch and at the tiller. Carlotta alternately slept and wandered; but she uttered no word to indicate consciousness of her sad bereavement.

"Sister Ethel," she said once, "we met a young gentleman in our travels, he was, oh, so kind! If I had been young I should have admired him. We told him about you."

Next morning a sail was in view and they tried to signal her by every means available. At length she made toward them, and they felt that deliverance was near. They were rescued and received every kindness and attention. The relieving vessel was the good ship *Waterloo*, bound from Havana to Quebec, and they were within two days of the latter port. Lord Bolton looked at once after the comfort of his friends. Mrs. Roberts was convalescent; he pressed her hand and left her without speaking. She understood his emotion and burst into tears.

"Oh! my lost sister," she said, "why could you not have lived to make him happy?"

Carlotta did not recognize him, but addressed him as "Mons. le Curé," and upbraided him for his animosity towards her husband.

"If you knew him as I know him," she said, "you would mourn for your mistake in having crushed him. Maurice," she continued, "your mother has gone away. You must go and fetch her. Little Ethel is at home now with Nora. The sweet child! we shall see her to-morrow; and oh, Maurice, did I tell you, that awful day, that if you should die, I would lie by your side in the grave? And so I would, my precious husband; where you go, I must follow. 'Thy people shall be my people, and thy God, my God.'"

Lord Bolton left her in tears. "The first I have shed for years," he soliloquized. "I wonder when her eyes are opened, will her heart be as heavy as mine?" He found the Professor and Dr. Elmwood fatigued but comfortable; Col. Lyons had not accompanied him in the boat, and his young friends were about seeking that rest which all so sadly needed. He sought his cabin, and kneeling, prayed, "Oh, God, have mercy upon me! My punishment is greater than I can bear. Lead me to become the almoner of charities in her name, and to such a lifetime of good works as would have been pleasing in her sight; for I know that upon my faithfulness in these things it depends whether I shall meet her again." What vicissitudes these weary sufferers have experienced, within the last few hours, and yet what mercies have been vouchsafed to them! Which one of them will remember all and profit by them to the end?

And now our travellers have retired. The great

strain has been removed; exhausted nature yields to the reaction. Poor Carlotta, left to the care of her maid and the surgeon, passed the time between stupor and wandering, and the day and the night were uneventful. The next morning broke bright and beautiful. The hills were visible in the distance, for the ship was navigating the broad bosom of the river. Telegrams would be sent from the first station to the friends of the rescued. Lord Bolton had sent inquiries after all his friends. The condition of the invalid continued without change, but the others of the party were refreshed and comforted.

"That scene yonder is magnificent," said Dr. Elmwood, pointing to the shore they were nearing, "if one had the heart to enjoy it. The altitude of the mountains seems prodigious, and how beautiful is the variegated foliage with which, here and there, they are adorned."

"Beauties will multiply as we ascend the river," observed the Professor, "and reach the bounds of habitation and culture. On either side are rich lands, possessed by thrifty *habitants*, who maintain there the habits and customs which they brought from France generations ago. These settlements were originally founded under the feudal system. There were the Lord and his tenant, the *seigneur* and his *censitaire*. The latter paid various tributes, and could not even take a bushel of corn to be ground, except at the mill of his master."

"Is not all that changed?" asked the Doctor.

"Yes," was the reply, "but you cannot in a moment change the consequences of an old aristocratic system. It educates a people to the idea of superiority on the one side and to dependence on the other. One class is born to command and the other to obey, and when you destroy this system you may only have changed the yoke. The people so trained are still waiting to obey, and would fall an easy prey to illegitimate masters. Poor De Luynes had large property down here, and he often spoke of these conditions; he complained that the system of education was not calculated to elevate the people, and he despaired of improvement while matters remained as at present."

"He was rather hopeless of Lower Canada," said Dr. Elmwood, "and he was a man of great parts and wide reading."

"Yes, Maurice De Luynes was an accomplished man," remarked the Professor. "I knew his father by reputation, and had even met him in London and in Paris. He was a man of rare gifts, which his son seems to have inherited. His talents might have been of great service in a country where there was independent public opinion; but here there was no field for them in politics. Science, art, belles-lettres and benevolence, father and son might have pursued with their ample means, and their cultivated, charitable tastes, had the restrictions been less galling. But the scope was too narrow, and their *penchant* was for public life. The father died of a broken heart, and the son seemed to have inherited his despondency. I had formed an exalted opinion of him and of his fitness for the highest occupations. The broad views which made him unacceptable at home would have recommended him in more tolerant circles. The Imperial service might have profited by what his own country lost. I hinted as much to him, but he did not seem ambitious of distinction, and said that he was too old to begin a new life. So my views did not prevail."

"He has entered a higher service now, poor fellow," said the Doctor, sadly, "and from what I hear, his wife may soon follow him."

Tom and Miss Winthrop met for the first time since their rescue, that morning, and at sight of him she burst into tears. "Pray forgive my weakness," she said at length, "but I am not strong yet, and everything has been so dreadful. What shall I say to my brother? How can I comfort him?"

"Great griefs are not assuaged with words," replied Tom, "and perhaps you will find guidance when you have need. His trials might have been sore, even if no accident had befallen us. He must suffer as others have suffered, and he will find strength and aid where others have found them. Am I a clumsy comforter? And yet I can pity him, for I know what desolation would have overwhelmed my heart if I had lost you."

Miss Winthrop bade him be silent, but gave him her hand. "We must not be selfish," she said; "if our burdens are lighter than those of others, we have so much the more sympathy to spare. But what can I say to my poor brother?"

"Wait," said Tom, "till he comes; the occasion will inspire you."

"Will he come here," she asked, "on board the ship?"

"No, that will be impossible, but he will not lose time; if he does not meet you at Quebec, I shall go with you to Boston; but, ah, I had forgotten your uncle."

"You shall come, my friend," said the young lady,

"if my uncle and my brother are both there. Who can be nearer to me than you, who have shielded me on this terrible voyage of death?" she added, passionately.

Tom saw the change with delight, but he did not notice it openly. "She loves me," he thought, enraptured; "but I must not press her now."

All the other young men were in a group around Mr. and Mrs. Roberts, but their sympathy was conveyed by looks rather than by words.

"That is a touching picture," said Dr. Elmwood to the Professor, as the sad group caught their attention. "But where is Bolton? He was on deck this morning to inquire for us, but usually he has clung to the solitude of his cabin; his heart is terribly wrung."

Holt, catching the last words, said, "Yes, poor fellow; he is dreadfully broken and has entirely given up at last. He mastered himself with a strong will while his responsibilities lasted. I never knew his fine qualities as they have been displayed in this great trial, though I have always admired him. But it is pitiable to see him now."

"You should go to him," said the Professor to Dr. Elmwood.

"I was with him last night," was the reply. "He was full of reverence and resignation; it is better to leave him alone now that his marvelous self-command has yielded to a natural grief. He will find relief and composure after giving way to it. I will seek him by-and-bye. He is one to gather strength from spiritual consolation. He feels himself crushed, but he speaks beautifully of his trust in Divine aid, and his longing to lead that better life which he knows will draw him nearer to her whom he has lost." "He is less resigned now," said Robert; "he regards his bereavement as punishment, and incessantly mourns that it is greater than he can bear."

"But his sense of duty will make him strong again," observed the Doctor. "There are other sufferers, and Bolton is not the man to give way to what he calls selfish griefs, while others need his assistance."

"Yes, we are all sufferers," remarked Robert, "and we have all been objects of his solicitude. But he blames himself about the De Luynes. He says that but for him they would have remained on the *Alaric*."

"And both have been lost," said a voice.

"Then, in grieving over the loss of Miss Roberts," continued Holt, "he fears that he over-persuaded her; and says that her brother, until finally pressed by her, seemed unwilling to go in the life-boat. Sometimes he feels that he was reckless and wonders does Roberts blame him."

Roberts overheard this, and said to his wife: "We must go to him, poor fellow; he has behaved so nobly and now he needs us."

"Miss Roberts was a noble character," Holt continued.

"And both noble and lovely were the De Luynes," added the Doctor.

"Yes. I was intimate with Maurice for days, and we spoke of many things which I am now glad to have discussed with him. It is strange how I at first misjudged him, but toward the end, as I knew him better, he inspired me with a tender regard which one man rarely entertains for another. He was too sensitive and deprecatory of himself; he regarded his life as a failure because he had not won success in a single path, but he said that, in his circumstances, there was nothing left for him of political usefulness, and that public opinion was too superstitious and credulous to afford him a fair field. He was brought up under the eye of his father, who had delegated to an old friend, a Jesuit, the duty of instructing his boy. De Luynes' quick perceptions revolted against some of the lessons he had been taught, but he found a strange delight in others. He had a taste neither for exaggerated humiliations and self-denials, nor for the unreasoning obedience which he was taught. His imagination was fascinated by pictures of celestial purity and by the mystic philosophy he learned; but such was the natural and outspoken frankness of his character that he was in little danger of ever acting upon such teachings as would lead him, for any cause, to pervert the truth, or to do evil that good might come. The old Jesuit loved him, but, of course, subordinately to the interests of his Order; and he marked out for him a career in life very different from that which the young man actually followed. Maurice's father watched the progress of his son with satisfaction, for he saw that he was gaining knowledge without imbibing a spirit of hostility to liberty. Finally, when he went to Paris to complete his education, he was carefully guarded from extremes, and was trained to be, at once, a loyal son of his Church and an earnest advocate of freedom. He loved the genius but deplored the skepticism of the popular *littérateurs;* and he would have restrained the people through the influence of a holy faith and the spiritual teachings of the Church, which left them room to think and act for themselves in matters public and secular. I suggested that there might be difficulty in drawing the line, but he said, 'No, there could be nothing incompatible between the service of God and an independent and conscientious devotion to one's country. The Church might denounce free-thinkers in religious matters, but she must not interfere with free speech and free opinions in the service of the State.' He read law in Paris, but he frequented society at the same time, and perhaps learned more of the world than of jurisprudence. There, too, he met Carlotta Lytton, of Connecticut, whose father had, at one time, been attached to the American Embassy. Carlotta was a New England girl, but had spent some time in France with her mother's friends, and was a favorite of society there. The year after, he married her, and they took up their residence on his estate in Canada. About this time his father died and left him a large fortune. He was ambitious to serve his people, and was elected to parliament. But you have learned from his own lips that he was overmatched and crushed by his enemies. He made no secret of his disappointment, regarding himself a victim of intolerance and bigotry. The rest you know. His young wife, as you have all seen, is worthy of him, and may soon rejoin him. If she lives, what sorrow and desolation await her! There is a strange romance about their child, the shock of whose loss killed De Luynes' mother; but I believe the child is safe and will soon be restored to her desolate home."

"Truth is stranger than fiction," said the Professor. "What a sad romance it all is!"

Mr. and Mrs. Roberts had sent a message to Lord Bolton, desiring an interview, and he had promised to come to them in an hour. He entered their presence with a firm step and an air of self-control.

"I have sent for you," said Mr. Roberts, "because my wife and I felt that we must see you; but not to indulge in any formal expressions. Perhaps, in view of our terrible loss, words are more trying than solitude. You, who have loved her so much, ought to know that she was not indifferent to your attentions. You may have divined as much, but she felt that in her position she could not tell you all. After a short acquaintance last winter my sister became engaged to an excellent and most promising young man. He was impatient to be married at once, but though she loved him, she sought to postpone the marriage. His letters were importunate, however, and she finally consented to marry him shortly after our return. After her acquaintance with you, she began to have doubts about herself, and of her real love for George Winthrop; 'but I have promised him,' she would say to me, 'and I must discuss this matter with George before I harbor a thought of being disloyal to him. He is noble and generous and would release me, but I am bewildered and miserable. George and the world might think that wealth and position had influenced me, and I am bound in honor to be true to my pledge' Her one idea was to hide her heart and be worthy of her *fiancé*. Had she lived, she would have told you all this, but now it becomes my duty to do so."

"I knew it all," said Lord Bolton, "and I was selfish to press my attentions; she acted the part of a true woman. Under the discipline of the last few days, I might have learned unselfishness; but as things were, I never could have given her up to another. Was it to rebuke my assurance that she was snatched from me in this dreadful way? Does the hand of a kind

Providence rule over these things? Oh, God! Why couldst Thou not in some other way have afflicted me?" And overcome by his emotions he sobbed aloud. They all wept; and after a pause, Mrs. Roberts, recovering herself, placed her hand upon Lord Bolton's shoulder and said: " My dear friend :

> "'There is no Death! What seems so, is transition——.
> This life of mortal breath
> Is but a suburb of the life elysian,
> Whose portal we call death.
>
> "'In that great cloister's stillness and seclusion,
> By guardian angels led,
> Safe from temptation, safe from sin's pollution,
> She lives whom we call dead.'"

The scene on either side of the river was beautiful; but nobody was in a mood to enjoy it; and when night set in, everybody gladly retired for the last time during this untoward voyage. Next morning the roofs and spires of the old city were visible, and as the ship finally came alongside of her wharf, Miss Winthrop espied her brother, and there was mutual recognition. Ethel Lytton, with friends, was also in waiting and prepared to board the ship for her sad interview, though not prepared for the shock produced by the condition of her widowed sister. Carlotta, still wandering in mind, recognized no one, but spoke plaintively of her husband and child. She was taken in loving arms to a carriage, and was driven rapidly to her desolate home, which she called an hotel, and in which she expected Maurice and little Ethel soon to join her. Lord Bolton and Holt followed to make inquiries and to offer assistance, and met Miss Lytton, who was strangely calm and self-possessed. The doctor was with her sister, and had less fear for her life than for her reason; but all thought unconsciousness a mercy, so dreadful would have been her condition had she realized all her loss.

At this moment a cable was handed Miss Lytton, addressed to Maurice De Luynes. She was overcome for the moment. Robert's quick eye caught the situation, and he asked politely to be allowed to read it to her. It was from Gustave. Little Ethel was found safe and well, and would return with him by the next steamer.

"Be tranquil, I can explain it all," he said, and he told her of Gustave's interview with Maurice and his own relations to the child.

"She will be here in a week," said Miss Lytton, much excited. "You have saved her; pray remain with us till she arrives."

Holt readily assented.

"You will stay with me, Bolton," he said.

"With all my heart, if you desire it," and addressing Miss Lytton, he added; "I have a superstitious faith that the arrival of the child will restore the mother; I have known such things."

"God grant that it may be so," she said, nervously.

As the visitors were taking their leave, Miss Lytton and her friends pressed them to take up their lodgings at the mansion.

"This is no place to accept hospitalities," considerately remarked Lord Bolton; "we can remain only if we may be of service."

"If it would not incommode you," said the young lady, "you would gratify me by remaining. I cannot regard you as strangers."

So it was arranged that they should return later. Their luggage was lost, and a fresh wardrobe must be provided. But that night they slept under what had been the roof of Maurice De Luynes.

There was no change in Carlotta's condition; the first impression of the physician was confirmed, that her life was not in danger but that her reason was overthrown. A severe illness, a sudden shock, or, time might restore her; but at present quiet and good nursing were all that were needed. An uncle and aunt of De Luynes were in the house with Miss Lytton, and occasionally friends and relations stayed for a few days at the mansion, but the care of the stricken household fell upon her. The young lady was equal to her responsibilities. She had been carefully trained for such emergencies, while, at the same time, her polite education had not been neglected.

"What a beautiful girl," both her guests exclaimed as she retired, and left them for the first time alone together.

"How she resembles her sister," Lord Bolton said. "Except that she has a younger and more cheery look, I would swear that she was Madame De Luynes."

"Yes, Maurice told me that," Holt observed, "almost the last time we spoke together on the *Alaric*."

"Poor Maurice!" said Lord Bolton; "how little he dreamed of what was in store for his 'dear Carlotta,' as he called her."

CHAPTER XV.

"DE LUYNES HONORED IN DEATH."

WE left Miss Winthrop and her brother at the ship. Their meeting was quiet but affectionate, and they reserved, till they should be alone, the sorrowful explanations which he expected. George Winthrop was a tall, handsome young man, with fine features and a commanding presence. Miss Winthrop presented him hastily to the Professor and Tom, and they all went to the hotel together.

"As we have no baggage," said Cuthbert, "Boniface will require a deposit in cash."

If this observation was intended as a joke the remark fell unheeded. George explained to his sister that his uncle Horace was in Washington, but could not come for a day or two, although he had telegraphed kind greetings. The whole party was anxious to leave, though none of them had been in Quebec before; they were in no mood, however, for sight-seeing, and had little desire to remain. They would all travel together as far as Montreal, where they would separate, some going to New York, others to Boston. Dr. Elmwood decided to accompany his niece, and Tom determined to go on with his father. "They could go up the river to Montreal," Tom said, "which they might reach by steamer in the morning, or they could go comfortably by rail in five hours."

"I vote for the cars," cried Miss Winthrop. "Let us have variety, even in our perils."

"Yes, just for once," said Fred, aside; "I'd rather be shattered than smothered."

It was agreed that Tom should pay his respects at the De Luynes mansion, to make inquiries, and after that they should leave in an hour. "It is such a short job to pack," said Fred; so they left without seeing anything of the classic and historic city.

That night they rested safely at Montreal in a magnificent hotel, which could not be surpassed in comfort by any hostelry they would afterwards visit. Early next morning they pursued their journey, and the following night, Dr. Elmwood, with George and his sister arrived at their uncle's in Boston; while the Professor, with Tom and his friends, took fashionable quarters in New York.

The newspapers were filled with sensational accounts of the loss of the ill-fated *Alaric*, and the trials and escapes of the rescued passengers. A few days later, the safe arrival of the *Thiers* was telegraphed from Havre, and all the passengers were reported well. The worst was now known, and a sense of relief followed.

We must leave the Professor and his friends to the quiet and rehabilitation they needed. Meantime, Lord Bolton and Robert were still at the De Luynes mansion, whose mistress continued in the same unsatisfactory condition.

Ottawa is the capital of Canada, two or three hundred miles above Quebec, and there the Vice-Regal family generally resides; at some seasons, however, the old military castle or citadel of Quebec, is occupied by the Queen's representative. Lord Lester was there now, and had tendered hearty hospitalities to Lord Bolton and Robert, which they, for obvious reasons, had politely declined. They called to pay their respects, however, and found the Governor full of sympathy. Her Excellency, the Countess, though a person of very exalted rank in her own right, was full of womanly sympathy and went herself each day to inquire after Madame De Luynes, and tendered Miss Lytton every assistance possible. At first, she had insisted upon visiting the patient personally, but Carlotta did not recognize her, though they had known each other well.

"The city, with its environs, is beautiful," said Lord Bolton to Holt, one fine morning, as they were strolling together, "and we ought to visit some of its principal sights."

"It is classic ground in North America, but I have no heart for all that," replied Holt. "To my mind it is chiefly distinguished, now, as the home of the loveliest and most unhappy of women."

"You are right," said his companion; "when will the child come? My prophetic spirit tells me that the little one will restore the mother. But, upon what desolation will she open her eyes! The ship is due to-morrow, and we shall soon see the little Ethel. With what charming tact Miss Lytton manages everything; she was made for such occasions as this; she has a strong head and a tender heart."

"I am told that the tone of the press here, French and English, has been generally friendly to De Luynes," said Lord Bolton, "while, what they call the *Rouge*, or Radical press, is full of encomium and panegyric. Two or three newspapers, it is said, however, have heaped obloquy on poor Maurice in his watery sepulchre; but human nature is nowhere altogether free from meanness, and you may everywhere find some vile creature who would be willing to carry his animosities beyond the grave. There is to be a public funeral, I learn; they were a little slow about it, but the people are now taking it in hand, and so the authorities are beginning to move. There is an article, I should think very full and fair, on Maurice De Luynes, in the morning paper, which fell into my hands last night. It concludes by quoting these beautiful lines:

" ' Tender as woman; manliness and meekness
   In him were so allied
That they who judged him by his strength or weakness,
   Saw but a single side.
Men failed, betrayed him, but his zeal seemed nourished
   By failure and by fall,
Still, a large faith in human-kind he cherished
   And in God's love for all.
But now he rests; his greatness and his sweetness
   No more shall seem at strife;
And death has moulded into calm completeness
   The statue of his life.' "

The next day Gustave arrived with little Ethel. Who cannot picture to himself the delight of the friends who welcomed her, or the terrible shock to Gustave himself, when he heard that De Luynes was no more. They had been cousins by blood as well as brothers in affection. He was so stunned that the state of Madame De Luynes scarcely interested him, and his solicitude for the child for the moment ceased; but he was soon aroused again.

Little Ethel shrank from the transport of those around her, but responded to Holt, and clung to him. All were overcome with emotion, and yet, the greatest trial was still to come—the presentation to the mother of her child. Carlotta sat in an easy chair; they told her they were bringing little Ethel to her. Holt entered with the baby in his arms.

"Here is your little Ethel," said her sister.

"No, Ethel is not here; she has gone with Maurice for his mother."

Holt came nearer, and the child made a spring for some flowers on the table at her mother's elbow, and the vase fell with a crash.

Carlotta sprang to her feet with excitement and vaguely regarded the ruin. Then, looking at the child, "*Les yeux sont beaux*," she murmured.

The doctor motioned them to take the child away, and she was not affected by its absence. For that day the trial failed. Robert returned to the library and declined all offers to relieve him of the little one.

"I have often caressed her," he said to Miss Lytton, "when I thought she was likely to become mine by adoption. I am very fond of her; I am glad to see her in her own home, and I wish that home were happier; but it will be painful to me to give her up. How the dear little thing nestled into my heart when I first found her in the police station in London."

"You have never told me about that," remarked Miss Lytton.

"I thought I had," said Holt, musingly, and then he remembered that it was only to poor Maurice he had related the full particulars. "When you have time I shall tell you all the sad story, Miss Lytton, and you will not be surprised that I grew to believe that this child's destiny and mine were strangely entangled."

"Tell me now, Mr. Holt."

Then he repeated to her the sad story he had related to Maurice, and the conditions under which he had told it to him.

"And did Maurice know little Ethel was lost?" inquired Miss Lytton.

"Yes, from Gustave, who met him at sea, but who believed she was saved, from what I told him, and from this portrait which he saw," answered Holt, handing her Ethel's likeness.

"How wonderful!" she said, thoughtfully, "and yet how dreadful! What joy there would have been in this house to-day if poor Maurice could have lived to welcome his child. No wonder dear Carlotta lost her reason with all these accumulated horrors."

"She knew nothing of the child's loss," said Holt, "or of its recovery. Maurice kept all that to himself."

"The noble man," she said; "and so he died with the secret locked in his heart, for the sake of her whom he would not let the winds of heaven visit too roughly, and yet his death was more dreadful to her than all. *'L'homme propose et Dieu dispose.'* But I must go to my sister. My more than brother," she continued, weeping, and giving him her hand, "in her name and for myself, I thank you."

The nurse took the child, and after dispatching a cable to his aunt, Holt left the house. He met Lord Bolton just returning from the Citadel.

"Lester tells me he has heard of Prof. Conant," said his Lordship, "and that New York is to give him a great public reception in a few days. Lester will be present and is anxious we should join him."

"It would surprise me if the Professor were not heartily welcomed in America," observed Holt; "his magnificent tribute to her greatness, in his speech the other day, and his life-long friendship for her institutions, should have endeared his name to that people. The Americans are not ungrateful, however, to their friends abroad, though they are perhaps over sensitive to criticism; but then, they are so often criticised in an unfriendly way at home by those who fear that our people may envy their prosperity and imitate their management of public affairs."

"England, too, suffers criticism at the hands of Americans," replied Lord Bolton. "The two countries are friendly, but each contains a class of busy-bodies and mischief-makers who live by propagating rancor and ill-will. The oftener there can be demonstrations in both countries calculated to promote mutual good-will the better. We do not quarrel with the man whom we are proud to entertain; and friendly intercourse may protect us from hostilities."

"Prof. Conant is the man for the occasion," said Holt. "I wish the President could be received among the people of every town and hamlet in England."

"I am of no use here, Robert, and I am ill at ease," continued Lord Bolton; "I propose to start to-morrow and join the Professor and Tom. Do you know it was my suggestion that Tom should come to America with his father? Life, as he will see it, will be so different from that seen by an ordinary traveller. From beginning to end, this trip will be full of lessons to him, with his father always at hand to modify and apply them. There is good stuff in that boy, but the life he is living is not calculated to make the best of him. Society has its uses, but with young fellows of promise the frivolous age should be short, and I think Tom ought to have passed it. He might aspire to anything in a political way, and make his visit to America his first step. Social and popular forces here present themselves as they do in England, but their activities may be witnessed from various points of view, and the same problems are solved in different ways. The 'why and the wherefore' he needs to learn, and his present experience should help him. A Britisher, cramped and prejudiced by insular restrictions, may have many good points, but let his views be broadened by contact with, and comprehension of, the world, and you have another and more civilized creature. This is doubly true of the Englishman, as he follows the institutions of his own country in America, where his own race has transplanted and nourished them. He studies the whole machinery of government, as it seems to have sprung from his own books, and as it has been enlarged and modified by the conditions of the New World. I wanted to impress all this upon Tom, but I have been prevented; it is no child's play the work he ought to do during his visit; after all, he will find such work more pleasant than the mere frivolities which otherwise might engross him."

"I expect Tom is likely to have pleasanter occupation in America just now," said Robert; "and even if things were serious, I would not forbid the banns. I believe with you that he has a career before him, which an early marriage with such a woman would not retard. His indolence is his only fault; you should speak to him, Lord Bolton. After his father no living man could influence him like yourself."

"I have always loved and admired him," was the answer, "and I doubt not he has force enough to form his career; his father has been too lenient with him; all he needs is an inducement; perhaps the examples he will see and the attachments he will form in America will help him. At any rate, we will talk to him and to his father too. I do not despair of seeing Capt. Tom Conant a great and useful man. I am convinced he has no taste for the army, Holt; it might be all right for him during the engrossing occupations of war, and Capt. Tom Conant on a peace footing would be a gem in society; but he would not too often adorn the haunts of the studious, nor pry into the mysteries which only intense application could solve. He will inherit great wealth on his mother's side, and that prospect will not push him to work." On the next street they met his Worship, the Mayor, who had come lately to office, and whom they had met casually before. That functionary, like many of his countrymen, was strongly impressed in the presence of an English Lord. He had grown rich in an humble way, and had some time before risen to the dignity of an Alderman. He was ambitious, without many qualifications, and he had the Commons and the Senate in his eye, but it had happened that a predecessor in office had been knighted and his dream, like that of his Lady Mayoress was, that some day he might kneel before the Queen's representative, and rise up, Sir Peter McGinn! And it was not at all unlikely that good Mrs. McGinn would before long flourish in society as 'My Lady,' and look down from her high eminence upon those who had been her companions in the service of a neighboring pastry-cook's shop, only a few years before. No doubt many cooks would better grace the position than some who have occupied it, and if these aristocratic distinctions are to be regarded as indigenous in our democratic soil, it would not be strange to see them fitfully conferred.

"Good morning, my Lord. I was going to your Lordship; I hope your Lordship is well," said the Mayor, approaching them cautiously. "I seen you coming this way and ventured to intercept you. I was dining at his excellency's last night, and his Lordship told me that your Lordship and his Honor, Mr. Holt, were about leaving the city. I wanted to speak with you five minutes, my Lord."

"Let us go to our rooms," said Lord Bolton, with just a perceptible effort at recovering his breath; "the morning is too cold to stand here."

"I expect my carriage," said the Mayor pompously; "would your Lordship join me in a drive?"

"Oh, no," said Robert, "it is only a walk of ten minutes."

"This dreadful business of poor De Luynes is what I come to your Lordship about," observed the Mayor, when they were seated. "The city council would not have allowed your Lordship (nor would your Lordship's humble servant have permitted them,) to remain in the city without any attention in ordinary times; but we have been overcome by those terrible things, my Lord. De Luynes was one of our foremost men, my Lord, though it was true there was them as went against him. The common people are excited; your Lordship knows they are more independent and difficult to manage in the cities than in the rural parts; but they say he was wronged and crushed, and they want to honor him, my Lord, by a public funeral, and a dozen societies of which he was a patron are moving, and we have decided that the city must give him a public funeral; and we want to know if your Lordship and his Honor, being as you was his friends and fellow-passengers, would honor the occasion by your presence as bearers."

Lord Bolton informed the Mayor that any attention to the memory of De Luynes would engage their sympathy; though it would be as a mourner only that he would wish to go. He added, however, it would be impossible for him to remain so long in the city.

Robert asked him, "Was there really a reaction in favor of De Luynes?"

"Very strong, yer Honor," said the Mayor.

"And would it strengthen De Luynes' political friends in the country?" Robert continued.

"Oh, no," said the Mayor, thrown off his guard (for he was not one of them). "There will be a short-lived excitement in the city, but the rural districts will be as solid as ever. Considering who were his enemies, M. De Luynes had undertaken impossible work."

"The time will come, as it has come in all countries," said Holt, "where abuses have prevailed under a smothered public opinion, that they will be destroyed. Some infuriated rabble will do it, perhaps, but if they had been fairly trained in constitutional matters they might have done better work in a less objectionable way."

Later in the day they met a Senator, an accomplished and sympathetic French Canadian gentleman. He spoke tenderly of De Luynes, of his many gifts and manifold virtues. They had been schoolmates and friends, and he was much affected at the harrowing misfortune that had befallen him.

"My countrymen will never cease to thank you, gentlemen, for the kindness and attention you have shown this unfortunate family. We all regret that the sad circumstances prevent us showing our gratitude in a more demonstrative way, but we all know the whole story and shall never forget you."

Our friends saw and conversed with other kindly people and were impressed with the tenderness of sympathy displayed for De Luynes and his stricken family.

The next morning, Lord Bolton and Robert Holt took their leave, having expressed the greatest anxiety for Carlotta's condition, the former persisting in his belief that her reason would be shortly regained. It was arranged that Miss Lytton would write to Robert informing him of the condition of her sister and the child.

At New York they found the Professor much refreshed and Tom full of enthusiasm about the city. Fred Cuthbert, they also learned, already knew many people, and had been installed at many fashionable clubs.

"If these are what you call vulgar people," said Fred, "commend me to luxury and vulgarity."

The Professor had accepted an invitation to a reception in one of the great hotels for which New York is famous, and the newspapers, by copious notes and comments, were indicating that the affair would be magnificent and enthusiastic.

"I have been telling Tom that I am a little nervous about this new character of the distinguished foreigner in which I am to appear," remarked the Professor, "and I am afraid I have not the ready tact to sustain it."

Lord Bolton and Holt reassured him, and both declared, what they had said before in our presence, that the Professor was the man, and America the country, for such a demonstration.

"You have paid so many eloquent tributes to these people at home," said Lord Bolton; "have defended them so bravely in former years when they were attacked; have shown such trust in their free institutions, and faith in their ability to maintain them, that you have contributed not a little to the enviable reputation which America bears among the European masses, and these people honor themselves by the honor they are to confer upon you."

"That is what I tell my father," said Tom, "but he is so modest, and laughs at the idea of a single man having been able to do anything toward earning the gratitude of a foreign country."

"I have made some charming acquaintances here and renewed some old ones," observed the Professor. "The great kindness I have received, so far, makes me feel that I have fallen among a nation of friends. But I have a letter from your aunt; would you like to read it?

Tom was greatly puzzled by its mysteries."

"You are a jolly old fraud, Robert," said Tom, "with your mysterious children and charities. Why did not you and mother tell me about that infant when we were at Brighton?"

"You were interested in a grown-up infant at Brighton, if I remember."

"But one does not like to be kept in the dark."

"Well, you know it all now;" said the Professor, "and it is too late to make amends;" and he handed Holt Mrs. Conant's letter. It was a kindly and affectionate epistle, full of social and domestic news. It contained tender messages to Tom, to whom she promised to write in a day or two, and then Robert's eye rested on the following:—"Tell Robert Holt, with my love, that his child has been tenderly nursed and is well, but a strange thing happened to-day; a Frenchman, who says he is from Canada, called at Robert's house this morning while I was there, and presented a scrawl in pencil, purporting to be from Robert on ship board. It was evidently in his hand-writing, bidding us let the stranger see the child, and deliver it to him, if he recognized and claimed it. The stranger declared that the child belonged to Maurice De Luynes, a gentleman of quality residing in Quebec, who was with his wife on board the *Alaric* with you all going out. He pretended that he had boarded your ship at sea, and had taken his orders from the father of the infant and from Robert. It seemed an improbable story, but he recognized the child and claimed her. The note might have been forged; why had not Robert sent me some token? Was it usual for vessels to lie alongside to allow passengers to go on board? And yet the young man seemed a gentleman, and if he demanded the child, what had I to oppose to Robert's order, which I must admit seemed to be genuine? I thought of cabling you, but there might be delays, and when I appealed to friends here they were unable to advise me. The child, moreover, almost seemed to recognize the stranger, and the likeness he had brought was perfect. Nevertheless, I was irresolute, and my dreams were disturbed. How did I know the motive which might prompt others in seeking to obtain possession of the poor little one? It might be another abduction; of course, the nurse would go with it, but what do I know about her? Well, I adopted the only course that seemed open to me. I gave up the child, but I will send our good old servant, John, on a confidential mission, with instructions to keep watch of the little one, till he knows it is safely delivered. Of course, he must go in disguise; neither the nurse nor the stranger must know it. Heigho! it has been a weary business; I dreaded to part with the little thing, though I do believe it is all right; but I shall send John as a precaution."

"Strange, I didn't see John," said Robert, looking up, to find in his abstraction, that everybody had left the room without his notice.

CHAPTER XVI.

THE FLAGS BLEND WITH GRACEFUL HARMONY.

MEANTIME, the visit of Prof. Alexander Conant, M.P., of England, was exciting wide attention and universal sympathy throughout the States. The newspapers were recalling how he championed the slave in former years, and upheld the cause of the North during the war, when friends were more needed and scarcer than now; and busy men, everywhere, seemed disposed to spend a day with an Englishman who had defended their country when she wanted aid, and to raise a national cheer for him. Letters of congratulation from leading public men, and invitations to visit various parts of the country, daily poured in upon him. These, owing to the shortness of his visit, he could not accept; but he responded to all alike in a tone of courtesy, and his work was expedited by Tom's ready assistance. The day was approaching for the reception in New York, and a leading Western journal thus spoke of it :—

"In a trying hour aristocratic Europe believed that the time had come to compass the destruction of this Republic. It was ruled, they thought, by the 'scum of the earth,' and was a bad example to the 'scum' of their parts of it. What cared they for the blood of brothers to be poured out like water in the conflict they prayed for? France, led by one despot, and aided by others, planted a hostile power on our borders to harry us, and the ruling classes of England, our own kin, gloated over our desperate situation, and bullied and threatened us. We knew we were the masters in our legitimate fight, but we could not hope to overcome the world in arms against us. Then it was we found the truth of the assertion of a great man, that there are two Englands; our friends then came to the surface, as, misled by our enemies, our mother was about to declare cruel war against us. There was a man in England whose teachings contributed to thwart these machinations. He was Alexander Conant, then an Oxford Professor, and now a leading member of the British Parliament. His burning eloquence, which marked him for obloquy at the time, has since won him a foremost place in the House of Commons of England; and after all these years, his last great speech, which the other day electrified England, and challenged the admiration alike of friend and foe in that country, was marked by an eloquent apostrophe, full of sympathy and good-will to us and our country.

"Alexander Conant came to New York, the other day, without parade or ostentation; he is merely seeking rest, after the pressing work of a trying session. Americans! let us make him at home on this side of the water; let us open our hearts to this great scholar, philanthropist and statesman, and let us show him that he has not hoped for democracy in vain."

A leading city morning journal after reciting Prof. Conant's friendly services to "this country," added: "It may be that we have given too much occasion for the want of confidence which certain classes in Europe have felt for us. Could we present, for example, the great American city of New York as a model of self-government? The frauds we denounce, sometimes justly and sometimes with wild exaggerations, would these inspire foreigners with confidence and respect? They can know us only by what they see and hear, and perhaps our press has not been altogether blameless. Among ourselves, we know that these spots are only excrescences, and that they do not really endanger, though they embarrass, our Republican system. But when men like Prof. Conant are willing to study and understand us, and for the sake of the masses, who generally so much profit by these labors, trust us to the end, what attention too great, or what honor too pronounced, can we render them?"

There was, of course, some journalistic dissent to the strain of eulogy generally indulged in, for there are always two currents of opinion; and excellent Irish friends of America doubted whether she could afford to forget that Englishmen were her traditional enemies. But the tide was too strong, and the malcontents subsided.

On the evening of the reception, the great hall was ablaze with illuminations, and the walls were profusely decorated. The dais, upon which the guest of the evening was to be welcomed, was ornamented with flowers, and tropical plants, and overhead the Stars and Stripes and the Union Jack blended with graceful harmony.

When Professor Conant entered, the great multitude rose as one man, and he was greeted with enthusiastic cheers. An eloquent address was presented to him, through the ministry of a distinguished committee. It recited his relations to science and to literature, and his eminent services to freedom. It acknowledged the obligations and the admiration of America, and proffered him a hearty and universal welcome. The address was supported by able speeches, full of compliment, from eminent men, and when finally the Professor rose to reply, the cheers were renewed and the ovation was magnificent.

"Ladies and gentlemen," he modestly began, "ten years ago I paid a quiet visit to your great country, believing then, as I believe now, that its organization was an incalculable benefit to mankind; and I can see how the institutions of my country, transplanted here and tended and cultured by my own race, have multiplied and improved under altered conditions, and become indigenous in a fruitful soil. Englishmen can never be indifferent observers of what goes on in America. They have made some successful experiments as promoters of constitutional liberty, but good men among them had been cautious and dreaded the distribution of power among the people, whom they loved, but dared not trust; and you Americans might have thrown free England back a hundred years if you had proved unworthy to play the *rôle* of freedom. As it is, you have not wholly met with success, but you have surpassed the attempts of all ages to confer freedom upon the people, and encourage industry and thrift. As compared with other people, it may be said that you did not make the country, nor create all the conditions of its marvellous development; but it will be sufficient for you, as a people, to establish that you have loyally improved your opportunities. You had from the first a great problem to solve. Could the people govern? And no doubt your vast and rapid, and shall I add, unexpected growth, had multiplied obstacles and created dangers, which the enemies of your political system were not slow to exaggerate. You might be all right enough in peace, they admitted; but what of peril? If the national life were in danger, who would care for or protect it? How could you expect a rabble to submit to restraints and self-sacrifice? It was a fair question, and your friends in Europe hoped that you would answer it well. In all time it had been said we might trust the masses with anything but self-government; and the privileged classes were always willing, if they did not usurp the right of government, to undertake it. There was, moreover, a deep blot on your system, which nobody could justify. Claiming that all men were free and equal, you held some of them in bondage with the sanction of your laws and the concurrence of your people; you ostracised the black man and you hunted the slave. At first, we in Europe tried to be your apologists. 'They inherited the system,' we said, 'they are not responsible.' But for a long time we were embarrassed by the fact that you took to it kindly. When we wanted reform, to extend the franchise, and thus to gain more power for the people in England, our enemies and yours said to us, 'Look at America, which you imitate, with her social color-lines and her bloodhounds on the track of her slaves!' What could we answer beyond expressing our hopes? But a little later, 'with malice toward none, and charity toward all,' you did the great work of your national life; you emancipated your slaves! I never saw Mr. Lincoln, except in my dreams, but by that one act he won immortality. Whatever his motive, the fact remains. Then it was that you, as a people, showed how you could fight to maintain your liberties and your nationality;

and then the world, rather tardily, perhaps, recognized you as a brave and independent nation. But there were more unprecedented events still in this succession of marvels; the North and the South, shaking hands over the bloody chasm; the leaders of the great Rebellion engaging unmolested in ordinary pursuits, and under the very government they plotted to ruin; the vast armies, on both sides, peace having been restored, returning voluntarily to the farms, the mills, the mines, and the work-shops of the country. And this last follows from the universal franchise you have adopted. There should be no mercenaries where all are masters, and where each personally loses or gains, as it goes ill or well with the country. If the people of America will recognize this in their administration of affairs, and continue true to the precepts of their great teachers, mankind will be the gainers, and the masses of Europe, will ere long become in their own homes, what the Americans are to-day—the free citizens of a free country."

He deprecated great individual wealth and luxury, as carrying with them corresponding poverty and squalor, and besought the people never to forget this, when advised by kindly people in his own country or in theirs, to abandon simplicity and organize a government of aristocratic landlords and hereditary senators, with all which that change would imply. He adjured the great British and American people to love each other. In the main, they were the same stock, and, at any rate, they owed the same fealties to freedom; and, barring petty rivalries, their interests were the same in their relations to the world. Twice they had been at war, and a third and more terrible conflict had been averted only by the alternative of arbitration. He hoped the alternative would be repeated, and whenever national disputes threatened, that arbitration would be the result. He continued, in words which we cannot repeat, and with an eloquence we cannot describe, to express his confidence in American Republican progress. He wanted America to stand side by side with England, among the foremost nations who were displaying the torch-light of liberty to the world; and, thanking them all, he invoked the blessing of God upon the two kindred nations, mother and child, desiring that they might go on in unity, and multiply the advantages which each had conferred upon the world.

There was renewed enthusiasm when the speaker took his seat, and a large number of ladies and gentlemen were presented to him. There was room for only casual, though kindly words, and at length the great throng moved slowly into an adjoining hall, where a splendid collation had been prepared. The Professor's friends were chiefly in the body of the hall; Lord Lester had thought better of coming down, and Lord Bolton, for reasons about which the public speculated, though we can understand them, declined a conspicuous place. The young men, as the chairman had said, would soon be all right; once presented to two or three ladies, they would swim without help, or, as Fred suggested, "like ducks in deep water." The latter young gentleman had made the most of his time in New York; he seemed to know everybody, which was not difficult, as he was well accredited, being the son of Sir John Cuthbert, Baronet, as well as a favorite member of the Professor's party.

"I have been telling these gentlemen," he said, nodding to Tom and Holt, and addressing a pretty brunette, the daughter of a late Secretary of State, "that I want to become an American citizen. I suppose there may have been no end of reasons for it, these hundred years back, but the Professor's speech puts us in mind, that it is the thing to do ; first of all, you govern yourself; then you do it with so much personal credit to yourself; you do honor to your country, and your country does honor to you ; and all the world looks on and applauds. And when you say, ' *Romanus sum,*' the effect is terrific."

"Don't be facetious at our expense," said the young lady; "we might refuse you the freedom of the city."

"I was never more serious," said Fred; "and besides you are not an American citizen."

"I might be that sooner than you expect," she retorted, "when women get their rights ; and I am strong-minded enough to defend Prof. Conant any time."

"Oh, I didn't attack the Professor," said Fred ; "I only *orated* a little about citizenship."

"Is 'orated' good English ? " she asked, mischievously.

"Perhaps nothing English is good," he replied. "Can't I celebrate my new allegiance by coining a word ? Has such a thing never been done here before ? "

" May be you think it is the fashion," she interrupted. "Now, tell me, Mr. Cuthbert, do Englishmen ever boast ? "

"Never."

" Hardly ever ? "

"To tell the truth, they haven't much chance," said Fred. "England is an effete old monarchy, and she is outshone by her eldest daughter. An Englishman can't boast much of his titles, because they are about to abolish the House of Lords; nor of his fortune, because his cousins over here outstrip him. John Bull never did boast of his younger sons like me, but they say the lower stratum is coming to the surface, and that may afford a chance to utilize waste material; so I think, Miss Douglas, we shall have to conclude that Englishmen never boast except of their relations over here, and these are sometimes the wife's relations, as Artemus Ward used to call them."

"Mothers-in-law, for instance," said Miss Douglas, "and he would 'sacrifice' them."

"Artemus only spoke of sacrifice to the Juggernaut of war; our intentions are peaceable. But I have been reading, and I find the Americans are not always good historians. For instance, they were whipped at Bunker Hill, but Boston has celebrated the anniversary of that fight for a victory ever since."

"Oh, our people did not escape reverses," said Miss Douglas, with a laugh. "We got along very well, but we lost a beautiful and highly cultivated island with chalk cliffs, that would have been part of our booty if our triumphs had been complete."

"That is no doubt a pleasure to come," Fred rejoined; "but do let us move away from the band, the noise is deafening."

They were soon lost in the crowd, Tom and Robert going off in another direction.

Five minutes later Tom and his friend encountered Mr. Roberts walking arm in arm with Lord Bolton; Mrs. Roberts was convalescent and had gone to Washington. He had come to the entertainment expecting to see without being seen, but his Lordship's quick eye detected him, and after all why should he not seek distraction in this way?

"You have seen a New York gathering of the best people," said Roberts. "I do not mean the richest, though great wealth is represented here; but people of culture and refinement, such people as would naturally be attracted by a great reputation like that of Prof. Conant. I presume, you will have observed little of the vulgar parade and over-dressing which some of our critics attribute to American society. The people you see here, so far as they are traditional New Yorkers, are chiefly descended from old Dutch and English families, added to that larger class of men who came here from New England in search of fortune, imbued with that firm and masculine self-reliance, and devotion to the old political ideas, born of New England training. Indeed, the western part of this State has been almost wholly settled from New England. The English vastly preponderate in the interior, but the city population is a medley of races, and its political and city government is altogether in the hands of men who were but lately foreigners."

"I suppose you have still a good many of the old Knickerbocker families," observed Holt.

"Well, yes; we have old families like the Schuylers and Van Rensselaers. They were landlords, and maintained a local jurisdiction. Their descendants may be found in New York society to this day, but I do not think they call themselves 'Knickerbockers.' A Knickerbocker was originally a cracker-baker; that is the literal signification of the word, I believe; and how Washington Irving wove his fancies about it, and made the wide world accept them, has always been a mystery to me."

"Well, that's new to me," said Tom, "and destroys half a dozen romances that have found a lodgment in my brain."

"But, can you swear to that?" inquired Lord Bolton. "I have always understood that the old Dutch families accepted this Knickerbocker distinction."

"You may be right," replied the other; "but a 'Knickerbocker' was a 'cracker-baker' all the same. This is of consequence, however, only for the sake of accuracy. In spite of the old families the social 'gates are ajar,' and men, who sprang from the toiling masses, are daily gliding through into the charmed circle."

"That is as it should be," remarked Robert. "Why should social distinctions be monopolized by an hereditary class?"

"But will they be desirable distinctions," observed Tom, "if they grow cheap?"

"Ah! that's an old question," rejoined Roberts; "but I see the Professor is moving away, and I must follow him, as I wish to whisper a word in his ear."

An hour later, the great hall was deserted. The morning journals would announce that the reception to Prof. Conant had been a splendid success. Holt had received letters from Miss Lytton, which were merely a pathetic diary of what occurred from day to day in Carlotta's rooms, with an added account of how the child grew and prospered. It had not then been recognized by its mother, though she had sometimes noticed and petted it. The name of little Ethel seemed to awaken no interest in her, and she always repulsed friends by saying, "No, it is not Ethel, she has gone with

Maurice to bring his mother." The doctor saw hopeful signs of restoration. Sometimes she seemed to falter and hesitate, as if her intellect flickered. But these symptoms were succeeded by a return of the mental paralysis.

CHAPTER XVII.

THE JESUIT AND THE ORANGEMAN.

NEXT morning, Holt received a telegram from Miss Lytton, with this startling intelligence: "Child badly burned; Carlotta conscious, but prostrate; calls constantly for you." Without loss of time, Holt despatched the following answer: "Will go to you by next train."

"May I go with you, Holt?" inquired Lord Bolton after Robert had explained the nature of these communications; and it was agreed that both should return together.

They took up quarters at a hotel in Quebec, on their arrival, but hurried at the earliest moment to the De Luynes's, where they found Gustave and Miss Lytton waiting for them.

"She is conscious and knows all," was Miss Lytton's greeting; "but the child's recovery does not compensate for the loss of poor Maurice. Tuesday night little Ethel was in Carlotta's room and for the moment they were alone. Playing about the grate, the child's clothes caught fire, and her screams roused the mother, who rushed toward her, and, wrapping her shawl about the little one, extinguished the flames in a most rational manner, but the dear little thing was badly burnt. Its cries seemed to distress Carlotta, whom we found pacing the room with it in her arms, and striving to soothe it. She helped to dress its wounds and to nurse it, and was often noticed gazing into its eyes with an interested and inquiring look. Presently, she said, 'It is little Ethel; but where is Maurice? Oh heavens!' she screamed, 'I remember it all now.' And with these words she fainted.

"Carlotta was soon restored, however, but suffered great prostration; she seemed conscious, and I thought she realized everything. She moaned for Maurice and called urgently for you. That was the state of things when I telegraphed. The child is better, and Carlotta seems conscious. I shall notify her of your presence, and I hope your visit will strengthen her."

Returning shortly, Miss Lytton said, "My sister is eager to see you."

The interview was short but affecting. Why should we recite what was said by the pallid sufferer, or expose to the curious gaze the wailings of a broken heart?

What could Holt say? Words could not comfort her; he bade her be strong for her child's sake, and for the sake of friends who loved her. He spoke of trust in God, to whom Maurice had gone, but she answered, "No, it was too cruel; God could not have taken him. Why should he be snatched from me, while so many less worthy are left?"

"God knows best," observed Holt; "not a sparrow falls to the ground without His notice."

"If I could pray!" she said sadly. "But how can I return thanks when my brain reels, and my heart is broken?"

"Ask for help," Robert replied soothingly.

"Oh! I need help, and it is for that I sent for you, who had been with us in the last days we spent together."

Carlotta seemed exhausted and fell into a gentle sleep, and Holt noiselessly left the room and found her sister at the door.

"She sleeps," he said; "I shall return if I am needed." He found Lord Bolton in earnest conversation with Gustave. They were going over the history of the De Luynes family.

"In most countries my cousin would have had a career," said Gustave, "but here we all have to bow the knee to Baal. He commenced his political career by refusing to accept clerical support, and was crushed by clerical animosity. It was never the aim of the clergy to defend the Church, which neither Maurice nor his father assailed; on the contrary, they were its most generous patrons and defenders. The clergy were madly allied to one party, which they knew they could control, and the principles of Maurice led him to affiliate with another. The Church, of which he was as true a son as any of them, had fairly nothing to do with the controversy. His name was denounced, and it pleased them to magnify one of her children at the expense of another. History will put us right, but we can expect little from the present generation. Generally, the press is an agency of freedom, but these men can forbid their people to read a certain newspaper; that crushes it, of course. There is a Liberal press, but on these topics it must be silent. They are only discussed in the by-ways, and with bated breath. The English papers are as prudent as the French, and the politicians are still more careful; so that nobody ever hears of this great abuse which goes on under the very eyes of liberty, and nobody dares to speak about it. You will meet these men, and they will be models of politeness and toleration; but independence of thought among their own people, there is none. They assume to think and act for all, and in the name of religion endeavor to crush every obstacle which may oppose them. The men who enjoy their confidence in Parliament are merely their overseers. You would think the press, the great champion of those who think for themselves, would aid us, but upon all these topics the press is muzzled. Now and then some adventurous journal makes a dash, but the people are forbidden to read it, and, after a bitter experience, it collapses. There is a good deal of independent criticism in secluded nooks, but the press of Quebec, French and English, is too prudent 'to beard the lion in his den,' and as for the politicians, bless your soul! if there have been a few who took the risk, they have been crushed like poor Maurice of unhappy memory. There is no hope of public opinion, left to itself, but our people are a minority, and the other provinces may awaken to the danger. I would rather we could seek another remedy, but I believe the madness of the hour will be checked from Rome, and that the Propaganda will decree that our priests shall abstain from partisan politics. If that happens, they will, at least, profess to obey; but I know them well, and they will be more loyal to the Pope, proclaiming the programme, than to the Pope, cultivating the freedom of political opinions for all. Lower Canada is a little corner of the world, but she is the paradise of the reactionaries. What is possible among her simple and uninstructed people, will be attempted in every corner of North America. To study our troubles is to be warned in time. The policy pursued among us is faintly resisted by the best instructed and more liberal among the clergy, but they are powerless. The traditions of our good old priesthood are despised and forgotten, and the power of the curés, which was intended to lead the people aright in spiritual matters, is sometimes degraded to the lowest work of the most mercenary politicians. The path of our public life is strewn with the carcasses of those who have striven to resist, and the readiest tools of this uncatholic slaughter are the men of your race among us."

"How bitterly they all seem to feel this clerical interference," remarked Holt after Gustave had retired.

"No doubt it is a great power," said Lord Bolton. "One wonders would they have resented it as much if it had always been exercised in their favor; in great emergencies the Church always appeals to the loyalty of the people."

"Ah! but that is when questions which affect the interest of the Church are concerned," observed Robert.

"Do you think that when no great question was involved, Cardinal Manning would encourage his people to interfere in an election, simply because one of his priests had preferences for one side or the other?"

"Oh! I don't know," rejoined Lord Bolton, "and I can't bother to think about it; yet it is a pity if the priests carry the consciences of their people in their pockets. But what can we do when the people want to have it so? As to our own race here, politicians have not much conscience, and so, I suppose, not feeling much interest, they ally themselves with the stronger side."

"Yes," said Robert, "that's the view of the practical politician; but if it goes to the extent I am told it does, of making the Jesuit and the Orangeman brothers-in-arms, it does not suggest anything very noble to my mind."

Shortly dropping this conversation, Robert explained to Lord Bolton the touching interview he had had with Carlotta, and the ground of his hope for mother and child.

"We cannot remain long," Robert said to Miss Lytton in the course of the day, "on account of other engagements. I would not leave Madame De Luynes so long as I could cheer her; but, do you know, I fear my presence summons sad thoughts to her mind, and that she will thrive better among those who have not witnessed her great bereavement."

But presently Carlotta sent for him again, and he found her more composed and self-reliant.

"You did me good this morning, my dear friend," she said, "but I must not detain you here. I see it all now, and though I have many friends, I must tread my desolate path alone. At first, in my helplessness, I involuntarily turned to you who had been near to us and were my husband's last friend. Now I must release you, and ask pardon for the trouble I have given in asking you to come hither." Extending her hand, she added, "You interested my husband, you saved my child; what recompense can I offer?"

"I did little at best," replied Robert, "but I did nothing for reward. To feel that I was the friend of Maurice De Luynes, or that I could perform the least service to his widow and child, would be a satisfaction to me more than words could express. If I can serve you, or give you strength at any moment, you have but to command me, and my delay will be measured only by the distance I have to travel."

Later in the day she received Lord Bolton, and was more calm and self-possessed than they expected. Robert spent much of his time with the child, who evinced a fondness for him, and a day or two after, with many tender adieux, he and Lord Bolton took their leave.

CHAPTER XVIII.

THE PROFESSOR VISITS BOSTON.

ONE morning Dr. Elmwood called on the Professor at his lodgings in New York. He had just returned from Boston, where he left Miss Winthrop well, but weary with her efforts to reconcile George to his fate. At first he had been inconsolable, but they had thought it better not to disguise anything from him, and had expressed their belief that poor Miss Roberts had not been indifferent to Lord Bolton's attentions. They told him what they knew, and what they surmised, which amounted to this, that Miss Roberts had been loyal to her engagement with George, but had not been sure of her affection, and that had she lived, she might have asked him to release her altogether. As the story was told him, there was left no cause for resentment; hence he felt that his mourning was more for a beautiful woman and a dear friend than for her whom he was shortly to marry. As his thoughts became more rational, he felt like reproving himself for indulging in any violent grief. He understood that Miss Roberts had discouraged Lord Bolton's suit because she was pledged to himself, and not because it was disagreeable to her. "She was a noble girl," he would say. "Our engagement was so sudden that she did not know her own heart. I have nothing to forgive, but it would have been dreadful to have found out our mistake when it was too late."

His sister was full of kind words for the memory of the lost one, and he clung to her more than ever.

The Doctor had explained all this to the Professor, and had politely expressed satisfaction with the reception accorded him. "I knew there would be enthusiasm," he said, "the moment it was known you had set foot upon our soil. My brother Horace will ask you to spend a few days with him in Boston, and you will find an equally kind, though somewhat different, welcome. Boston is more distinctively an American city than New York. It is one of the old landmarks in our history, and a great centre of Republican thrift and refinement. My brother is an eminent lawyer, but he is a statesman and a man of letters as well. He is eager for your expected visit; I hope Tom will go with you, and I shall try to drop down while you are there."

"Your brother is very kind," said the Professor, "and we must go. I want to make his acquaintance and to see Miss Winthrop; besides, a visit to America, which does not include Boston, would be like the play of Hamlet with Hamlet left out."

They spoke of New York, of its marvellous growth and ever-increasing facilities, as one of the wonders of the world. "She is the mistress of our commerce," said Dr. Elmwood, "the centre of our wealth, and her activities are an unfailing index in denoting the expansion or decline of the national prosperity. Here are found representatives of every race and creed which our diversified immigration confides to us. Wealth and squalor, education and ignorance, and all the extremes of the overburdened and strained social conditions of the countries from which our immigrants come, are to be found here; but the great multitude walk the peaceful paths of industry, and quietly reap their legitimate reward."

That morning, in Boston, Miss Winthrop received a letter from Miss Lytton; it was dated Quebec, and was an answer to a note of inquiry about Madame De Luynes. It told her all we know of Carlotta De Luynes, and of the recovery and condition of the child. It drew a sad picture of the life they had led at the De Luynes mansion, which was now brightened by Carlotta's convalescence, and by hope of her early recovery. It contained a photograph and thus explained the enclosure: "Something Carlotta said to me this morning made me wonder could her friend Miss Winthrop, of whom she speaks so lovingly, have been the little Aggie Winthrop, whom I knew and loved at Madame Charland's school, on Beacon Street. Pardon the photograph, which is sent, if indeed you are the same, to help your memory in recognizing your old friend. I do not think I am mistaken. I remember the honest gray eyes so well; they always looked lovingly into mine, and what romantic stories you used to tell me about your home, and about your big brother who came for you every Saturday! I can scarcely tell you how I cling to this theory, which would make Miss Winthrop the accidental friend of my poor sister, my own sweet little Aggie Winthrop of the old days." The letter continued, "My sister speaks often of you; she seems always reaching out to those who were with her in the last days of her poor husband. Could you not come and see us? If you are, as I believe, my little Agnes, accept a kiss, and my imperative order to come here at once."

"Dear girl," said Miss Winthrop, "I had lost sight

of you, but I have not forgotten to love you, for your kindness to me in those old school days. The likeness is perfect, though the face is a little older. It is more like Madame De Luynes. I always thought she reminded me of some one; I will go to them both for a day, and George shall take me."

The young man heard the story.

"Will you come, George?" said his sister.

"I am not invited, little one," he replied.

"Trust me for a welcome;" and they went to Quebec together. Miss Winthrop was received warmly by her friend, and George was pleased with her beauty and grace, and particularly with the cordial greeting. There is this compensation for the stricken in heart, that grief yields to reaction; were it not so, the thread would break under a constant tension. The three chatted pleasantly of old times; even Carlotta received them with a smile, and seemed for the moment to forget her own great sorrow.

George and Ethel compared notes, and remembered having met before, and as the day advanced they all seemed like a family reunited. Thus, sometimes, even in grief, we tread lightly over the green sod that presses our loved ones, and take in exhilaration and strength from the warm earth and fresh breeze.

In the afternoon Miss Winthrop remained with Carlotta, and George and Ethel drove out round the city. She showed him where Montgomery fell, and the castle on the "heights," and told him something of its classic history. They saw the Plains of Abraham, where Wolfe and Montcalm won immortality, and the falls of Montmorenci, distinguished for their height and volume. The frozen spray of these waters, she told him, formed a huge cone of ice in winter, which was covered with snow, and down whose precipitous sides pleasure seekers were fond of making swift, but perilous voyages. At its base, she had known large rooms to be skilfully cut out, with furniture exquisitely carved in ice. There was a bar, with a counter ornamented with bottles and glasses; there were saloons furnished with sofas, chairs and tables, and figures of men and women grouped, as if in conversation, and liveried servants, all cut and carved from solid ice with marvellous skill.

"The tale would seem incredible," said George, "if one heard it in any ordinary way. How much one loses when one travels without an intelligent guide."

"But the story must be at least founded on facts, for I have seen all myself, and more than I have described to you, except the figures of men and women, and these would not be more difficult than the rest." They had a long drive home, but the way was beautiful, along the high ground overlooking the great river and the old city. They talked pleasantly together, as if neither had seen trouble, and as if they were old friends who had come together after a long separation.

"I have to thank you for a very pleasant afternoon," he said, as they turned in at the gate of the De Luynes mansion.

"The pleasure has been mutual," replied Ethel; "I suppose I shall condemn myself, by-and bye, for having escaped from the dark cloud into the pleasant world again."

"You ought not," George answered; "in great bereavements those who go first are perhaps most fortunate, but those who remain cannot always keep their hearts in the grave, else mourning would be the business of life; and as everybody has been stricken, we should all be Rachels refusing to be comforted." If Miss Lytton had known the truth, she might have thought he was taking comfort early, but as it was she agreed with him and determined to cultivate, at least a reasonable self-control.

"They seem more cheerful," thought Miss Winthrop, as she welcomed them in the hall, but she only asked, had they enjoyed themselves, and declared that, strange as it might seem, she, too, had spent a pleasant afternoon. Carlotta had been in a calmer mood; she had caressed the child, and chatted cheerfully, and they all expressed hopes that verged upon cheerfulness, as if a black cloud had been lifted from the house. Little Ethel was in gay spirits, which tended to dispel the gloom. In the evening, Carlotta asked them to sing some hymns; they reminded her of Maurice, she said; and when they rendered the "Sweet by-and-bye," and "Nearer my God to Thee," she melted into tears, and spoke calmly of that night on the *Alaric*, and what she called the heavenly enthusiasm that prevailed among the passengers. It was a quiet, pleasant evening, and gave promise of restoration that unconsciously cheered them all.

"We must go to-morrow," said Miss Winthrop. Ethel persisted, and George thought it reasonable that they should remain another day; but Agnes explained that her uncle expected friends, and it was agreed that they should go the following night. Both George and Miss Winthrop urged upon Miss Lytton that the whole family needed change, that is to say,

Madame De Luynes, Miss Ethel, and "baby Ethel;" and they won a conditional promise of a visit later.

"Now that Madame De Luynes is so much improved," said Agnes, "we should try to engage her attention with new thoughts and new scenes; our home in Boston will be quiet for some time after the Professor has left us, and you shall meet no one whom you do not wish to see, and will be as completely at home as you are here. Little Ethel shall have command of all the pets, and you, poor, weary Ethel, shall be my especial care. Here, nobody will know where you have gone, and there, nobody will know who you are; and the change will do you as much good as if it were altogether fashionable and orthodox to go."

Carlotta bore up bravely as they took their leave, and spoke almost cheerfully of returning their visit. Miss Lytton, however, promised nothing, though she said that the visit would be grateful to her, but she must watch and wait a little. To Agnes she said the visit had given them new life. Uncle Horace Winthrop was not advanced in years, though he was a Senator, and he was not worn by hard work, though he stood at the head of the bar. He was a great student and led a laborious life, but there was always a corner in his heart for his friends and for any innocent recreation; and the wish of Agnes was law with him. He was proud of George, who had inherited his gifts and his enormous practice, and he was as much their confidant in all that interested them as if he were of their own age. He was a great scholar, and Massachusetts admired him; a great orator, and so she lent him her ear. It was fitting that he should entertain Prof. Conant; they were a distinguished host and a distinguished guest. The Professor and Tom were the guests of Mr. Winthrop, but their friends took lodgings near by. The first day was spent in visiting the sights of the city, and in driving about the suburbs, which are among the finest in the world. The next night, Senator Winthrop was to give a grand reception in honor of Prof. Conant, and the *elite* of Boston were to be present. Modern Athens would be seen at her best that night. Her statesmen and scholars, her poets and *littérateurs*, would be well represented, in honor of England's foremost thinker—a great orator, a rising statesman, and a good man.

Everybody, and especially George, was pleased with Capt. Tom Conant. He was full of spirits, and displayed the greatest interest in and admiration for everything American, so far as he had seen the country and the people, and was thus accepted as a most liberal and intelligent Britisher.

"Do you know," said Tom, in conversation with some callers, "this visit of mine to New England is the realization of a long cherished dream? In the early days, the story of your people was so full of trial and tragedy; there was so much human nature in first fleeing from persecution and then exercising it, such heroic sacrifice of everything to principle, that one recalls with pride the fact that one belongs to the same race. It may be a question whether a modern softening of the severe and rigid morality of those times has been really a blessing to mankind. Be that as it may, the hardy, honest and uncalculating devotion to principle of the early settlers, makes one almost regret that he had not descended from the Plymouth fathers."

"*Nous avons changé tout cela*," said a voice near him.

"Well," said Tom, taking up the remark, "history

changes, conditions alter, but principles are for all time. You may restrict or enlarge their application, or modify it in a hundred ways, but the people who have followed the Puritans as teachers, must, indeed, have fallen, if they have ceased to be independent and self-reliant, and fail to put honesty of purpose before success in life."

"Ours is a comparatively short history, but it is instructive," said a city editor who was present, "and in the main you interpret it aright; but you do not allow for the fact, which is growing every day more apparent, that the people of New England are not all descended from the Puritans."

"Then I should think those who are not would envy those who are," remarked Tom.

"From envy, hatred and malice, and all uncharitableness, good Lord deliver us," said the Professor, coming to Tom's relief.

"The population of America is so diversified, you have so many classes in your broad country (I use the word for convenience, for I know, constitutionally speaking, you have no classes here), and they have all in their own way contributed so much to your prosperity, that it would be invidious to discriminate; yet it cannot be denied that the Puritans displayed great qualities, though others have done the same, and nobody need be called upon to envy them."

"The descendants of the Puritans claim so much," observed the editor, "that they do not give others fair play."

"It has been well said that a Puritan cannot be an aristocrat, nor could he conceive of heaven as an aristocracy," remarked Mr. Winthrop, epigrammatically.

"Yes," said Robert, "Green has that idea in his essay

on Paradise Lost. He says it is time God ruled all, but He demanded obedience because He is pure goodness. This is not our idea of the ground of imperial rule; Milton nowhere gives the Imperial title to the Almighty; He is the Almighty Father, the King of Heaven, but never the Emperor. That title is reserved for Satan. The heaven of Milton is a Republic under the dominion of goodness. Satan rebelled because the Son was placed over the angels, who were free and equal. Abdiel allows the equality and the freedom, but defends the supremacy, the Son is the 'Visible form of God, and is at one with Him.' The only change is that now through the creation of the Son, through God himself, becoming as an angel, he has lifted the whole angelic body into higher dignity. And of our dignity—'How provident He is, how far from thought to make us less, bent rather to exalt our happy state under one Head more near united.' History has given the Puritans a high niche among those whom she makes famous in the service of liberty, but they did not live in tolerant days; they prepared the way for freedom rather than conferred it."

"Their influence is still great in New England," said the Journalist, "but I think even Mr. Winthrop will admit that it is fading."

"I am sorry if I misapprehend," said Tom. "I am a stranger, but I thought New England was a Puritan stronghold, and that though she did not applaud their severities, of either doctrine or discipline, her institutions were chiefly moulded after their teaching. Right or wrong, I have been a great admirer of their history in my own country, and I was prepared to admire it here."

"Oh, you are to a certain extent right," said the Editor, who was descended in a direct line from a neighbor and friend of Miles Standish, "but we must never forget what we owe to Americans whose citizenship, if more recent, has not been less conspicuous."

The conversation now sought other topics; but at lunch Tom, who was not altogether satisfied with his part in it, alluded to the incident, and his regret that he should have given matters a controversial turn.

"What you said was true enough," said Mr. Winthrop, "but one or two citizens of foreign descent were present, and our friend Taylor of the 'Press,' saw his chance to pay them a compliment, and he took advantage of the occasion."

"I said just what I thought," said Tom, bluntly.

"It is best to be guarded in mixed company," moralized the Professor.

"It is not worth remembering," rejoined Mr. Winthrop. "You expressed your opinion, Taylor improved his chance, and the gentlemen of foreign descent will vote for him."

"These gentlemen are becoming a great power with us," said George. "The politicians pander to them and they are very exacting. The streets are full of people who seek opportunity to speak for and flatter these gentlemen of foreign birth or descent; the Irish-Americans, the French-Canadian-Americans, and other Americans of promiscuous foreign stock—the Indians, if they had votes, would be included—but the poor descendants of the Puritans, and in general the real Americans are growing silent about themselves, or are struggling, like Tom Taylor, to win favor with the men who are becoming their masters!"

"Well, America owes a great deal to these people,"

observed the Professor; "she invited them to her shores, the poor, the halt and the lame, and promised them employment and citizenship. You asked them to come over and help you to develop and govern the country. Most of them were needy and ignorant, and had never been trained to govern themselves. 'The mills of the gods grind slow.' They are hewing down your forests, cultivating your farms, and building your railroads. But you must wait for the full fruition. Train their sons in your admirable schools, and the second generation will be intelligent and patriotic Americans."

"Many of them sneer at our schools; they prefer the system they have cultivated for ages, one that has made them what they are," said George. "At least half a million of one foreign nationality in New England to-day, and one which is increasing largely, came to us instructed by their teachers at home, and are constantly exhorted to abstain from intercourse with us, like the Chinese; not to intermarry with us, nor become citizens; and if these things have roused some of our public men to denounce immigration of this class, and recommend its discouragement, they raise a cry of persecution, and declare that we are false to the traditions of our government. God forbid we should discriminate against the foreign-born population; but they ought not to discriminate against us."

"To a great extent you may expect narrow and ignorant views to prevail with the first generation of these people," observed the Professor. "They are your national raw material; but your system of universal education, and the atmosphere of thrift and intelligence they will breathe, will make good citizens of the second generation. Meantime, it may be awkward, considering your extended franchise, that they should exercise power over matters they do not understand. But they are adding constantly and immensely to your national wealth. The statement is startling, but it has been computed that during the four years of your civil war and all the terrible destruction to be expected from two millions of men in arms, the total wealth of the nation did not decrease, owing chiefly to the vast volume of immigration that bolstered it. In fairness you must credit these people to that extent, while they are chargeable with whatever they do in the way of lowering the standard of public morality among you. But we are making things too serious for the ladies," he added, bowing to Miss Winthrop.

"Oh no," said Miss Winthrop, "I am sure we are all delighted, but you must give us your views about women's rights," she added laughingly, as they rose to withdraw.

"Yes, we have talked enough about 'men's wrongs,'" the Professor responded good-humoredly.

CHAPTER XIX.

"WE ARE MASSACHUSETTS FARMERS."

The Professor and the Senator were to drive, but we will not accompany them, for what could they see in or around Boston which has not already been described by a hundred facile pens? They would see landmarks and recall traditions enough for scores of romances; but have not all these been written and illustrated in a hundred ways in the chronicles for which literary and artistic Boston is famous? The young men, with the exception of George, joined the ladies, and for the first time in their lives they found themselves entertained by half a dozen jolly Boston girls in a fine old Boston house which overlooked Boston Common. Of course, they had seen Miss Winthrop, but they found her first in Europe, and they claimed her as belonging to their party. Alas, how evanescent are preconceived notions! There was not a pair of eye-glasses, nor a pert blue-stocking, in the room. There ought to be scores of the latter in Boston, and no doubt they are very charming people, wherever they are to be found; but Miss Winthrop's friends were all quiet and pleasant young ladies like herself; most of them were older, and had seen more of society; many of them had travelled, and all had enjoyed such advantages as belong everywhere to young gentlewomen; in conversation, they were sparkling, lively and entertaining; and our young friends had not spent a happier afternoon since they came to America. Not that they were so misled as to have expected vulgarity; they had rather been taught to look for hypercritical culture, and they had a half-defined idea of a Boston girl as a philosopher and a mathematician, who was never without a book under her arm. On the other hand, these young girls had equal occasion for disappointment. They had read, though they had travelled and knew better, that Englishmen abroad were always churlish and disagreeable; that they were impatient with American women, because they called a "jug" a "pitcher," and tolerated too much crust under their tarts. If the truth must be told, they were glad to meet these young Englishmen. They were surprised to see nothing brusque in their manner; and that they were always agreeable and careful of the comfort of others. On the whole we must say, that the afternoon afforded mutual delight and mutual disappointment; because they had found, on the one side, that the young ladies were neither frigid nor strongminded, and on the other, that the young gentlemen were not upstarts nor bores. So they soon forgot their apprehensions, and became as thoroughly acquainted as if all parties had been brought up together on one side or other of the water.

Among the young ladies was a cousin of Miss Winthrop, a Miss Mattie Elmwood, from Bloomfield, a small suburban village near by. The young lady was midway, as she told Fred, between the eldest and the youngest of nine children. Her parents were humble people, and they lived in a quiet way; but she hoped Agnes would fulfil her promise of driving Fred out to see them.

"If you want to understand America, Captain Conant," she said, "you must extend your observations to the poor, who are an important element of this commonwealth, but who, like all true Americans, think themselves as good as their neighbors. We can't give you a practical lesson from an extreme point of view; but we are Massachusetts farmers, and, in that quality, belong to a class which one of your countrymen, who once travelled among us, described as 'the finest peasantry on the face of God's earth.' I should like to take you among the farmers whose lands are smaller than ours; but who sleep under their own roof and cultivate their own soil. Do English girls never speak of such things?"

Tom hoped they did speak of them.

"Well," she added, "we hear so much of the diffusion of the good things among the people, not altogether of wealth and culture, but comfort and intelligence, which the higher classes—for we *have* classes—used to absorb more than they do now; and we are so taught to find the solution in the fact that each man cultivates his own here, that even to children it all seems rudimentary, so my father says, and he worships your father. He says you can't exactly understand our system, unless you see it in a prosperous community of farmers with small holdings. It is not very hard to get the idea, or I should not myself have got it; but father's heart is set on having you come to Bloomfield, and stay until he has shown it all to you. He says your father has been teaching him for twenty years, and now he wants to return the compliment. He says the farmers of Bloomfield are what the English agricultural laborers ought to be."

"I am sure my father will go if he can," said Tom;

"it is just in the line of his studies, but I shall be more diffident. You ought to teach me."

"You are joking," said Miss Elmwood; "but I think I could teach a new-comer, for I have been among these scenes all my life."

Robert had found a young lady, familiar with art, who knew "Kingsmere," his estate in Scotland, and who had in her own house sketches of landscape she had taken there. "You must come and see them, Mr. Holt," she said.

Robert politely promised to call the next morning. To himself he said, "After all, how small the world is! Here I am, away in America, and I find among strangers sketches of my old home. I wonder shall I recognize them?"

Fred Cuthbert's attentions had been general as well as delightful to the young ladies, and they declared him to be a most agreeable young man. The Professor immensely enjoyed his long drive behind Mr. Winthrop's fine bays, and he found out for himself, what others indeed had told him, that his host was an able man. At dinner that night there were, besides the Professor's party, only three or four distinguished men. One was a fashionable preacher, though a man of great eloquence and high spiritual life; one was a poet, whose wit and genius were proverbial, and whose muse for forty years had been appreciated on both sides of the Atlantic; another was a learned and well-known philanthropist, somewhat up in years, an advanced radical and an orator of great versatility and power.

"I knew you were fatigued," Mr. Winthrop had said after the guests retired, "but I thought I must present to you a few of our remarkable men."

Miss Winthrop extolled the clergyman, eulogized the "dear old poet," but was more guarded in her praise of the eloquent philanthropist, who, though she admired him, she wished was less rancorous and exercised more charity. "I remember when his life was not safe in the streets of Boston, because he sought freedom for the slaves," observed the Professor. "By the way, Agnes had an uncle, a little way out of town, who has always been a bosom-friend and a firm supporter of our philanthropist. He knows him as well as any man living, and says that he is at heart full of benevolence and tenderness; that his scathing satire and extravagant denunciation are only tricks of his rhetoric, and that his private life is full of sweetness and charity."

"To have met these men is ample recompense for my journey across the water, perilous though it was," said the Professor politely. "I shall always be your debtor, Mr. Winthrop."

"Pardon me," was the reply, "America is honored by that journey and is hastening to say so. My guests are honored by their experience to-night, and, I have no doubt, you felt yourself to be surrounded by kindred spirits, and that an unseen magnetism circulated among you."

"I am sure your compliments are kindly meant," continued Prof. Conant, "but you exaggerate. What have been my puny efforts compared with the services of those who struck the shackles from the slave?"

"If my admiration and gratitude have led me astray," rejoined the Senator, "my countrymen have all fallen into the same error."

That night George and his sister gave Tom and Holt an account of their visit to Quebec, of their recognition of Miss Lytton, the recovery of the child, and the improvement in the condition of Madame De Luynes, and of their expected visit to them in Boston.

"You must both come and see them," said Miss Winthrop. "As was proper, we have promised them to have no company; the visit is only an experiment to try what change of scene will do; but we will, I am sure, with their consent, treat you as members of the family. George is more cheerful," she said aside to Tom, "and I do what I can, without shocking him, to keep his mind diverted. Don't you think Ethel Lytton beautiful?"

Tom assented, but he thought he knew a fairer than she.

"Ethel was kind to George," she continued, "she talked and drove out with him, and at times seemed to make him forget his own sorrow. It is all so distressing though," she added. "Do you know, Capt. Conant, there is a lost link in my life, and I only found it out lately?"

Tom pressed for an explanation with great interest, but was a little disappointed when she exclaimed, "Oh! if George could have known Ethel before he met poor Miss Roberts! Is that wicked?" she asked.

"No," said Tom, "time flies; in a few short months what may not happen, which you and I tremble to speak of now!"

"I thank you," was all she said, but her manner seemed to add, "I must lean on you for advice." And he answered with a kiss.

"You have done wrong," she said coquettishly; "let this never happen again."

When Tom bade George "good night," he was so

much at peace with the world that he congratulated him on his seeming more cheerful, and said, "If you ever want a friend, your sister will tell you that you may trust me."

Next morning Robert called with Fred to see the sketches, and found two or three young ladies waiting to receive them. The artist had done her work well, alike in choosing her company and in selecting her landscapes. They admired the one and applauded the other, and spent the morning in a most delightful way. Fred became convinced that no one in England, save perhaps his sister Alice, could compare with a young Boston lady, and Robert, candid Robert, was inclined to admit as much, though, as usual, he kept such thoughts to himself.

The Professor and the Senator were fast growing inseparable friends. They talked of politics, of books and statecraft, as if they had been born to agree; and some of the young people, though less learned in their conversation, seemed equally fascinated and drawn together. Some were serious; would they be constant? and others, alas! were just flirting *faute de mieux*.

During the day, many of the élite of Boston called to pay their respects to the Professor—magnates from the State House, savans from the colleges and schools— and thus the day passed and the night came which was to witness Prof. Conant's first reception in Boston. It was private and select; only such as were invited guests attended. But "the solid men" and their wives and daughters were there—men eminent in theology, law, medicine, commerce and letters; do we put the first last?—but in that congenial atmosphere they were numerous and distinguished.

The Professor and his friends received an ovation that charmed and delighted them, and accepted it in the highest of good spirits, and for the whole week Boston threw wide open her homes and hearts to greet the great English statesman.

The Professor had already made the acquaintance of Gen. Enoch Elmwood, of Bloomfield, and the whole party had promised to spend a day with him. Dr. Elmwood, his brother, would join him there. Agnes was in high spirits about the visit, till she found it would be impossible to persuade George to go. The last time he had visited his uncle, he said, had been to confide to him the secret of his engagement and approaching marriage. To revisit him now would be to recall painful memories.

Tom endeavored to persuade him with cheering words, and his sister besought him to yield; they all expected him, she said, and everyone would be disappointed.

"Don't press me, little one," George answered, "it is hard to refuse you, but I should only be a cloud upon the spirits of the whole party."

Enoch Elmwood was an only brother of the Doctor. He was older by several years, and had struggled with poverty in early life; but he now enjoyed a comfortable competence, though he had always snatched from the pursuits of his frugal life time enough to study public affairs, and to comprehend the principles which he thought should guide them. He was earnest and intense in his convictions, and was a typical Puritan in his exacting devotion to duty. He was kind and tender-hearted toward all who suffered; but he could hold no truce with wrong-doers; so long as they were perverse, he was intolerant, and would smite them hip and thigh.

He loved his country, whose government he believed was the best in the world, and which had been established after much persecution and was maintained in the midst of many trials. He had been conspicuous in the anti-slavery controversies of Massachusetts before the war, and had gone to the front when, finally, the sword was drawn and the scabbard thrown away. He had raised a company of the three months' men, first called out by President Lincoln; but he had continued in the service as long as he was needed, and adorned it with many brave deeds. He had gone out a captain, but returned a general of brigade, "thankful," as he said, when his country's enemies had surrendered, "to return to the quiet cultivation of the farm." "I went with two sons to the war," he remarked; "they both fought at my side, and laid down their lives there. Tens of thousands did like me with no thought of gain, and yet our critics called us mercenary, and said that we had shown our patriotism by hiring foreign substitutes to carry on the war. I was in the Massachusetts First Regiment," said he to the Professor, "and their time had expired, and we expected to have been mustered out, just before the battle of the 'Wilderness;' but we remained till after the engagement, and suffered seriously in dead and wounded. The troops were then transported to Boston direct, but I came in before them. It was a touching sight as those worn and shattered veterans marched through the streets of the city. I think there was a public welcome; but what touched me was the manner in which the common people, whose battles they had been fighting, mingled with, recognized and embraced them. Discipline was almost impossible. There had been no accurate news of the casualties in the last fight, and the friends of the brave soldiers did not yet know who were returning to them. Fathers, mothers, sisters and brothers, from the door-steps, from the wagons, from every elevation, were peering into those serried ranks for the sight of some dear one whom they expected and whom sometimes they found, but who as often had fallen by the way. It was a touching sight, but war is full of such pathetic incidents."

General Elmwood was a religious man, his soul was full of reverence, but he had not preserved the severe orthodoxy of his Puritan fathers. Punishment, to his mind, was sure to follow sin, but he hoped it was to be a beneficial discipline; he dwelt most, however, upon God's goodness, and Christ's sacrifice for all men, and his kind nature was agonized at the thought that any soul could be lost. "Our fathers would turn in their graves," he said, "if they could realize how the New England of to-day is softening the rigors of her austere theology; but I have given the subject much thought, and cannot believe we are the worse for it."

Bloomfield was a tranquil New England village, clean and thrifty, such as everybody has seen, and General Elmwood's hospitable farm-house stood like a country bungalow, on an eminence above the town. Some people, of local importance, had been invited to lunch, and altogether they were a large party, but the long dining-hall, which, at the busy season, was used to serve meals in to those whom the General usually called his "helps," was made to do service, and there was ample room for all. One feature of the entertainment was especially noticeable to Fred Cuthbert. When they all sat down to their mid-day meal, what he would have called the "servants," took their places at the table with the family, and, more than once, the farm hands contributed to the conversation. It was a new departure for our friends, though they were too well bred to notice it; but Fred whispered, "we have all men free and equal at last."

The Professor listened more than he talked. He drew out the village schoolmaster on the subject of graded schools; the county sheriff on the causes and expenses of land-sales; and a bright little woman, who was understood to write for "the Press," told him what she knew of the kindergarten and Chautauqua systems. The village editor discussed the temperance question, and expressed the hope that his friends would make it a party shibboleth by-and-bye.

"Yes," said the General, "that is one of the great questions of the future. Is the State to furnish poison which induces crime, and then punish the people for committing it? Another question of the near future, is that of woman's rights; it is making its way, though I confess I don't see through it in all its bearings as yet. I have no doubt about a woman's right to vote; what troubles me is to know whether its exercise would elevate or degrade her."

"Male politicians are not a great success, but you would not take the franchise from men on that account," said the Professor. The conversation soon became general, and everybody seemed to take an intelligent interest in it. After lunch the Professor received a committee of farmers who called to present resolutions of a public meeting held the night before, and who at the earnest solicitation of General Elmwood remained after their business was over.

"I wanted you to meet these gentlemen," said the General, "because they represent important interests in this country of the agricultural class, as the proprietors of their own farms, who are neither pestered by landlords nor by rents; who are sheltered by their own roofs and till their own acres. If a feudal, instead of a democratic society had grown up here, its revenues would have gone to the lords, who would have become rich, while these men would be correspondingly poor. Now, if you will visit a hundred farms about this place, you will find reasonable comfort, a surprising intelligence, and a general independence of thought and action, which come of having been trained to call no man master."

"The statement is full of interest," said the Professor; "the relations between the land and its tillers furnish in my country what has hitherto been an insolvable problem. In America you have solved it as you suggest, but at home, where we are required to uproot a bad system of great antiquity, the obstacles are incalculable."

"The difference is," said Holt, "that here the people own the land and enjoy the revenues, while, there, they seem born only to pay tribute to noble holders. I could name less than forty families of the titled aristocracy of England, who govern that country. It has been claimed that each of these families averages a supply to every House of Commons of three members, not to mention their seats in the Lords and their hold upon every department of administration. Look at this American picture, and see what might happen if all men could enjoy equal rights as to the acquisition of land in England."

"Bloomfield, though a model town," observed the Senator, "I am afraid does not fairly represent the whole range of agricultural prosperity. The West is the great scene of settlement now; individuals are holders of large tracts, and railway companies have been granted areas broad enough for kingdoms. A good many things may happen before the settler of to-day is quieted like these Bloomfield folk in their independent holdings."

"That would not affect the matter, so far as I am concerned," replied the Professor, "though it shows that in some parts of America there are still some lessons to learn."

The committee vouchsafed their views like men who understood whereof they were speaking. The schoolmaster said there was a new study of American history, which ought, for the sake of accuracy, to be mentioned, and which to some extent controlled current ideas. The Puritan organization was not original, nor was it precisely in old time as it is now. New England towns were but a survival of Teutonic customs, which Tacitus had described, and which could be traced in Germany to this day. The Saxons carried them into Britain. They survived the Conquest, and the founders of New England brought them here. He had just been reading a book which dealt with this subject, and the agricultural community of the Middle Ages, and was said to solve the old puzzle of the English lawyers about certain customs of village land-holdings, which antedated the feudal system. The New England towns originally were founded on the idea of a village community of allied families, settled near for social intercourse and defense, but there was a common street. Fields were allotted in the same way to individuals, but they were fenced under the communal plan. These customs were inherited from the Saxons, and have not altogether faded away. Vestiges of these common properties are still to be found. In Plymouth there are two hundred acres now known as town-lands. A company of twenty-four proprietors, heirs of the first settlers, own a hundred and thirty acres, called the town-neck, in the old town of Sandwich, on Cape Cod. Every year the proprietors meet to regulate the pasturage, attend to the fencing, and to elect a moderator and a clerk, with jurisdiction over the property. And a recent writer, speaking of Virginia and New England, may have had something of this kind in his mind while supposing both to be the most strictly English parts of the United States, and that the mixture of any foreign element in the original settlement must have been very small; he adds, "the two lands represent two different sides of England. Virginia more nearly followed England at the time of the settlement, and New England, the England of an earlier time."

The Professor assured them that their position shed light upon the controversy. "A young man studies law," he said, "from musty books in a dingy hall; there is a dry statement of principles, but he does not understand them very well until he enters the courts, follows the practice, and applies a procedure; in short, sees how it all works, then all becomes clear, and he comprehends it. Just so with us, who theorize in our relations to you, who show us what you are doing."

"A general proprietorship is a strong conservative element in any country," remarked Dr. Elmwood. "What civilization has most to dread is communistic teaching among dissatisfied masses of people. It is comparatively easy to convince the man with nothing that the acquisition of property is a sin; give that man a home of his own, with the blessings of comfort around it, and he will change from being the enemy of society to being its friend and defender."

"And now I must interrupt you, gentlemen," said the General, "for *apropos* of agricultural enterprise, I must show the Professor my flocks and herds." They examined the capacious barns, and inspected the broad and highly cultivated meadows, in which occupation the young people, in high spirits, joined. They saw choice breeds of cattle, and the enthusiastic owner explained their best points, and made practical suggestions. Before they returned to town, it had been arranged that the General and his daughter should visit them the next morning. Dr. Conant was to dine with the Governor of Massachusetts, an eccentric man of great parts, who had commanded at important posts during the war, and whose military record was still a subject of dispute. He had won his present position by one of those reactions which sometimes befriend popular leaders, and his administration had given rise to controversies in the State, more varied and more bitter than Massachusetts had known for years. Our Senator had declined an invitation, but he told the Doctor he was to meet a remarkable man whose military record had been cruelly misunderstood in England. 'Few men have a better knowledge of public affairs, and you will find his conversation brilliant and instructive.' The young people were to attend the theater, where a celebrated play had been running a hundred nights, and all the actors, men and women, were Americans. Dr. Elmwood and George spent the evening at home with the Senator. They discussed the events of the week, and all agreed that the visit of Professor Conant and his party had been a rare treat to the good people of Boston.

"I am in love with Tom Conant," said George. "I believe there is the material for great things in him."

Both uncles cordially assented, and shortly after withdrew for a game of billiards, leaving George alone.

"What a strange thing is the human heart," said George, thoughtfully. "A few weeks ago all these people were in the midst of death, but now they have gathered up the threads of life again, and who would dream that they had ever known disaster? And should it not be so? for, if a single grief should darken a whole life, there would be no room for poignancy in our later bereavements. And what am I? Is my heart, which was so stricken, retaining the sting; or do the mists lift, and are the clouds floating away? Did she love me, or had she turned to another? I can never know. Could I mourn for her if she loved me not? Lord, lead me aright that I may not cast away grief unduly, nor mourn beyond the measure of my loss."

The next morning Tom received a letter from Lord Bolton; he thanked him for an invitation to join their party, spoke of the honor paid to Tom's father in Boston, more cordially, according to a morning journal which he quoted, than had ever been paid to an Englishman in this country. He said the day was "beastly," dark, rainy and cold, and, after a few like commonplaces, added: "I suppose you will be here to-morrow. I am awfully seedy, and I am dying to get away. I think of going to the Pacific coast. It would be rest, and, in any case, distraction. My dear boy, come with me! I am always happier when I am with you."

"I must go to him, father," said Tom, and he glanced furtively at Agnes, whose color came and went. "Poor old Bolton is in trouble and he needs me."

"You won't go to California, Capt. Conant?" Agnes inquired.

"No," replied Tom, with a look that reassured her.

"We must all go to-morrow," said the Professor, "my time is drawing near."

In the meanwhile Dr. Elmwood, with the General and his daughter, arrived, and there was an excitement of welcome and greeting. The General was in high spirits. "I reckon you don't have such sunshine as this in England," he remarked to the Professor as he wandered off with him in a conversation about the weather, the crops, and other topics, into which we shall not follow them.

Tom was deprecating the acceptance of hospitalities for such a "crowd," as he called the Professor's party.

"My uncle says he never enjoyed a week so much in his life," observed Agnes.

"Well, we can all say that," Tom replied; "but I don't know how it would be if we had to bear the burdens of the host. The fact is, I don't think I can judge for the others."

"Why?"

"Because my circumstances are so different."

"Tell me how," she inquired coyly, pretending not to understand him.

"Well," said Tom, "I have 'a friend at court.' My

dear little friend is a fairy; I have only to wish and my wish is gratified."

"You will have to be more explicit if you want me to understand you," Agnes responded.

Then he made his meaning so plain to her that she comprehended it all. "You are my fairy," he said.

"No, no, not that," murmured Agnes; "let us be serious. Have you enjoyed your visit to Boston?"

"More than I can find words to express," Tom answered.

"And your friends?"

"They have all been delighted beyond measure."

"What do you think of the people you have met?"

"Men and women, one could not find their superiors anywhere."

"Dear old Boston seems very charming to me," Agnes said, absently.

"Why, I should have thought myself in an English city," observed Tom.

"Do you still believe it is so very essential that a city must be English in order to charm you?"

"Well, no," replied Tom, "but to find it English would be the highest compliment I could pay it. You know England is my home, and I haven't been long enough in America to forget my attachment to it; but every day I am here I find something to surprise and delight me. When I came to Boston I at once felt at home. My opinions are of small consequence, except perhaps to you. What I say, I feel. Would you ask me to say more?"

"Oh, no!" she responded; "that you and your father have been pleased with your visit is gratifying to us all, and to no one more than to me."

"Some time you will be English," he said, caressingly.

"And would that involve forgetting Boston?" she asked.

"Oh, no!" was the reply; "all our lives we will together love and admire Boston."

"My darling!" he continued, "places go for little in the calculation I invite you to make. Could you leave Boston and come to London?"

"I know what I could do," she said; "but we won't speak of that now. Let us be happy and not think of such startling changes."

"But when may I speak? You know we are to leave in the morning," urged Tom. "I can't keep silent forever."

"Speak when you are bidden, sir," she answered; "and now come to the drawing-room with me."

Tom gently tried to detain her, but she bounded away with his hand in hers, and thus ended another attempt to declare himself.

Fred Cuthbert and Miss Elmwood had been enjoying a tête-à-tête. The latter had been giving Fred her ideas of American life and manners. "I have never been in Europe," Miss Elmwood remarked; "but I suppose you are ever so much wiser and more polished there."

"Well, no," Fred answered; "we are older, and of course that counts for something. I used to give England credit for greater superiority before I came here. And as for Bloomfield, I don't know what could surpass the interest one feels in those old farmers and their wives and daughters whom we met there. Do you know I begin to think that we attach too much importance to mere geographical distinctions? It isn't because a man is English or American that he is refined or agreeable. Gentle manners everywhere denote the same thing. In England we have titles and wealth, and here you have wealth without titles; but they all mean little without the adornment of cultivated minds."

"Well, it appears to me that is a very democratic statement," said Miss Elmwood. "To the aristocracy of intellect we all subscribe, but I never expected to hear such doctrines from you."

"Perhaps I am a little off the beaten track, and I may have seen America through the ministry of unusual fascinations; but you and I shall never get far apart if all you ask me to believe is that mind should be more powerful than millions; and if the common people, as we call them, were fairly represented by some of the gentlemen we have met here, who escaped early from their ranks, and have been for a life-time undergoing the polish of study and thought, then even that distinction might be abandoned."

It was to be the Professor's last night in Boston; a good many friends were calling to take an unceremonious leave; and that good man was warmly thanking everybody for the generous welcome he had received. "It is not strange," he said, "that England and America sometimes find it difficult to understand each other. There are rivalries of commerce, opposing fiscal systems, and many men in each country hostile to the other; but as to our great mission of freedom we have a common work to perform. We have each our national faults and failings, which require a season of peace and prosperity to get rid of. It is the interest of each that the other should grow freer and stronger. There ought to be a united English-speaking race throughout the world. I do not speak of a union of treaties and alliances, but one of common aims and purposes, which spring from sentiments of universal brotherhood, and a sense of common duties each has to fulfill.

The young people had been busy in paying calls and bidding adieu to friends, but now that they were at home again, the parlors were thronged with Boston folk who had "just dropped in" to say good-bye; and there was in the appearance of things a suspicion of impending change and the obvious din of preparation, as if one's engagements had been fulfilled, and the hour of departure were at hand.

"To-morrow will be Evacuation day," said Fred to Miss Winthrop, "and then the weary may rest."

"Are you studying our patriotic nomenclature?" she inquired.

"One may learn without study here," replied Fred. "Everything is in such big print, you can read it like Sam Slick by moonlight."

"Then you shall read to me by-and-bye," she said gayly, "but you must read to my guests now."

As he mingled with the bright throng and was lost to view, she remarked to Robert who approached her: "How saucily he carries himself; what a fund he has of humor and wit!"

"He is a fine fellow," said Robert, "and full of good nature, though we call him 'the cynic.' But really if he was intended for a wit I think his make-up is rather feeble."

"Oh, you are serious, Mr. Holt; you are not in a mood to appreciate funny things."

"Well, I sometimes laugh, at any rate, as I did at poor Fred's expense this morning. We were driving along the river-side, and found a countryman lazily fishing from its banks.

"'What are you fishing for there, my man,' asked Fred, with an air of hauteur, which the countryman resented.

"'I'm fishin' a'ter Britishers,' he answered quizzically, "but 'taint no kind o' use. They don't bite here's as they did in '76.'"

George had responded to Tom's invitation, and had unreservedly given him his full confidence. "She was so good, and so beautiful," he said; "I thought her the loveliest of women. My sister spoke of another man's brilliant and dazzling suit. Something in her last letter had almost prepared me for it. Would she have asked me to release her? Agnes does not help me. She knows nothing, she says."

Tom knew that Agnes refrained from defending the memory of Miss Roberts, because she saw in George's doubts a mitigation of his grief.

"It is not all clear, even to me," she had said; "she was loyal to him, but did she love him?"

"That is what we can never know," Tom answered; but he gave no hint of all this to George, as silence had been enjoined upon him by his sister.

And then they spoke of Agnes, whom both worshiped, from different points of view; and George related how, since her return, she was devoting herself to charities, hunting out and relieving the destitution of the poor; and Tom's big heart throbbed quicker as he recognized in Miss Winthrop an early follower of his good mother's example.

"Now I must go, George," he said; "but if you ever need a sympathetic friend, you will always know where to find Tom Conant."

He sought Miss Winthrop and was distressed to find

her in low spirits. "Why are you sad, my darling," he inquired; but she gave him her hand without heeding his question.

"Has something happened?"

"No."

"Then why are you sad?" he persisted.

"But something is about to happen; are not you going away?" she asked, and her gray eyes filled with tears.

Tom rendered his answer as he had done before, but this time without reproof, and she nestled in his strong arms for a moment, as if she were unable to break away.

"Sweet one," said Tom, "let me speak to your uncle, now that my father is here."

"Not now," she replied; "I have been weak, but we must wait. Is that dreadful? You have known me but three months," she added, smiling; "but you will come to me again soon and we shall learn to know each other better."

"Do you doubt me?" asked Tom.

"My dear friend," she responded caressingly, "when you are with me, I doubt nothing; I forget that you are not mine, and that your good heart might change; but when you are gone my faith relaxes, and in your absence I tremble lest I may not see you again. You think I am weak; well, strength is not born of this strange new influence under which I am falling. I must resist it, and we must wait; but my uncle says you may write me sometimes. We shall not see each other alone again. We will go to the others. Good-bye," and in spite of all, they embraced like young people who almost understood each other.

"Good-bye," Tom repeated; "you are a cruel little

darling, but God bless you." And as they rejoined their friends the great pictures on the walls smiled upon them in the gaslight, as if their choice was approved and their secret safe.

Next morning our travellers returned through a rough but beautiful country, flanked with small villages and thrifty towns. The press had given notice of the train by which they would journey, and all along the route crowds of people beset the station and thronged the cars, eager to catch sight of the great Englishman who stood by their country's cause in her hour of peril. Everywhere, as the train approached and departed from the stations, the Professor was welcomed and cheered on by the heartiest salutations.

On his arrival in New York, Tom found a note from Lord Bolton, saying that he was too restless to remain, and had gone to Canada for a day or two. They all found "letters from home," full of congratulations on their escape from peril, and abounding in kind wishes for the homeward voyage. Letters from home are as the "bread of life" to the far-off wanderer; and these letters cheered our friends and they passed their evening happily together.

CHAPTER XX.

"THE PEOPLE'S KING IN AMERICA."

Next day the Professor called to pay his respects to the President of the United States, who was spending a few days, like any private gentleman, at one of the leading hotels. He was cordially received, and was struck by the absence of ostentation and parade in the going and coming of the people's king in America. Among the Professor's callers was an old gentleman, well stricken in years, a famous philanthropist, who had spent millions in benevolence, himself superintending the administration of his gifts and securing the best results, "instead of," as the Professor observed, "clutching his filthy lucre to the end, and then, perhaps, leaving his vast estates to some extent burdened with charitable bequests, which interested neither his heirs nor his executors, who would be only too ready to set aside his charities altogether if they could."

The same afternoon he was waited on by a deputation of "the Irish National Land League of America," to congratulate him on the noble sentiments he had from time to time expressed, and to ask his good offices in their behalf, who were seeking "Home Rule for Ireland;" so much had this good man opened his great heart to all the people, that he had won them all. Such things would oftener happen if public men were more sympathetic and sincere.

That night the party was to be entertained by the Hon. Mr. Douglas, a former Secretary of State, who had flourished in earlier days, when the native population had organized to check the influence of the foreign element, and claimed "America for the Americans."

"And we were right, too," he said to the Professor, as they discussed this subject; "we violated no traditions and we preached no intolerance; but we, who were Americans by birth, whose all was at stake here, found ourselves in many places outnumbered and outvoted by foreigners, who knew nothing about government, either of the country or of themselves, and who could hardly read the Constitution in the vulgar tongue. The movement was not a success, and brought down the vengeance of the foreign population upon those who promoted it. It was a conspiracy against them, they said; but had we not a right to conspire? The classes at which we aimed were always against us, in a solid body."

"This is all very dangerous in a mixed population," remarked the Professor. "I suppose, for example, our Irish friends who honored me to-day, and would at least be included among those you discriminated against, were influenced chiefly by the labor question and the possibility of rivalry from the negro."

"Well, yes, but not chiefly," said Mr. Douglas; "their hostility dates farther back. When our government was in its infancy, the followers of Washington and Hamilton dreaded such immigration as came over to us, inflamed with the passions of the French Revolution; party strife ran high, and party spirit was rancorous. The Whigs sought to impose restrictions, and the Democrats defended these people. Their resentment on the one hand, and their debt of gratitude on the other, have moulded their politics to this day; and the Republicans inherited from the Whigs. No doubt the dissension has been kept alive, as more recent antagonism developed, but the negro question has been only one of many."

"We must always expect human nature to develop two currents of opinion," observed the Professor, "but there is positive danger to any community whenever the wrangles of race and creed underlie the differences of party. They may smoulder but they are not to be quenched; it is moreover the manifest interest of demagogues to keep them alive."

"At the worst the pressing danger is confined to the cities," said Mr. Douglas. "The immigrant who settles on the prairies or in the nearer rural districts, has quiet and steady occupation, and speedily becomes a good citizen. He is not educated as his son will be, but he has a house to be taxed and defended, which gives him an interest in good government, and he is removed from the worst schools of vice and dissipation. So there is a chance for the first generation, and the country will have a stronger hold on the second."

"Yes, your safety lies there," remarked the Professor, "in the distribution and assimilation of foreign comers, and in the thorough adaptation and efficiency of your schools. But I am afraid I am a sad trial to you ladies," he said, rising, and bowing to Miss Douglas, "my time is so short, and I have so much to learn, that I set every body speaking to me of public questions."

"I am sure Papa is not unhappy," was Miss Douglas's answer; "I have enjoyed so much, when I have heard you speak, but I did come to interrupt you. His Excellency, the President, is here, and desires me to present his compliments to Professor Conant, and to you Papa, which means, I expect, that he wants to see you both."

"Your Republican King abroad among his subjects!" said the Professor, briskly.

"Not his *subjects*, but his *people*," interposed Miss Douglas. And they withdrew to meet the great man who helps fifty odd millions of people to govern themselves.

They found the President awaiting them, and after cordial greetings, he led them into conversation about ordinary topics. A new interest had been lately given to the question of Civil Rights, as it affected the colored people; "Were they to be recognized in law as the equals of white men? Could they be discriminated against, as guests in hotels, as passengers on the routes of travel, or as worshipers in the churches?"

The Professor would have been glad to know the President's views, and he introduced the subject cautiously.

"Oh, we have spent blood and treasure enough for the negro," observed Mr. Douglas; "he must let us rest."

"In all we have done for the negro we were really serving ourselves," said the President; "as to his social status he must help to make that. A gentleman is a man of intelligence and refinement, black or white; men stand with each other, all things being equal, according to their work as men. We must not insist on privileges for the negro which we deny to the white man, and which he is unfitted to enjoy. His wrongs while he was a slave have directed great sympathy toward him. But he must not force impossible issues; there is an unjust prejudice against him now, which is gradually fading away. We may let it fade, but we cannot obliterate it by force. The Civil Rights question will settle itself. This discrimination against race on account of color will disappear. Public sentiment is tending that way. The negro will be a guest at the same hotels, and a passenger on the same trains, as the white man. Some white men will, and some will not, invite him to dinner. That question of social inequality may involve hardships, but it is only a relic of greater hardships which have been wiped out. It, too, may go in time and perhaps sooner than the negro himself could have believed emancipation would come, a few years ago. By attempting to force it now we might perpetrate another tyranny. *Festina lente*, in this, as in most other things, is the safe motto."

"Yes," rejoined the Professor, "among mixed populations iron rules are dangerous pacificators. Some respect must be paid to the habits, and even the prejudices, of a people. We must have reasonable patience and sooner or later the right will prevail."

"Y-e-s," observed Mr. Douglas, "but we are dealing with old enemies. We must not imitate the dough-faces, and for the sake of quiet, plead for delay."

They all went to the drawing-room, to find the guests. The President was a familiar figure, and had gone in and out among these people for years. The Professor noticed that they greeted him respectfully and cordially; but there was nothing abject or servile in their manner toward him. To the eminence he now occupied they might all aspire.

Fred Cuthbert was in his usual good spirits. He had been catechised by Miss Douglas, as to his opinion of America. We, who saw him falter in Boston, might expect him to capitulate to Miss Douglas, but he was more wayward, and peals of laughter were provoked by his hits and drolleries. As he was taking his leave, he said to Miss Douglas, "the one thing I do envy America is her young ladies."

"You might have spared us that," she said, curtly.

"Upon my honor," Fred gallantly remarked, "I have never met in any society before such a proportion of brilliant and fascinating women."

"Good-night, Mr. Cuthbert, I shall expect you at eleven. You should go and study your part for to-morrow."

Next morning Tom received a letter from Lord Bolton, who was the guest of the Governor of Canada at Quebec. It reasserted his Lordship's intention to visit the west, and his desire that Tom should go with him. "I cannot give you any gossiping news," the letter went on, "but what seemed to me a strange thing happened last night at dinner. There were covers for fourteen. One of the guests at the last moment sent an excuse on account of indisposition; this left us to be thirteen at table! Lord Lester refused to be seated till a young officer had been sent for and had been given time to array himself. 'You know the superstition!' he said to me. I laughingly told him I had heard of it, but never saw it officially recognized before. 'Well,' he said, 'a painful case greatly shocked society here lately. A gentleman, whose hospitalities were proverbial, here, found himself and thirteen guests about sitting down at table, when one of them was peremptorily called away. 'This leaves us thirteen,' said the host, carelessly, 'but if it means death, I shall be the victim, for I am much older than any of you.' They made an unsuccessful effort to fill the vacant seat, and the party was constrained and gloomy. Next morning the host died of apoplexy. The sad circumstance created a profound impression. I am not superstitious, but I would not risk making my guests uncomfortable.' I was in the mood to be impressed, and I brooded over the superstition long after I had retired."

"Let me say about that, before you proceed," interrupted the Professor, "that this mystic superstition dates back to the beginning of the Christian era, and there is a legend that good King Arthur's Round Table was provided among others with thirteen seats to represent the Apostles of our Lord; twelve for the faithful, and one for Judas, who betrayed Him. The most valiant knights occupied the twelve, and if one of these died, his seat was unoccupied till some Knight of equal distinction could be found worthy to take the vacant place. An unworthy candidate was repelled by magic. Only once was the thirteenth seat taken, and then the haughty Saracen Knight, who intruded, was rewarded by the earth yawning beneath and swallowing him. From that time, thirteen hundred years ago, men have dreaded the thirteenth seat, and the disasters which from time to time have befallen its occupants have multiplied into fatal precedents, and taken the place of the lost tradition."

All were silent till at last Tom asked permission, and resumed his reading. "But you will want to hear from the De Luynes. They are better and less wretched there, and I visit them daily. I have long conversations with

Madame De Luynes, which seem to do her good, and she bears her bereavement better as time passes, and speaks beautifully of death and the hereafter. Miss Ethel Lytton is her sister reproduced, which means everything complimentary of a woman. Tell Robert, little Ethel progresses finely, and the child's mother wants to add Holt to the name she is called by. She says she dreamed Maurice bade her do so, and she knows the idea would have pleased him as it has pleased her. In that case he would have to address his little *protégée*, as 'Ethel Carlotta Holt De Luynes.' 'Carlotta Holt' would sound well, but the whole name does not euphonize."

"Strange! the child must have been christened," said Tom.

"Oh, yes," added Robert, "but another name might be used conventionally."

"He has thought of that before," remarked Tom to his father, when next they were alone. But the Professor saw nothing astray in Carlotta's suggestion, nor in Robert's willingness to lend his name to the child.

"Yes," observed Tom, with a faint smile. "The child is dear to him, and its mother feels the warmest gratitude toward Robert Holt, while she suffers the deepest of human afflictions. Bolton wrote, though I did not read it aloud, 'Miss Lytton will shortly visit the Winthrops in Boston, *quietly*,' whatever that means, and as if one could be quiet in that hospitable old mansion."

"I suppose Madame De Luynes will accompany her," said the Professor. "I understood the journey was merely for her, and to try the effects of change. Of course they will be quiet and will not receive."

Father and son read for some time in silence. At length the Professor handed him a letter and said, "Tom, your dear little mother seems disquieted about you."

"About me!" Tom answered, astonished.

"Well, she gathers from your letters that you have formed an attachment, but you do not seem to have shown her any purpose in your suit. She thinks this unfair to yourself and to the young lady. As usual, she is right. Read the letter, and we will speak about it again. Your mother made an early marriage, and she believes in it."

"I have had no secrets from you, father. When I learn more, you shall know it; if I am not to be married early, the fault will not be mine."

"You know I must leave America now in a few days," observed the Professor. "I suppose you will remain."

"Yes, if my leave can be extended," replied Tom.

"We must see to that," the father answered; and they went out to pay calls.

An hour later Tom returned alone; he picked up the evening paper, and his eye caught in flaring headings over a British cable, "The *Times* demands reorganization and a dissolution. Professor Conant to be Chancellor of the Exchequer and Leader of the Commons." As usual, the real text was a little milder than the flaring caption; but the *Times* did urge that dissolution was desirable, and stated that no Liberal Cabinet would be acceptable which did not include the Professor.

"Things seem almost settled," said Tom, after his father came back.

"It is only a newspaper paragraph," observed the Professor, modestly.

"But Bolton says it is sure to come," said Tom with confidence.

"And when it comes, my son," slowly replied the Professor, "it will add loads of care and burden to your father's life. But if all this fleeting popularity would sustain me, I might do good; yet, perhaps, ere my feet were in the stirrups the people would abandon me, and be found running after new idols."

Tom had just now received a letter from Agnes, which he hastened away to read, and which put him in great spirits. The letter was promptly answered, but we will not disclose the secrets of the correspondence further than this, that it announced Carlotta's expected visit in two weeks with Miss Lytton and little Ethel. The visit was a secret, known only to Uncle Horace and George. But Agnes felt very sure that Madame De Luynes would forgive them if Tom and Robert should come, and she notified them to govern themselves accordingly.

That night, Lord Bolton arrived, and was full of his projected visit to the West, but disappointed that Tom could not go. He took leave of his friends, and was to undertake the journey next morning.

Tom parted from him with regret. His Lordship promised to write often, and to return in a few weeks.

The Professor, on the invitation of the British Minister, was to pay a flying visit to Washington, and Mr. Winthrop was to meet him there: the party was to be absent for a week. There was an extra session of Congress, so that the Professor met some of the great men, and saw all the politicians in Washington. Of course current political topics engrossed attention.

Professor Conant listened to the debates and was instructed in the theories of those who see prosperity for the poor man in high prices. He was astonished to learn that England was scattering gold throughout America, to bribe the way for the starvation of the toiling masses here. He did not believe the theory, but he was prejudiced, perhaps, and his ear inclined to those who pleaded for such fiscal provisions as would enable them to buy in the cheapest and sell in the dearest market. "I am a free-trader, but theories may be plausible, and even practicable here, which in our different circumstances we could not tolerate in England. Your vast resources leave you room for waste, which we could not afford in my country," said Dr. Conant. When his attention was called to the enormous national surplus, he simply observed, "I suppose all the money is derived from the taxation of your people. It might have been a half more, or a half less, as the taxation was increased or diminished. But your vast resources, and varieties of climate and production, especially in your prosperous days, will accumulate wealth, in spite of burdens. I suppose you must have revenues here for the general expenses of administration. Your people would not bear direct taxation, though that would be cheaper and more logical, so that in this country it is not a question of whether you will impose duties, but at what point you will draw the line."

The Professor attended a reception at the White House that night, and when he saw how the crowd persecuted the poor President with their loyal attentions, he laughingly said, "It might be worth a battle or two to fight democracy back a little, and put the President on an elevation, as to the familiar greetings he encountered, so that everybody could not unceremoniously reach him."

He was delighted, in conversation with high dignitaries, at the freedom they indulged in the discussion of affairs, and he specially noted some remarks about a case which involved bribery.

"Other crimes," said one of the Judges, "according to the popular idea, may involve greater depravity, but nothing can be more dangerous to the public welfare. We have lately emerged from a great war, and as it has been among other people in similar circumstances, the plain truth is that corruption abounds. It carries a dagger aimed at the national heart, and is full of danger to our liberties and a menace to the existence of the government; the people should combine to crush it as one man. You cannot reach it in the ordinary way; it is so often exercised in the interest of one or other political party."

"Bribery is common among us in England," the Professor said to himself, "but its putrid breath is not perhaps so often detected in high places."

And so, from group after group, as they passed and repassed each other, he learned something new on subjects which he might have read or thought of before, but which he had never heard discussed by human lips on the threshold of Democratic authority. Men were not less honest here, he thought, even if corruption were more extended, because in this country every man has a voice, though some men might be open to influences that would silence it; but in older countries, the voice of the same class is silent, and having no influences to sell, these people are not liable to be tempted. It was the old story over again, of Democracy and the tempter abroad.

The young men had met kindred spirits among the

Civil Service, at the Embassy, and among young officers of the Army. Tom's position, as the son of his father, would have given him the entrée anywhere; but he was not less run after because he was an officer of the Guards; and Robert and Fred were not less esteemed chiefly on their own merits, let us hope, and because they were pleasant and entertaining gentlemen; but it may have entered the heads of their entertainers that the one was the son of a rich Baronet, and the other well connected—himself a young man of fortune. However it was, they were petted and pampered by the simple Republican society of the capital. They received callers, and they returned calls. Hops were fashionable, and they attended them, and to their seductive influence, they all, more or less, succumbed, and Boston ran the risk of being forgotten as Fred's responsive heart glowed with admiration of the women he met in Washington.

The Professor, with his friends, drove about the beautiful city next day, but everything they saw has been so often described by cunning pens that we abstain from following them. There was a dinner at the British Embassy, and Attorney-General Burrows, who had parted from him under duress, was a fellow-guest, as he had been lately a fellow-passenger. He was full of the disasters of the *Alaric*, which had grown an old story with the Professor, and he listened to it as to a twice-told tale; when Mr. Burrows recalled his acquaintance with De Luynes, whose accomplishments and brilliant talk he admired, the Professor's sympathies were excited, and his eyes were moistened with tears.

"He was a fine fellow," said Mr. Burrows, "gentle, with a heart full of kindness, and mental faculties of a rare order." He explained that his own family and friends had arrived safely, and listened with interest to what the Professor told him of the experiences of himself and party. "Poor Miss Roberts," he added, "she was a lovely character; I knew her well. For the last two years she had adorned society here."

The Professor sat at the right of the British Minister, and for some time they spoke of home gossip and political affairs. At length his Lordship said, "The Americans are striving to correct a great abuse, and I hope not with indifferent success. They are reforming their Civil Service. As things have been, this service was a creature of the party patronage, and its reformation was difficult to approach. The rule here has been 'to the victors belong the spoils,' and many civil servants knew that their appointments were not for fitness, and that their successors would have their places when their enemies came into power. Their party levied on them for a percentage of their emoluments wherever expenditures were required. They knew that in that way the party disbursements were really paid out of the general public fund, so they might naturally say, why should not these funds contribute to our convenience as well as theirs? If they became dishonest public servants, here was the entering wedge; and they knew, moreover, no matter how distinguished their services, that they were likely to be bundled out with their party when its time came. There was little encouragement for honest service, and it was, to a great extent, both dishonest and inefficient. We understand the question at home, and we know how important it is that the Civil Service should be removed from party patronage. They are trying the experiment here now, because there is a clamor for a change; but it may be doubted if either party is honestly ready to promote it. Political patronage," added the Professor, "is a great source of corruption if dishonestly dispensed; there are many things to be said against us, but in this particular we are moving in the right direction."

"Our politics has this great advantage," observed the Minister. "There are multitudes in this country to whom politics is a trade. With civil service reform, the occupation of these men would be gone; so, you see, it will not be really accomplished without a battle."

"It seems to me very plain," remarked the Professor, "that the civil servant is an officer of the State, and should be the henchman of neither one party nor the other. His services should be rendered as is his fealty, which is due to the whole country. He should have no favorites, he should hold office only during good behavior, and should neither look for, nor accept a favor. The public service could not otherwise be well conducted. On what other principle could the affairs of a bank or a private corporation be administered? How could a merchant conduct his business with ignorant clerks, who are never to be depended upon and who are always changing?"

"These are questions which in this country the people have to answer," said Lord Gough, "and the nation can never have an honest service nor an efficient administration till they have settled them."

"It will all come in good time," said the Professor. "Fifty years ago we could not have dreamed of the purity of administration which we have since achieved in England."

"Do you think it fair," inquired Mr. Burrows, "that

there should be no rotation in office? Is one man to be forever preferred, and his neighbor forever debarred, from enjoying it?" "Assuredly," replied the Professor, "unless the public good requires a change. Office is not one of the privileges which the State undertakes to confer upon the citizen. If it were so, every man would have a claim, and there is no safety except in the country's demanding the best service and the highest qualifications from her men in office." "That is a plausible doctrine," remarked Mr. Winthrop, "but under its teaching parties would be shorn of half their strength."

"Then the sooner the better," responded the Professor. "Petty patronage is the curse of parties, and their selfish exercise of it is a menace to the free institutions of any country."

"What a pity it is that the subject could not be as summarily disposed of before the country as we can treat it here," observed the Attorney General.

The conversation here grew more diffused; they spoke of Mexico and the labor strikes, of research and the exploration of the Polar seas; of Germany and her massive concentrations; of Republican France, her strength and her peril; and of Ireland, her progress and her reaction, her desperation and her hope.

"Why do you not give her Home Rule?" said a voice. "My countrymen would grant that if she would be satisfied," replied the Professor. "The disposition to do Ireland that measure of justice is growing, but the effect of extreme and violent courses is to retard it."

There were to be no toasts, and the host, who evidently dreaded an explosion, rose from the table and his guests followed him. They found Lady Gough with several distinguished ladies in the drawing-room. Meantime, His Excellency the President had dropped in unceremoniously, and the kindly interchange of thought and of courtesies continued until a late hour.

"I ought to apologize to your Ladyship," said the Professor in taking his leave, "and to the ladies everywhere during my visit; for I suppose it is altogether my fault that the conversation wanders among dry political subjects."

"Nothing could be more interesting in this country," said an American lady. "You won our hearts by appreciating our public affairs at a critical period, and it is fitting, now you are among us, that we should enjoy your counsel and criticism. We can always discuss society, the balls and the opera, the latest novels and plays, or the more recent flirtations and engagements; but Prof. Conant is not always with us, to shed light upon graver questions, and besides, they are fuller of interest to us all than you imagine."

"Well, yes. If I were to write a book of my travels, and describe all the startling incidents of my tour and the accidents we have encountered, I think perhaps some serious talks on popular subjects might be tolerated as padding; and besides its being instructive, my story would be relieved by it."

"Yes, you ought to write such a work," urged Lady Gough. "I know you would speak racily of many things and prosily of none; not dwelling too long on descriptions, and thus magnifying the author at the expense of the reader."

"When I send you an advance copy of my book, you will see that your hints have been remembered," laughingly remarked the Professor.

Fred Cuthbert had been, as usual, one of the evening's entertainments. "He is so full of good nature, and so determined to please," said one of the ladies. "And everything he says is so sparkling and *piquant*," added another.

"Do you think him a wit?" asked a young officer, who was half inclined to be piqued at the attention Fred received from the ladies, or, as he put it more tersely, at "the infernal noise he made."

"Oh, dear! I am not a judge of wit," replied the lady addressed, half startled at his tone; "but what he does and says is funny if it is not witty. His manner is so droll, when he chooses, and all his hits are good-natured and make us laugh. Don't you like him, Capt. Strong?"

"Oh, immensely!" was the latter's reply.

Fred had said some frivolous thing at the club that afternoon which had been misunderstood, and he frankly apologized. He forgot the incident soon after, but Capt. Strong remembered it. "These Englishmen," he had remarked, "are churlish and unbearable." There was nothing more of it then, but a year afterward Fred would heap coals of fire on his head in London, and he would tell Miss Alice in a mood of confidence how much he admired her brother here, and how little he had understood him in America. We shall violate no confidence by informing the reader that the handsome young officer would not have said so much, but that he and Miss Alice, with Fred's consent, had been cultivating great interest in each other.

Robert and Tom had not been idle observers of the evening's picture. They were accustomed to society, to luxurious rooms and magnificent decorations, and they were no strangers to the social elegance in which they mingled; but it did happen that they saw here a man and there a woman blazing in diamonds and in dress at once ill-fitting and extravagant, while they expressed eccentric views in a version of the English language which Lindley Murray would never have recognized.

"Wall, I done it once for them fellers," said an old Bonanza Politician in their hearing, "and I ain't agoin' to do it agin."

"And 'tain't no kind o' use," said his pretty young wife, whose diamonds fairly dazzled Tom. "They don't know nothin' about society, and English folks is kind o' pa'tic'lar, and wouldn't want 'em; if 'twant that you're a Politician, you might a run after him for a week and Lord Gough wouldn't 'ave asked 'em."

"And they ain't no ornament when they git here," said the husband haughtily.

"They're good but they ain't cultered," added the wife, "and I don't see why we should carry 'em into good society if they did vote for us. I guess they got paid out o' that one hundred thousand dollars it cost."

"They'll be darned mad," said the Magnate apprehensively.

"Well, let 'em," rejoined the woman, "you can buy 'em agin."

Tom laughed and turned away. Democratic as he was, it was too much even for Robert. "Who are they?" he asked a young attaché at his side.

"They are a product of American Democracy," replied the latter. "A rich mine, vulgar ambition, and corruptible electors did it all. I know the old man well; he is pursuing a claim upon an estate in England,

and sometimes comes to talk to me about it. It cost him a great deal to get here, but he has no idea of his unfitness or his vulgarity. He says public life is a great burden and expense, but he intends to reimburse himself. He tells us that the lobbyists won't get much out of him if they don't 'chalk up,' and if they are stingy, he'll 'jine the anti-monopolists.' He is an accident; there are not many such men."

"One is enough," quietly observed Robert.

"His position gives him the *entrée;* we have to invite such people now and then," said the attaché. "His pretty wife has friends among the newspapers, and the British Lion would fare hard if she were slighted by the British Minister. There are only two or three such people here to-night. They are too feeble to pervert the ways of fashion. Everybody expects to meet them and they disturb nobody."

"Oh, it's nothing strange," said Tom, "though the language in such a place as this did startle one a little, as the whole coarse broadside came down upon us. Such a scene would be impossible in such surroundings in England."

"Yes," observed Robert, "because the same class of people would not be represented at all there, and it is only politics anywhere which would throw a man of this kind among such people, but probably twenty years from now, or less, you may meet his sons as educated gentlemen. Everybody votes in the United States; but in the United Kingdom a population of thirty-five millions furnishes a constituency of only four millions, because the poorest classes are not included. That saves us some exhibitions of coarseness, though poor people are not always vulgar; but what about the material prosperity? Do you think the ignorant, unenfranchised poor in England contribute as much to the national wealth as the people this old man represents do in America? And don't you think the elevation of the poor, in the same way in England, would create an element of national strength there as it does here? The people, long degraded, may sometimes stagger under new responsibilities, their backs unaccustomed and their muscles untrained. But depend upon it, on our part, we might train them for citizenship, and they, on theirs, might contribute vastly more to the wealth and prosperity of the state."

"Oh, Holt," said a voice, "you are always finding excuses for the Yankees and damning England with faint praise; you are like John Bright, a friend of every country but his own."

"I have often thought myself," said Tom, "that Robert resembled Mr. Bright; but I don't think this uncomplimentary to him."

The next morning the Professor received among his callers several leading workingmen, who expressed pride in his career; and a deputation of colored citizens signified their appreciation of his good work and their hope that he might long be spared to pursue it.

To each of these deputations the Professor gave the same advice: "Elevate your people; educate your children; in no other way can you join the aristocracy of intelligence, or enter the charmed circle of refinement. You must study public questions. Ignorance will be a barrier for all time, and in all countries. I do not urge you to pursue the difficult paths of profound scientific and classical learning; you have not perhaps the time, the opportunity, nor the inclination. But you may have access to books, and all you need will be found in these, if well selected. You may be poor, but so were most of the lights of your country. What they accomplished you may imitate with more or less success; and if you never cast a vote until you have studied its consequences, nor support a measure till you understand it, and believe it will work for your country's good, you will follow the best examples and reach the highest rewards." He told the laboring men that America was their paradise, and reminded their colored brethren of the oceans of blood and treasure the nation had expended for them. No record more glorious had been written for any country, and no people more than they owed gratitude and fealty to their government.

"These noble sentiments will be recorded everywhere, sir," said an enthusiastic son of toil, "and will endear your name to the people. In the past few weeks you have done more than any Englishman, since Chatham, to win for the masses you represent the sympathies of the workingmen of this country."

"Would that the public men of both countries did more such work as this," said Mr. Roberts.

"It would be more than difficult to do it in the same way," observed Mr. Burrows. "The people of this country are now ripe for such lessons; and Conant is the man from whom they want to learn them."

"With such men to lead both countries," remarked Mr. Winthrop, "we should become practically one people."

"Do you think England is likely to go back to protection?" asked a rich manufacturer, who had been waiting his chance.

"I do not," said the Professor.

"We hear a good deal about fair trade."

"Yes, that has been spoken of," was the reply.

"I suppose by fair trade they mean protection," said the other.

"No doubt," said the Professor, "but they dare not say so. I think that English people are free traders; we all know what they were in the last generation, under the teachings of Cobden and Bright. But they were instructed on a large scale then, and could all give reasons for the hope that was in them. The subject has not been much treated of late years in a popular way. Nearly all the writers on Political Economy have been free traders, but their books did not reach the people as did the literature of the great agitators in Cobden's time. The masses of the present generation of Englishmen have not much studied the question. There may come a wave of popular discontent, and there may be extraordinary changes. We have become so democratic now, and it is so hard to tell what popular opinion is on abstract questions, till you have counted the votes, that it is dangerous to prophesy. Notwithstanding all, you may class England as a free-trade country. We should be glad to say as much of yours; but we can afford to wait. The late Mr. Webster was a free-trader in early life. Some of his finest speeches defend that theory. When reproached for inconsistency in after-life, he said in effect, 'Yes, I advocated free trade, and my State prospered under it. But you forced us into a protective system, and now I strive under that system to make the best terms possible for her.' I think he still believed in the old doctrine; but I am not here to provoke controversy, and we may each prosper walking our separate ways."

CHAPTER XXI.

HOMEWARD BOUND.

THEY were all to take a quiet tea next evening with Mrs. Roberts, whom they found greatly improved, though a touching sadness pervaded the house, and on the morrow they left Washington for New York by an early train, through Baltimore and Philadelphia, cities which the Professor regretted to pass without a visit. He was anxious also to visit Chicago and the great West, but pressing cablegrams and letters admonished him that he could not claim his own time further. So he arranged to sail by the Wednesday steamer.

Professor Conant's occupations were henceforth engrossing, and he was obliged in consequence to decline all invitations. The night before he left, however, he gave at his hotel a dinner, followed by a reception, which was made a notable event in New York society.

Mr. Winthrop, and Dr. Elmwood and his niece were among the guests. George declined an invitation, though he wrote a kind, sad letter of farewell. The uncle and niece were to leave for Boston by the early morning train, and as the Professor said, his instructive visit to America would soon be over.

At the dinner the Professor was profuse in his expressions of gratitude for the welcome he had received, and his guests were warm and sympathetic as to the pleasure his visit had given them.

"It has been a month of unusual interest to us all," Dr. Elmwood observed, "and will be followed by happy and far-reaching results."

Tom and Agnes had only a moment together, but she reminded him of Carlotta's hurried visit next week, and he promised for himself and Robert that they would join them. Agnes reminded him that Carlotta's friends were only seeking change for her, and that nobody must know she was there. With the near prospect of bidding adieu to his father, and with the sad scenes which the name of Madame De Luynes suggested, Tom was moody and ill at ease. He explained all this to Agnes, who admired him for his tenderness of heart, and told him so; and though their parting was sad, each knew, without saying so, that the other was nearer and dearer than ever before. So the evening passed, and the great party separated, more like the members of a family saying farewell, than like fashionable strangers who might never meet again.

Next morning at breakfast, and just before the Professor was leaving, he received a letter from Lord Lester at Ottawa, expressing regret that he should not have the pleasure of welcoming Dr. Conant at Government House. "You ought to have come, if for nothing but to show our people that they are within the range of a British statesman's sympathies." The letter continued, "Your visit to the States, your sayings and doings, and every incident of your stay on this side are regarded by us with the greatest interest. We all feel pride in your success; but, if I might take such a liberty with an old friend, I would say that some of your compliments might have been paid to your own colony. I fear this pompous gallop on the Democratic horse may raise hopes among the common people at home, which, as your responsibilities increase, you will find it difficult to gratify. But as we began to disagree at college, and have never been the worse friends for disagreeing, I suppose we shall go on to the end, differing as to the best way to govern, but always happy in our esteem for each other. What else can I say but to wish you *bon voyage*, my dear old friend, not only across the water, but throughout your noble and laborious life, for I know that you are going home to heavy work as well as to high distinctions. As you are giving me the slip, however, I want your son to make a point of coming to see me. I dare say we can amuse him, and I shall give him *carte blanche* to bring his friends."

"What a gorgeous ass!" said Fred. "He has been sitting alone up there in the cold, till he is positively jealous. The idea of his subjects being hurt because you have said America is a great country! Though I *do* think it was a pity you could not go to Ottawa."

"Yes," said the Professor, "I have missed a great deal, but I came here to take a rest."

"Which you have not done," observed Tom.

"Well, I should not have improved matters by taking on double labor," remonstrated his father. "You must write Lester, Tom, and visit him."

They drove to the wharf and found a number of friends already aboard the steamer waiting to say good-bye to Dr. Conant, and, as the boat steamed slowly away, they sent after her hearty and repeated cheers.

"God bless him! he has done good work here," cried Mr. Douglas.

"And he goes home even better fitted to be a leader of the people," a voice replied.

"Trust him, oh, my countrymen!" said Robert, "for he dedicates a noble life to you!"

Tom returned to his lodgings weary after a restless night, and the still more restless excitement of the morning. His father was gone, to tempt again the perils he had only lately escaped, and if he reached home safely, which the son did not doubt, for he believed there was still a great work for him to do—to re-enter the turmoil of politics, under conditions which would make him a conspicuous and responsible figure. Tom knew how much of domestic sacrifice this meant; at another time his regrets would have been chiefly for his mother; but to-day he was worried and lonely, and he felt that his father was making a great personal sacrifice to the state. "What would home be without him?" he asked himself, "and yet all his faculties will be absorbed now in what they call higher work. Perhaps his love for us will be as great, and his devotion as tender, but it will be only an abstraction; the living man will be occupied and absorbed in public affairs. To me he has been everything, my father, my brother, and friend. There was always a kind word and a leisure hour at my service. I shall only know him now on the hustings, in the newspapers, and in Parliament. He will be a distinguished statesman, and his head and his heart will be enlisted in the work of his country. General Elmwood spoke with pride of his two sons who fought by his side. Why should not I fight by the side of my father? He discourages me because he would give me an easier life. Have I no duties? Would it be ignoble to throw aside my profession of arms and enlist under his banner? He says I have the necessary gifts, but advises me to shun the hardships of public life. Why should I shun work? I am but a creature of society; why might I not do good, win honors, and perhaps carry forward the prestige of my name? I am not altogether ignorant of men or of public affairs. There will be a dissolution. Why not win a seat in the Commons? That would afford me opportunity. Why not make a career? But I should require to imitate my father's industry, his honesty, his devotion to duty. I could do that, and I might fall far behind him in many things, and yet be the equal of men who have been useful and famous." After a pause, he added, "No, marriage would not retard my career; it would aid me. She is clever and good, and would grace any position. But I must win her first, and the way will then be open and clear before me."

Tom fell asleep in his easy chair and dreamed that he was at sea again. Far away, in a waste of waters, he saw Agnes buffeting the waves and calling to him for help. He was riveted to his chair by an unseen force. He suffered agonies, but could neither move nor speak. By-and-bye, a great white cloud gathered and rested above the fainting and exhausted girl. Then the forms of De Luynes and Miss Roberts emerged therefrom and turned their smiling faces toward him. Agnes was rescued and brought to his arms. He woke to find that the grate was cold, and that a chilly blast was entering the open window.

CHAPTER XXII.

"THINE AND MINE."

Our friends had all been invited to spend a few days with Mr. Douglas at Newport. Robert and Fred would go, but Tom was too dull, he said, and wanted to commune with himself a little. The custom was growing to prolong the summer at the watering-places, and many families still remained. The young men were favorites in society, and saw life in new colors. Robert, as usual, enjoyed it all in a quiet way, but Fred was as rollicking and boisterous as ever. He was in search of pleasure and it abounded; he desired to please and he succeeded; his droll conceits amused his friends and his sunny disposition shone for all. "His nature seems changed," Holt wrote Tom; "we called him petulant, but his good-nature is inexhaustible; a cynic, but he never snarls. He was to reform abuses, he used to tell us; but he has fallen in love with everything he came out to condemn."

"Poor Fred," mused Tom, as he read this, "Robert never understood him. His attempts at ill-nature were always affectations, and since he has been here kind feelings have been so much at high tide that he has floated away from the old shoals; and as for liking what he sees here, all Englishmen will condemn America less as they understand her better."

No doubt our friends were all disposed to see things *couleur de rose;* faults and misfortunes common to all countries were passing every day under their eyes; peculiar abuses and prevailing extravagances, such as could only exist under a system of democratic rule, were not unobserved. Some, or all, of these were open to improvement, or perhaps, to be reformed altogether; all around them lay abundant work for the statesman and the philanthropist. They criticised as they went, but their criticism was more in sorrow than in anger; and they meant it to be just and fair. If they saw an abuse, they asked could it not be remedied? If they encountered suffering, they looked for the means of relief. Other critics, less fair, had fastened eagerly upon whatever they could unequivocally condemn. Was there vulgarity? Was there crime? Was there political maladministration? Their work was done *con amore*, and they saw none of the conditions which might explain or extenuate the evils. But our travellers, like Dr. Conant, noticed what they saw amiss, and they studied the true cause and sought out the true remedy. They had no prejudice against the government by the people, and they hoped and believed the experiment would not fail.

Tom had spent nearly a week alone at his lodgings; his despondency was wearing away among the good old books he had been reading, many of whose ideas were fresh to him, and dozens of whose heroes had undergone greater trials than had befallen him. He had just received a hurried letter from Agnes, which announced the arrival of the De Luynes the day before. Of the party there were, she said, Madame De Luynes, Ethel Lytton, and the baby, and they were accompanied by Gustave

Lamothe, who would only remain a day longer, and had taken lodgings at the hotel. Carlotta was still improving. It was touching to see her habited in deep mourning. She was all grace and loveliness, but *so* frail, that a breath might blow her away. Uncle Horace took a deep interest in her sad story, and she seemed to turn to him as if for rest and help. George had greeted Ethel like an old friend, and seemed to be his old self again. She, dear girl, was stronger and more cheerful, and then the baby came in for a paragraph of tender caresses. Mr. Gustave Lamothe, she said, was last but not least, for she liked him. Ethel had told her he was a man of great worth, and had been, not only the cousin, but the most trusted friend, of poor Maurice De Luynes. He seemed worthy of all that; and Agnes wanted Tom to know him, because he should know all good people. "After all," she continued, "he is not half so good as somebody I know, who shall be nameless, and why should I care? Ah, but I do! there must be a reason, do you know it? And I have never explained it even to you. To-day some ladies called on Madame De Luynes, but they were told she did not receive. I hope that will finish the callers. But she joins us all in wishing to see you and Mr. Holt; she spoke of him much to-day, as she fondled little Ethel. 'Dear Robert Holt,' she said passionately, 'where would my darling have been now but for you?' And now I must close, and you will come at once, won't you? Uncle says you should take the morning train. Dear good Uncle Horace! he has promised to spend the week at home, and help to entertain my friends. Is he not kind?"

"Is he disinterested," thought Tom, but he was alone, and said nothing. "Horace Winthrop is still a young man," he went on musing, "full of poetry and of a fascinating presence. His high position and his great gifts should not tell against him. The human heart is unfathomable. Is it true that sometimes great bereavements dispose us to new friendships, and that, as time passes, these ripen into tenderness?" Robert, he was sure, would meet him in Boston next day.

Tom rose the next morning full of new purposes in life. He thought he saw the way, and he had already written his father; he knew the Professor would not persistently dissuade him, if he was really in earnest. He knew, too, if he decided to go to work, it was because he would have a helpmeet who would profit by his exertions. That Agnes loved him, he never doubted, though she had never told him so; she knew his love, and she encouraged it with her innocent and girlish ways, but when he was serious, she parried his questions; yet he had not dreamed he could live without her or that she expected him to do so. Perhaps their lives had run too smoothly and their intercourse had been too unrestrained for the exercise of exaggerated romantic feeling. He expected her to take her seat at his side in the new English life he was proposing, and he knew she would comfort him with her love, and sustain him with her sympathy and good sense. They were both young, would it be wise to delay? Not as Tom accounted wisdom. Agnes Winthrop was his idol and his ideal. Without her he could not live, and with her all things would be possible.

Absorbed with such thoughts he journeyed to Boston alone, and arrived at Mr. Winthrop's in time for dinner, where he found only the De Luynes and Holt. Agnes welcomed him in high spirits; all their friends were so much improved, she said, and George and Ethel had just returned from a drive. Madame De Luynes's welcome was sad but cordial, and as she went into dinner on the Senator's arm, Tom thought he had never seen more sweetness and grace. "I have just met your friend, Mr. Cuthbert, on the street," said Agnes; "he has been staying with my uncle in Bloomfield a day or two, and they came up to the city together. I ventured so far to relax a certain rule as to ask them to call in the morning, and Madame De Luynes has forgiven me," she added, smiling.

"Yes," explained Robert, "he tired of Newport, and went to pay a promised visit to Bloomfield."

"Queer," said Tom, "I did not know of his promise."

"I dare say my cousin will make it jolly for him," observed Agnes, "and he is sure to make it pleasant for them all."

They were interrupted by the laughter of little Ethel who made her way to Robert's knee. His face wore a look of triumph, and everybody had compliments for the child. The conversation was at first quiet and restrained, and each feared the suggestion of painful thoughts, till Gustave inadvertently replied to some observation in French, and then the others all followed his example, and the good old English was banished for the evening.

The Senator understood the language, he said, yet from want of practice he was not an expert talker; but Gustave declared his pronunciation was perfect, and Madame De Luynes observed that all he said he said well.

"Oh! you are a nation of flatterers," the Senator said laughingly; but the diversion relieved the restraints, and the conversation was once more lively and general.

Madame De Luynes recalled her school days in Boston, and inquired for her early friends, and Mr. Winthrop gave charming pictures of Boston life and manners twenty years ago. He spoke of his home and his work in Washington, of society there, its elegance and its eccentricities. There was magnetism in his manner, and grace and humor in his descriptions. Robert delivered himself of his impressions of Newport, which were pleasant, and he spoke of the great kindness he had received from many cultivated people there. What struck him unfavorably, he said, was that some of the people of great wealth seemed engaged in a struggle as to who could display the greatest number of ducats in the most ostentatious and extravagant style.

Tom and Agnes remarked to each other that George and Miss Lytton were speaking English, but as they made no accusations the offence was not noticed, and the fact has not been established to this day. Gustave was a good talker and took an active share in the conversation.

"Canada affords peculiar facilities for acquiring the French language. I have wondered that Americans do not more generally patronize our schools. For such a purpose they are as good and more convenient than those of France and Germany." Miss Lytton suggested that many Catholic children were sent to Canada from the States.

"And do you think that but for religious difference more Protestants would study the language there?"

"It may be so. But the chief cause is to be found

in the belief which prevails more or less in this country that the French in Canada speak and write a *patois*."

"Ah! we are provincials, of course, but they have these in France, and they differ in their pronunciation. The Greek has dialects, but we have not corrupted *la belle langue*. Do you remember that our young Poet Laureate received an ovation from his countrymen in New England the other day? Well, during his brilliant speech, he apostrophized the native-born American, and alluded especially to this subject. He had just attained high literary distinction, and had lately published two additional collections of poems for which he had been crowned by the French Academy—an honor, I believe, not hitherto conferred upon any other American. He said: 'There is a class of people who would teach you that French can only be spoken in Paris, or by those who have been educated there. I would not sound my own praises, but I must meet slander with truth. I never studied in France; I was educated at the Quebec Seminary, and I speak and write French as it was taught me there. I offer you the opinion of the French Academy which recognized merit in my works, and honored me, an humble Canadian poet and student, against the teachings of those who would disparage the literature and the scholarship of my native land.' Depend upon it," Gustave continued, "that Harvard is not more adept in the graces of the English than is the University of Laval in the belles lettres of her mother tongue. All the conditions are so different that it is only in this respect I should dare institute a comparison."

He gave his ideas upon the opera, the drama and other subjects of more or less practical interest. To him oratory was the highest gift, and music the most divine art; but sometimes, he said, the great masters failed to impress him, while humbler performers often enthralled him. He thought humor an outcome of genius, and wit a scintillation from a higher life. He related how, years before, he had loitered alone in the streets of Boston, and had wandered aimlessly into the Boston Museum. Poor John Brougham was producing an Irish character, which was new to him. He had no doubt the piece was now forgotten. He could not recall either the incidents or its name; but partly, perhaps because it was good, and it may be chiefly because his mood was propitious, he had all the time been convulsed with laughter, and had never enjoyed a play more.

When the ladies were about to withdraw, the Senator asked permission to waive ceremony and accompany them, and they passed the evening cosily in the little parlor like a quiet family, at peace with themselves and the world.

Next morning Gen. Elmwood, with his daughter and Fred, came, and Agnes noticing their hilarity bade the young people remember in whose presence they were. They promised obedience, but Fred seemed to treat the restraint as an excuse for closer communion, and they consequently did not lose sight of each other. The General was full of the glories of the exhibition, which was being held in the city, and to which he was again hastening, and the house continued as quiet as it had been the day before. Tom had spoken seriously to Agnes; she was not indifferent to his overtures, but they were young and they could wait, she said.

"Do you love me, Agnes?"

"Yes, with all my heart and soul," was the reply.

What could he do? What did he do? That afternoon Mr. Winthrop had given his consent. "She is too young," he had said to Tom. "But your father and I have spoken of the matter, and I am acting for him as well as for myself. Agnes is the apple of my eye, Capt. Conant; but I don't fear to give her to you."

"May God so deal with me as I shall deal with her," said Tom with emotion.

He caught her in his arms; "My darling," was all he uttered, and she, permitting his embraces, whispered, "Thine and Mine!" From that hour Tom Conant and Agnes Winthrop were to be all and all to each other. It was arranged that Tom would return to England and come back for her in the summer; but the engagement was to be a secret until after the holidays.

Presently the young couple sought the seclusion of the park, where they were alone among hundreds of people. For a time they were too selfish in their happiness to care for the presence of others. Language to them was no longer a symbol of ideas, and they made scant use of it. The vocabulary of love is not made up of spoken words; a look, a pose, a smile, a pressure of the hand may express unnumbered lights and shades of passion. Words of endearment were too faint and expressionless to paint their deep and overpowering attachment. They had just entered a new life, a paradise of bliss, a revelation, a beatitude; they did not for the time understand that others had been there before, and that still others would follow them. If he called her, "my darling," and she responded "my love," what were these but common words which all the world had used? Theirs was a grand exceptional passion. There was no other man like Tom to love, and no other woman like Agnes to love in return, and yet these raptures must consume themselves and they must see the world moving about them.

Let the artist who copied the sunbeam portray the rhapsodies of love, and leave us the simpler pleasure of wishing God-speed to the young lovers!

> "So the multitude goes, like the flower or the weed
> That withers away to let others succeed.
> So the multitude comes, even those we behold,
> To repeat every tale that has often been told."

Tom was to write at once to his father and mother the joyful news which they were both expecting; and Agnes, who remembered to have met Lord Lester in London, would try and persuade Uncle Horace and George to accompany her on her visit to his Lordship in Canada. George she thought would go, if Ethel could be induced to join them. Tom took the hint and promised to do his best to bring about this arrangement.

Meantime our prudent young lovers had permitted no word of their new and happy relation to escape them; but perhaps if the others had been less absorbed, signs might have been detected; as it was the day passed and the night fell without any suspicion among Mr. Winthrop's guests that unusual events were transpiring. Only George knew, and he seemed almost gay in his congratulations.

"I think I could have loved you before Agnes, Tom," said George, "if I had seen you as soon as she did. I began to love you from the day you set your foot here. Such things must happen, only it is hard to lose my little sister. But even yet I may take my revenge," he continued; "and I shall find compensation in a big brother. Take my blessing," he added, resting a hand upon each, " and as for you, dear Agnes, may your joys be as boundless as your brother's love."

"Oh, if you were happy, George!" she said, nestling close to his bosom.

"I dare not hope too much, little one, but it may come sooner than you dream."

George went to the library in answer to a message from his uncle, who awaited him there. "I have given our little Agnes away, George," said Mr. Winthrop in a tremulous voice.

"They have told me all, and you have done right," replied George. "She will leave us next summer. Tom was impatient of delay, but Agnes must study another year. It will all be over soon enough now."

"Yes, and ours will be a lonely house," observed his uncle. "You ought to marry, my boy."

George was silent.

Mr. Winthrop continued, "You have suffered, but with your temperament you should marry young; and you may even profit by the discipline of disappointment. The companionship of a good woman will be the sheet-anchor of your life; without it you may grow morose and misanthropic."

"This from you, sir?" inquired George.

"You allude to the great mistake of my life," observed the uncle.

"It is not too late to correct it," rejoined George. "You are not old, and you have all the qualities that should make a good woman happy."

"We will speak of my own case later," remarked Mr. Winthrop, "but I have lately dreamed of conditions which may in time render my case even hopeful; the example of dear little Agnes may make us a marrying family; but yours is more pressing; the prize is within your reach and should be appreciated."

"I know what you mean," returned George; "my position is equivocal; but, believe me, I am not indifferent."

"Your position will not distress a true woman; she will not love you less on account of your lost love. Any woman knows that

> "A stricken heart which loves anew
> May be more tender and more true,"

Gustave, pressed by engagements, was about to take his leave, and it was arranged that Madame De Luynes would return to Quebec, accompanied by Tom's party, on a visit to Lord Lester. Tom had received a cable from home, announcing his father's safe arrival, his finding all well, and that important letters would follow by mail. The week flew past like a happy dream to the young people and the hour of Carlotta's departure was at hand. They were all to go with her as far as Montreal, a common point in their journey, and from thence George and Robert would escort Mme. De Luynes to Quebec, the others ascending the river to Ottawa.

Ottawa is a prettily situated town on the river of that name, having some beautiful natural scenery, a commanding position, and distinguished by a magnificent pile of public buildings, of the Gothic style of architecture.

Government House, Lord Lester's residence, is situated in a fine park, some two miles from the town, but the residence is only remarkable because the Queen's representative lives there. It is long, low and rambling, and has been made up piecemeal as the growing importance of what has been miscalled Canada's court-life expanded and required further accommodations; but it has witnessed gay scenes and magnificent entertainments under the patronage of quasi-royal forms and ceremonies. A former Governor, whose successes in life have been remarkable, made the place distinguished for its princely hospitalities, and for the genial qualities and rare gifts of its temporary incumbent. More than any previous Governor he had endeared himself to his guests and to the people, while his lovely Countess lent grace and fascination to the scenes. As the successor of such an incumbent, Lord Lester's task was difficult, but he had proved equal to his work, while his august wife, bearing a sweet presence and a great name, added lustre to his administration.

The Parliament of the Dominion had been called early this year, and would be re-opened on the morrow by the Governor in person. The night before the opening, His Excellency annually gave a great dinner, to which his Ministers and Privy Councillors and the great officers of State were invited. Of course the dinner would take place that night, and Tom and his friends who had been invited, modestly asked permission to decline, as, being strangers, they would feel themselves out of place at a great state dinner; but they were told by the *aide-de-camp* in waiting that they must accept the invitation in deference to the wishes of Her Excellency, who had requested that ceremony should be waived in their favor.

The old house was *en fête* under the gas-light, and its tasteful decorations made the scene a gay one. As they entered the great dining-hall, Tom noticed that there were covers for a large party, and that no ladies were present; but he was told that the wives and daughters of the ministers and other guests would arrive later in the evening. A fine band discoursed music at a convenient distance, and a Highland piper now and then strolled majestically round the table, and contributed to swell the melodies.

It was a goodly company; the varied uniforms and decorations blended prettily, and it was all more like "home" than anything Tom had seen in America. "Poor De Luynes," he thought, "should have had a place among these magnates. I wonder which of them all does not at heart, though he may bask in the favor of the men who crushed Maurice, cherish the doctrines for which they proscribed him?"

There sat next to Tom a civil servant, an intelligent man who had been a Member of Parliament, and who seemed disposed to be sociable. They discussed the civil service, which Tom thought nearly perfect in England; but his neighbor only thought it better as it was farther removed from politics.

"But your civil service is not political, is it?" inquired Tom.

"Theoretically, no," was the reply; "but I suppose the incumbents generally owe their position to politics."

"Yes, they are all appointed on the recommendation of Ministers, no doubt," said Tom; "but the system is different here from that in the States."

"To this extent—we appoint for life."

"Are there ever dismissals for political reasons?"

"Such reasons would not be avowed," replied the other cautiously. "But there are advantages in having the sympathy of the strong side, and disadvantages in being known to have sprung from the weak one. Suppose I had been appointed by the last government, it would be a miracle if I should get favors from the present."

"That seems hard," observed Tom; "I should not think Lester would permit it. A great deal was expected at home from his administration here."

"Pardon me if I say," said his friend, "that there is misapprehension at home about the functions of the Queen's representative here. It is common to read in the leading journals of Lord So-and-So's (meaning the Governor's) successful administration in Canada. I do not discuss his constitutional powers, but if they gave him the right to mould the policy of his administration, it has fallen into disuse. Practically speaking, His Excellency is a figure-head; the government is that of his Prime Minister. Once in a while, if there happens to be friction, we hear of the Governor's constitutional powers; but in moulding a policy, any power he is supposed to have, is exercised so seldom that our people have forgotten that he possesses any, or that it amounts to much."

"He is one of the estates of the realm," said Tom.

"Yes, and as such he assents to bills, replies to addresses, and entertains by giving dinners and balls."

"Then, why not abolish the office?" Tom persisted.

"Because it is almost the last remnant of Imperial connection," was the significant reply. "We love England because we sprang from her and she fostered us; but year by year our relations have grown anomalous and illogical. Our people will not listen to the truth, and you Englishmen are too busy to consider it. But there would be an awakening if we should elect our Governor some day."

"This is plain talk from headquarters," Tom thought.

"One wonders to what extent this gentleman represents Canadian opinion. Oh! if there were an enchantment to disclose what the people want, what public opinion is, or will be, at a given time, what statesmen we might all become, and how many ruthless political disappointments might be avoided!"

When dinner was over and they had all sought the drawing-room, they found a large number of ladies and gentlemen, guests who had been bidden to come later in the evening, together with the ladies of the household, mingling among them. Her Excellency was in earnest conversation with Miss Winthrop. She signalled Tom to approach them.

"You can help us," said my lady. "Miss Winthrop is trying to explain to me your late dreadful experiences at sea." Tom answered her questions respectfully, and at length she complained of cold, and picking up a bit of wood from the corner in which she was standing she cast it into the grate as unconcernedly as though it had been the business of her life. She asked Tom if he liked the country, and remarked that she had herself been very fond of it since she came to it. Her physicians, however, had found it too cold for her health, and the newspapers had construed her absence into dislike. They had done her a great injustice, and she hoped her friends would everywhere contradict the story on her authority.

Mr. Winthrop enjoyed an evening's conversation on favorite topics with charming people, and Fred told of a high dignitary who had been polite to him, but was very rude to Lindley Murray. The dignitary in question had adopted a very aristocratic and exclusive tone, and had told him that he always regretted the Liberals coming into power, not on account of politics, but because it gave vulgar people the *entrée* to society, adding, with a confidential shake of his head, "I seen it much degraded thereby."

"He shall offset our Washington friend," observed Tom to Mr. Winthrop.

"He was more pretentious but not less vulgar," Fred continued. "He spoke to me of his daughters, and presented me to them. Would you believe it, they are not only pretty, but accomplished girls. I was curious to know about the father, and found he had laid the foundation of his fortune by keeping a corner grocery in one of the large towns."

"That explains his relation to politics," remarked Mr. Winthrop, "and clears his way to the Senate, no doubt. He would pass with you as a licensed victualler. No doubt the young ladies have been well trained and illustrate the Professor's hopes for the second generation."

"We meet most desirable acquaintances in both countries; there is no need to leave home to find vulgar people," said Tom.

"You are already beginning to feel the responsibility for your associates, Capt. Conant," said Fred, with a mischievous grin; "perhaps you won't be the only fellow with an American wife."

Mr. Winthrop laughed, Tom whistled, and they all thought it was time to retire.

Next morning there was a cable from Dr. Conant in these words: "If letter serious come home at once." "Which means," explained Tom to Lord Lester, "that if I have really determined to stand for the Commons, I ought to return and go to work"

There were but three days now to catch the outward-bound steamer, and they all understood that there was no time to lose; so the same afternoon saw them departing, Tom for England, and Agnes, as she told him, for her great, lonesome Boston home. Both Robert and Fred Cuthbert were to remain longer in America, but Tom sailed for home alone.

CHAPTER XXII.

THE BRITISH LION FONDLES THE PROFESSOR.

We must take a three months' vacation now, though, meantime, the world will move, and some things of interest to us will happen. Politics had been running high in England; there was a popular clamor against the Ministry, and a wide-spread demand for concessions; all the by-elections had lately gone against the Government. "It never rains but it pours." The health of the Prime Minister had been seriously affected, and the story of his early resignation was bruited about and believed. There were the usual intrigues and party defections; opposing interests were on the alert; rival factions were pushing extreme claims, and the nation was aglow with excitement, or apprehensive of impending danger. There was no real leadership, and the claims of personal aspirants were hotly discussed. Dr. Conant, who had hitherto stood well in the country, was now the idol of the laboring classes; public meetings were everywhere held to promote this or to denounce that set of opinions, and the kingdom resounded with the eloquence of local orators and budding statesmen.

In other countries such unwonted heat might have generated an explosion; but these Englishmen, arrayed for contest as they were, would fight their bitter battles at the polls. When victory was declared, or defeat assured, they would for the time accept the result as inevitable. A less stolid or more mercurial people might have persisted in agitation and precipitated disaster, but the English understood constitutional government, and they knew that majorities must rule. The Government were not indifferent spectators. They had asked for a dissolution, but it had been denied them. The people shouted for reconstruction and an amended policy, until finally Lord Bramley, broken in health and spirits, resigned. The great Whig, Lord Elton, was sent for by the Sovereign, and undertook the duty of forming a new Government, but his duties and his difficulties began together. He had given an unpopular Irish vote, and the Radicals dreaded his too conservative leanings. Finally, after a week of ineffectual effort, he abandoned the task as hopeless, and recommended that Dr. Conant be called. The masses were already demanding this, but for reasons, perhaps connected with the American trip, the advice was at first unheeded. After other trials and further delays, and still greater excitement, Professor Conant was sent for and accepted the high duty, on condition that a dissolution should take place.

There was a coolness at first among the more conservative Whigs, but, barring this, the popular enthusiasm knew no bounds; and his administration was formed without difficulty. The dissolution that followed, and the Prime Minister who appealed to them, were what the people demanded. It was a long struggle between mighty forces. But the popular star was in the ascendant, and the Government was sustained by an immense majority.

The new Parliament was distinguished for a large infusion of young men, and a well-known North-of-England County had returned our old friends, Col. Lyons and Capt. Tom Conant.

"Tom," his father said, "had developed into a wonderful stump orator, thanks, perhaps, to his recent visit to the States." At any rate, he had been indefatigable, and was prepared to enjoy the rest and triumph which followed his victory.

Parliament was immediately summoned, and the speech contained propositions which the enemies of the Government pronounced startling, but which were generally regarded as wise by the supporters of the Prime Minister, and were especially satisfactory to the Radicals. Caution and Conservatism are generally cultivated by the English people; but with their minds once fixed upon accomplishing progressive changes, they undertake the work with vigor, and with a confidence in the masses which is not often misplaced. Capt. Thomas Conant, as a young member, was to move the resolutions on which would be founded the address in reply to the Speech from the Throne. Nobody ever expects anything from the orator on such occasions. He follows a conventional form, and his style, to be orthodox, should be prosy and spiritless. The reply itself is usually an echo of the Speech from the Throne, and the mover and seconder follow the text without originality or amplification. In the first part of his speech Capt. Conant followed this rule in a tremulous voice and was supported by conventional cheers; but as he came to topics of interest his words began to ring out upon the Chamber, and he spoke like an enthusiast who believed what he said. "It is a glorious privilege," Tom said, "to sit in this hall and legislate for a great people. We are the successors of former Parliaments, in a long line and from the earliest days, which had moulded the policy and guided the destiny of the kingdom. To say that we have grown more wealthy and powerful, that the country is more free and the people are better informed than in the days of their ancestors, is speaking only the truth, and paying a just compliment to the liberty and progress which the British Constitution has gradually developed. Some people profess to be alarmed at the larger liberties which the Speech from the Throne proposes should be secured for the people; and in prophesying anarchy and revolution as a consequence of such concessions, they are but repeating the tactics of those obstructionists who, from age to age, as privilege has been gradually restricted and freedom enlarged, have made themselves prophets of evil, and foretold consequences which have never followed reform. Which of those ameliorations of the people's condition has been signalized by the people's abuse of the power given them? Which of the steps would you retrace that you have taken toward a nearer Democratic rule? Your confidence is in the rich," he said, his eyes resting on the Opposition benches. "You dread the masses as if they were the enemies of the State, but as history records our national troubles, can you fairly say that the great body of the people has been less loyal and devoted than the aristocratic and privileged classes upon which you prefer to depend? By multiplying their liberties you have made the masses an element of strength. Then why should we dread, in the light of such experience, these further concessions?" (A voice derisively: "Oh, America is the land of liberty.") "I am not sure," continued Capt. Conant, "that, barring the fact that her franchise is more extended, America *is* a freer country than ours; but this proposition of the Government will tend to equalize whatever difference there is. I have seen nothing in America, let me tell this House, to compensate for the tyranny which a four years' Presidential term of hostile estates might render possible. In this country, or in Canada, the power of the executive would be measured by its ability to control the popular branch of the Legislature; the balances are adjusted to a delicate touch, and the Government must fall the moment it ceases to command a majority. In Washington, the power of the President is assumed for a definite term. It is only incidentally that the people could reach their President during his term of office, even if he were in open or flagrant opposition to their views, as expressed by their representatives." (An honorable member: "It is a relief to know that there is something to criticise in America.") Capt. Conant—"There are wise men in America who court criticism and understand the abuses of their political system. There are others, no doubt, who, perhaps, like the honorable gentleman, believe that 'nothing good can come out of Nazareth;' but the fact remains that the teachings of American history enlighten and guide us, and that we in England are wisely borrowing from the store of American experience. I hope I did not detect a sneer in the interruption of the honorable gentleman. England and America have to teach each other lessons of liberty. Only the enemies of both countries could gloat over the embarrassments of either. Their people, mindful of the perils which in other times have overtaken liberty, should stand man to man for her defense, and should treat as a public enemy the incendiaries of either country, who would sow dissensions among them." Tom continued, passing on to other topics, but this episode we have mentioned pleased the House, whose enthusiasm was expressed in repeated cheers, and finally, when Capt. Conant resumed his seat, the manifestations of satisfaction were abundant, and several old members crossed the floor to compliment him heartily. He had scored a point, which it is not often the privilege of young members to do. He had moved the reply to a Queen's Speech, and, in any event, the journals would treat him to the conventional encomium the next morning, but he had done more; during the greater part of his speech he had been really eloquent; and he had gained what is tantamount to success in public life,—he had won the fastidious ear of the English House of Commons.

The Prime Minister made no attempt to disguise his interest and his emotion; for the moment, the father's heart gave way in the august presence of the nation, and his friends said he had not only consecrated his own life to the State but was giving a son, who was worthy of him, to her service.

Tom did not fail to measure his own success, but his first thought was for a little girl who was thinking of him far across the water. Could she know instinctively of this first triumph in his public life? Could he allow her to wait the slow course of the mail before she knew that the success she coveted for him had been won? It was the first step in his career. He was not an egotist, but he had triumphed, and he was in love. It must have been at his suggestion that the following cablegram was sent:

"House of Commons, London.
"Senator Winthrop,
          "Boston, Mass.:
               "For Miss Winthrop.
"Tom's maiden speech a great success.
                         "Alexander Conant."

CHAPTER XXIV.

GATHERING IN THE THREADS.

In the quiet of a Sunday morning breakfast, the Conants were speaking of the events of the past week. Tom described his diffidence at opening on the night of his speech. "At first you might have heard my heart beat, and seen my knees knock together," he said; "but that I felt as if I enjoyed a little official protection, because I was replying to the Royal speech, I might have failed."

"You did not fail," said his father; "some parts of your speech were very able. But your triumph consisted in showing that you can do better. You must not speak again till you are thoroughly master both of your subject and the occasion. The House listened and applauded to-day. You won its ear. You must do not only as well but a great deal better next time, and then you will have won your spurs."

"Thanks for your kind opinion," said Tom; "I will do my best."

Quiet Mrs. Conant was happy, but she was not proud; of course, distinctions were worth winning, and it was yet nobler to do good. But she had given her husband to the public service, and sometimes she pined for the old days when she saw him more and before he was so absent and absorbed. Was it her duty to give her son too, or would he be not so much lost to her?

In the midst of his triumphs Tom received a letter from Lord Bolton. There had been several short notes from that nobleman, from which it was gleaned that he had been passing his time pleasantly in California. His letter began by reminding Tom of the strange incident which had induced Lord Lester to avoid the dinner party of thirteen in Quebec, and of the Professor's explanations as to the origin of the superstition. "I have found here," it went on, "a strange society, consisting of the best people and organized in the form of a club, solely to rebuke this superstition. It is called the Thirteen Club, and its motto is '*Morituri te salutamus.*'

"The club is composed of thirteen original members, and it is incorporated by an act of the legislature of the state. The act of incorporation declares that its object, besides being charitable, is to combat by argument, by essays, and by example, the prevalent superstition against unlucky Fridays and against the prejudice in setting thirteen at dinner, a prejudice which is believed to be at variance with the enlightened intelligence of the age. The regular meetings are all held on the thirteenth day of each month. The dinners are to be served with thirteen courses at each table, non-attendance or non-payment of dues for thirteen months is made the cause of suspension of membership. The *menu*, the wine bill, and all the literature of the club are in keeping with this object. I sometimes dine there, and am supposed to have been fitted for initiation by the experiences which I have related to you. It is, to say the least, a coincidence, and I think the idea is original; perhaps it will interest our friends. This is a strange country, as is the history of its marvellous development. The city of San Francisco is beautiful, though the buildings are generally low to avoid the risk of earthquakes, which are not infrequent here. The society is cosmopolitan, and the business of the town is conducted by the people of all nations. Some of the most fabulous fortunes in the United States have been made here; and the palaces of men who started life a few years ago would rival in splendor the royal palaces at home. There is in California almost every variety of soil and production. At any season you may journey in a day from almost tropical heat to continual snow, including nearly all varieties of temperature. Of course, the country is young, but its progress has been magical. There is a great deal of refinement in this particular city, as well as over the state. I like the people. You find travelled men and women here, who would do credit to the drawing-rooms of our great capitals. I have spent some days in the mountains, and have visited several towns; two or three of which are beautiful. One little town of five thousand people nestling in a basin among the mountains, and inhabited largely by miners, has scarcely a house (if you except the Chinese quarters) which is not neat, surrounded by grounds well cultivated, and abounding in choice flowers. The people are intelligent, hospitable and law-abiding. I have never seen a mining town where the evidences of thrift and taste and contentment are so general. You approach the town, which is a county seat, by a unique little railway; a narrow-gauge road connects it with the main line, and passes over mountains, crags and cañons, which would make your head dizzy, and curves about in a way that would have generated lunacy among the railway engineers of a few years ago. I like the country, and have purchased a large ranch in one of the valleys, which I propose to stock with fifty thousand sheep in the proper season. I have reserved a place for you as herdsman, which I think you will grace, and I expect to make myself useful under your supervision. Seriously, you must arrange to come out next summer *en route*, perhaps, for China on a government mission. I shall return East in a week or two, and possibly spend some time with Lester in Canada."

A few days later, a letter was received from Miss Winthrop. She had to acknowledge the Professor's cablegram, and was profuse in expressions of thankfulness and congratulation. Robert Holt had lately returned from England, and George had met him in Quebec, but Mr. Cuthbert was not expected until summer. In the meantime, a correspondence, she thought, was going on between General Elmwood and Sir John Cuthbert, about which she only knew what her little cousin, Miss Elmwood, had told her, under a strict promise to keep it from Tom; so, of course, she could not tell him. But he knew it all from Fred, who only the night before had been raving about a certain event which was "to come off" at Bloomfield, as if it were really of international importance. "At any rate, it will make you and me cousins," Fred had said to Tom. "Is it not strange that I should have gone out intent upon slaughtering the Americans, and here I am a captive bound by silken cords?"

"George," Miss Winthrop reported to Tom, "had been two or three times in Quebec, and had met Ethel in Hartford; and Carlotta had lately written Agnes a long, sweet letter, stronger and more confident in spirit, and evincing earnest religious feeling." Then the letter took Tom aside to private thoughts whither we must not follow him.

> "My thoughts of thee too sacred are,
> For daylight's common beam,
> I can but know thee as my star,
> My angel, and my dream!"

Mrs. Conant thought it was strange Robert should have gone out again in mid-winter. "It can't be the child," she said to the Professor, "there must be some other, if not stronger, fascination. I remember that when I pressed Tom's example upon him, he spoke in a mysterious way of the only woman he could love being wedded to the grave. I knew what he meant, but it did not at the time impress me. Yet I should have known, for he spoke much of a life devoted to good works; and an ambition to consecrate himself to the priesthood of charity. I was so much occupied with my own cares, and so thankful for what it was my duty to regard as special mercies, that I am afraid I neglected the poor boy; but I had no idea he was going away then, and I felt that it was safe to put him off a little. Why did you not bring him into Parliament?" she inquired of the Professor.

"I sought to persuade him," replied Dr. Conant, "but he was averse."

"It is not too late; his own county of Kingsmere will be open presently. Nobody could well oppose him there."

"Then I must write him at once," remarked good Mrs. Conant. "Robert has great gifts; but what he needs now is absorbing occupation. I dread for a woman the character of political intriguer, but my husband will forgive me if I ask so much for my sister's only boy."

"It will be no gift of mine," replied the Professor; "the constituency is his own family stronghold. He can win it himself if he chooses. But whatever he needs shall be done for him. There would be no favoritism. A worthier member for Kingsmere could not be found in the kingdom."

And so it was agreed that Mrs. Conant should write Robert at Quebec, from which place his last letter had been dated. After explaining to him the chances, she told him that he needed work, and that there could be no nobler occupation than to sit with the first body of gentlemen in the world, and to help to administer the affairs of the freest and most powerful of nations. Benevolence would be still open to him, and public affairs need not stand in the way of the most far-reaching of his charities. Even if honors did not entice him, in no other position could he enjoy greater opportunities of doing good to his race; and she wanted him to stand for Kingsmere, and, if possible, to enter the House of Commons.

How could good Mrs. Conant know that when Robert received the letter he would be prostrate with grief, and regard himself as withered and blighted? So sudden and startling are sometimes the vicissitudes of life, and so rapid the accumulations of disaster! We must take the liberty of reading the sad tale which he told in his letter to his aunt. We may find love, hope, friendship, grief and despair illogically interwoven; but a sad story excites the sympathy and perhaps ennobles the purposes of the human heart, and here it follows:

"Quebec, ———, 18—.

"My own Dear Aunt:

"If my servant had asked me an hour ago, 'Could you write a letter to Mrs. Conant to-day, sir?' I am sure I should have answered, 'Not to-day;' for I felt so weary, so stricken and overcome that the task would have seemed impossible; but your letter has given me new life, though I cannot obey your wishes; and it makes me ask, 'What am I that I should set myself against fate, or by my repinings accuse the Inevitable?' You shall know all. The mysterious fascination of little Ethel over me is no secret to you. When I thought that her destiny was interwoven with mine, my friends found me superstitious and hysterical; others might have sneered, you were full of charity, though you feared my reason was giving way to my imagination. But explain it as you may, I was a prophet, and saw as clearly as could have done Elijah of old. When I met the poor father I was drawn to him as I had been drawn to the child, and I knew that the sweet woman, who is her mother, was in some way to absorb my life in hers. In two days poor De Luynes had become my dearest friend, and I knew that we two had something approaching fascination for each other. Was it superstition, or rather was it not a prescience? I had no idea what was to happen, but I was impressed that startling events, which would relate to our mutual interest and happiness, were pending. I pondered weary days and sleepless nights. Why did these people impress me so much? Why was my soul aglow at sight of this accomplished man? and my heart melted in the presence of this fascinating woman? Up to that time there was no thought of the child. By degrees it became plain to me that little Ethel was theirs. Here might have been, but was not, a solution. The finger of fate still pointed forward, the weird influence still permeated my being, and the nameless prophet still foretold that in some way this beautiful woman was unconsciously to mould and fashion my life. Then on that terrible night at sea, Maurice was taken, and by little less than a miracle, his wife was saved; but she struggled long between life and death, and yet I instinctively knew she would recover. I had an assurance which I could not explain, and of which I could not have spoken to others. She was to live and guide me. I saw that clearly. But in what way I could only conjecture. What wonder if my heart interpreted the mystery?—*She was to be mine.* The very thought was a profanation of grief; but I entertained though I would not have expressed it. She was drawn toward me because I had saved her child, as well as by the memory of her husband's friendship for me. Did I deceive myself if I hoped there might in time grow a stronger feeling? Since De Luynes's death she has been much with the Sisters, and I was jealous of the influence they exerted over her. The priests could not have reached her, I thought, because they had dealt unfairly with her husband; but the ladies were gentle, affectionate and pious, and they represented the Church that her husband loved. I thought they were propagandists before all things, and I dreaded lest she should desert the religion of her fathers. It was to guard her, to dissuade her, that I left England so suddenly in the winter. She admitted to me that her ideas of a woman's doing good were associated with conventual life, and that it had been an object dear to the heart of Maurice that she should worship with him within the same communion. She allowed me to expostulate, but she was not much impressed. 'Christ,' she said, 'would be found wherever two or three of His servants are gathered in His name.' She preferred Christian to sectarian work, and she regarded charity as the holiest of Christian efforts. She pictured to me the sweet, holy life of the Sisters; how they visited the sick, and 'bound up the wounds of the broken-hearted.' She spoke kindly and even tenderly to me, but I was not pleased with the success of my mission. Then a terrible blow fell upon us all— little Ethel was stricken with a deadly malady, which frightened the servants from the house, and we were left dependent upon the ministrations of the Sisters. Then I realized all I had read of the noble devotion of these holy women. They nursed the child night and day, and they gave strength and consolation to the mother. Little Ethel died; I was prostrate with grief, but Carlotta was calm, strong and hopeful. She had given the child to God, she said, and to its father. One night, when she fervently prayed for its life, she saw the face of Maurice looking reproachfully at her, as if he would say, 'Can you not spare me the child?' She had vowed to devote her life to the Church its father loved. In the presence of death I told her all, and she said, 'if Ethel had lived it might have been.' My dear aunt, is it a strange, unreal story? Could I have strength to face the world just as Carlotta De Luynes retires from it? Your letter was kind, and the prospect you hold out would once have been alluring. I cannot feel as if time will heal all things, nor as if old ambitions will return."

Mrs. Conant understood the letter and sympathized deeply with Robert and mourned for the dear little child, which had so recently left her, but it was at her suggestion that Robert was put in nomination for Kingsmere, and three months afterward, though he was still in America, he was elected to serve in Parliament. "He will thank us by-and-by," she said, "when the days of his mourning are over and when he finds himself face to face with great duties."

Meantime, Ethel had written George, and Tom had thus heard, that the illness of the little one had been terrible, but Carlotta had almost accepted its death as a relief, and was strong and brave afterward. "The sweet Sisters," as Ethel thought, "had given her strength and courage. They directed her to God and she trusted in Him." Perhaps she had been so stunned by the first blow that she was less sensitive to what followed; and there was no doubt the good ladies, and their ministrations, had smoothed her path and strewn the tomb with flowers. They taught her that afflictions were the admonitions of Heaven, and that a great sorrow was a privilege and a distinction. Ethel thought her sister's heart was full of noble resolutions, but she dreaded lest she might take the veil and be altogether lost to her. She spoke of Robert Holt, of his grief at the child's loss, and said Carlotta's composure seemed to disturb him. She thought it would be a personal bereavement to Holt if her sister should abandon the world. Then she spoke of her own loneliness, and of the comfort she found in her letters from George; of Lord Bolton and his kind and delicate attentions, and hoped Agnes was happy far away from the gloom she felt in the De Luynes mansion.

"What changes the year has brought us; how have our hearts been torn and our loved ones taken. Do we see the end yet? There *are* joys in life. Will it go on alternating between pleasure and pain? New friends and fresh bereavements, till we lay down the threads, and rest at the journey's end?" "Dear girl," Miss Winthrop wrote Tom (she had copied this letter for him), "Ethel has had her own trials. Only a day or two before the child Ethel fell ill, Lord Bolton, whom she greatly esteemed, proposed for her hand in marriage. He did not sue like an ardent lover; he told her frankly of his bereavements, but there was no one on earth, he said, whom he should so gladly call his wife. Ethel was surprised and pained; 'I wish this had not happened,' she told him, 'you are so kind, and you honor me so much, that I would not cause you a regret. What you propose is impossible, for reasons which you will understand, and which you will not desire me to explain. Forget this passing fancy, Lord Bolton, and honor me with your friendship which I shall highly prize.' 'May I ask if you are engaged?' said Lord Bolton, kindly. 'Yes, to George Winthrop,' she answered. 'George Winthrop, whom I have never seen,' repeated his Lordship slowly. 'How strangely we two have crossed each other's path.'"

CHAPTER XXV.

NOUS VERRONS.

Months have passed, and there has been high holiday at the Winthrop mansion in Boston. It is the anniversary of Tom's first meeting with Agnes, and the wedding day of Capt. Thomas Conant, M.P., and Miss Agnes Winthrop, and of Frederick Cuthbert, Esq., and Miss Elmwood, of Bloomfield.

Tom's mother and Miss Alice Cuthbert had come out from England to witness the nuptials. Agnes had desired that the names of a third couple should be added to the happy list, but George and Ethel felt that the days of their mourning were not over. The ceremony was strictly private, and only relatives had been invited. Capt. Strong was the only exception, and the sweet young life of Alice was pledged to him, but her father had said she was too young, and they must wait another year. Lord Bolton and Robert were in England. Uncle Horace had been indefatigable in his attentions during the day, but it was evening now, and the shadows seemed to have clouded his spirits.

"He has been unstrung for weeks," said Agnes to Tom.

"He mourns for you," he answered. "Yes," continued the young wife, "he will miss me; but he has another and deeper grief. We are not lost to him, but his good heart has refused to be comforted since Carlotta left the world. It is one short year since we knew each other; our love has made us so happy in spite of many trials! My dear husband, how mercifully we have been spared, while our path has been shadowed by the sad experiences of our friends."

"They would indeed make a book," he rejoined. "A sad story! Our lives have skimmed along social and national issues, and we have discussed them under the guidance of great and sympathetic minds. We have set an example to those who should strengthen the bonds which might bind kindred peoples closer together; while our trials have kept us mindful of the vicissitudes of life, and may thus point a moral and adorn a tale. The fascinations of romance are not wanting. Will you write, Agnes?"

"How dare I?"

"But it need not see the light."

"Some of the best characters would be unfinished. Where could I leave Lord Bolton and Robert Holt?"

"Oh, all our lives will go on, and if your book were a success, you might, by-and-by, follow it with a sequel."

"*Nous verrons*, my darling," said Agnes, "but if I wrote, I should say a great deal about you and our other friends, and with tears I should christen my book 'Maurice De Luynes.'"

Time has sped happily with Agnes, but absorbed with social and domestic care, she has not yet written; perhaps these hasty chronicles may touch her heart, and it may be, her more finished work will shortly follow them.

www.ingramcontent.com/pod-product-compliance
Lightning Source LLC
Chambersburg PA
CBHW031249250426
43672CB00029BA/1399